I0878477

WHARTON, HEMINGWAY, *and the* ADVENT OF MODERNISM

WHARTON, HEMINGWAY, *and the* ADVENT OF MODERNISM

EDITED BY

LISA TYLER

FOREWORD BY

LAURA RATTRAY

LOUISIANA STATE UNIVERSITY PRESS

BATON ROUGE

Published by Louisiana State University Press
Copyright © 2019 by Louisiana State University Press
All rights reserved
Manufactured in the United States of America
FIRST PRINTING

DESIGNER: *Mandy McDonald Scallan*
TYPEFACE: *Whitman*
PRINTER AND BINDER: *Sheridan Books*

Cataloging-in-Publication Data are available from the Library of Congress.

ISBN 978-0-8071-7048-9 (cloth: alk. paper) — ISBN 978-0-8071-7129-5 (pdf) — ISBN 978-0-8071-7130-1 (epub)

The paper in this book meets the guidelines for permanence and durability of the Committee on Production Guidelines for Book Longevity of the Council on Library Resources. ♾

CONTENTS

FOREWORD

In 2014 the sixteenth conference of the international Hemingway Society, held in Venice, attracted scholars from across the globe. A full, week-long program brought its own moveable feast. There were panels and papers on Hemingway and Italy, Spain, Africa, and on Hemingway and Japanese aesthetics. The conference revisited representations of war, trauma, and memory; delegates discussed race and ethnic consciousness, politics and ideology, genre and gender, alongside Hemingway in translation and reconsiderations of the author's modernism and its manifestations. Individual works discussed included *For Whom the Bell Tolls, The Sun Also Rises, In Our Time,* plus—perhaps a fitting, geographical inevitability—multiple panels dedicated to *A Farewell to Arms* and *Across the River and into the Trees.* Comparative studies addressed Hemingway and Sherwood Anderson, Gertrude Stein, James Joyce, Victor Hugo, and Prosper Mérimée, among others.

In this rich, varied conference program, one roundtable stood out, raised a few incredulous eyebrows even: Hemingway and Edith Wharton. *Wharton?* On paper the writers can look like the most uncomfortable of literary bedfellows: one renowned as the muscular, sparse, modernist innovator; the other mythologized as the genteel grande dame, at best ambivalent, at worst hostile to all forms of literary experimentation and change. The pairing was a bold choice by the roundtable convener, Lisa Tyler. Short, varied papers addressed Wharton, Hemingway, and the "architecture" of modernism, masculinist inertia and performing maturity, the writers' approaches to autobiography and reminiscences, nationalist ethos and American/European geographic, emotional, and literary epicenters. The session provoked vibrant, thoughtful dialogues that would prove a catalyst for this very welcome, fuller consideration, Tyler's edited collection *Wharton, Hemingway, and the Advent of Modernism.*

Among its other accomplishments, the collection charts the surprising number of common denominators in the career trajectories of Hemingway and Wharton. Living in Paris in the 1920s, at the epicenter of modernist experimentation, the writers could so easily have met—yet there is no evidence to suggest that they did so. In a letter of 23 May 1920, to her close friend, the art historian Bernard Berenson (who would later befriend Hemingway), Wharton described Paris as "a kind of continuous earthquake . . . with hundreds of thousands of U.S. citizens rushing about" (Lewis and Lewis 432). Gertrude Stein, T. S. Eliot, Ezra Pound, Sherwood Anderson, F. Scott Fitzgerald, Djuna Barnes, John Dos Passos, and Hemingway himself were among the many drawn to Paris early in the new age. Wharton, a generation or more older than most of the figures and at the height of her commercial and critical success, kept her distance. In "The Salons of Wharton's Fiction," Robert A. Martin and Linda Wagner-Martin suggest, "If young American writers could have gotten entry to Wharton, they would have flocked to her as rapidly as they did to the salons of Natalie Barney, Mabel Dodge, or Gertrude Stein. Getting to Mrs. Wharton was much more difficult." Martin and Wagner-Martin conclude "Hemingway would have been sitting at Wharton's feet, had he had the opportunity" (104). No such opportunity was forthcoming.

Though born almost forty years apart—Wharton during the American Civil War, Hemingway on the eve of a new millennium—the lives and careers of both writers were significantly shaped by their experiences of the First World War. For many young male modernists, war experience/injury was a hard-won badge of legitimacy; lack of it a lifelong marker of regret, even shame. The teenage Hemingway, volunteer ambulance driver with the American Red Cross, was wounded by Austrian mortar fire on the Italian front in the summer of 1918, an immersion a woman in her fifties would never share (though Wharton made five trips to the front in 1915 as part of her relief work). Her involvement was, nevertheless, full-blooded, far-reaching, and authentic. She founded hostels for fleeing refugees, workshops employing women who had been put out of work by the war, and convalescent homes for soldiers with tuberculosis, and she engaged in industrial-scale fund-raising, with "Mrs. Wharton's Charities" becoming the most diverse and second largest private charitable endeavor in wartime France (Benstock, *No Gifts* 313). In April 1917, the *New York Sun* introduced Wharton's special dispatch "In the Land of Death" with the line "No woman, probably no man not engaged in military service, has seen so much of the war" ("Edith Wharton Tells of German Trail of Ruin").

Tyler directs the volume to two fascinating sites of engagement: modernism and gender. Hemingway's work is renowned for, even defined by the former, yet his exploration of gender, particularly modern gender roles—while at times deflected by charges of machismo—can be equally profound. The opening of *The Sun Also Rises* offers one of the most remarkable, camouflaged meditations on early twentieth-century gender roles, and ensuing anxieties, in modern American literature. An entire, hidden narrative is disclosed by a passive rather than an active verb, or an unusual choice of preposition. Robert Cohn, we learn, "was married by the first girl who was nice to him," before being "taken in hand" by the "very forceful" Frances—the deliciously uncomfortable combination of passive object and awkward preposition speaking volumes about both the reticent Jake Barnes and newly contested gender roles. Wharton, meanwhile, is acknowledged for creating a remarkable cast of female characters, yet her male protagonists are often still sidelined in discussions. One early reviewer infamously highlighted her men only to label them "subtle and complex ladies wearing mustaches," wondering "whether the fault is with Mrs. Wharton's power of characterization, or in the material that she has for study" ("Mrs. Wharton's Nativity" 435–36). Yet Wharton was superb at exploring contested sites of "acceptable" behavior for both sexes, the straitjackets confining both women *and* men, often exposing the performativity of gender, while highlighting the double standards that defined women's lives in a world where women are judged and where appearance is all.

Both writers would fall victim to a certain posturing and mythologized self-image. Wharton struggled to escape the grande dame mantle. She came to loathe it, even while actively encouraging it, writing to Fitzgerald on 8 June 1925 that to his generation she "must represent the literary equivalent of tufted furniture and gas chandeliers" (Lewis and Lewis 481). Tyler charts Hemingway and his contemporaries' disparagement of Wharton, even as his library shelves told a clearer story. Both were writers of exquisite, polished prose—Hemingway confirming in *A Moveable Feast* that it often took a full morning's work to write a paragraph—but Wharton dismissed with venom any suggestion that he was "evolving" a new language. The timing was unfortunate. Younger modernist writers were an easy target for

Wharton—and vice versa. She felt threatened, her status challenged. The 1920s, when Hemingway's career was taking off, was Wharton's most successful decade, yet also her most vulnerable—a time when critics began to see her as a literary anachronism, a woman out of touch with the time. In her private correspondence, Wharton went full throttle. The writer made her now infamous comments about *Ulysses* to Berenson in a 6 January 1923 letter: "It's a turgid welter of pornography (the rudest schoolboy kind) & unformed & unimportant drivel; & until the raw ingredients of a pudding *make* a pudding, I shall never believe that the raw material of sensation & thought can make a work of art without the cook's intervening." In a swift all-encompassing broadside, she clobbered another: "The same applies to Eliot" (Lewis and Lewis 461). And so it continued: Faulkner's *Sanctuary* made her want to respond with an article "Wuthering Depths" (Lee 620), while Fitzgerald's *Tender Is the Night* appeared to deal "entirely with drunkards and drug-fiends" (letter to Edward Sheldon, 21 March 1934, qtd. in Benstock, "Landscapes of Desire" 41). Running alongside these pantomime performances, however, and as scholars such as Jennifer Haytock have noted, this was also a writer who read and appreciated Yeats, Gide, Huxley, Colette, Rilke, and Cocteau, among many others—a reading list suggesting a much more nuanced response to the age. (There are no works by Hemingway in Wharton's surviving library, nor by Fitzgerald, Stein, or Eliot—though there are two volumes by Joyce: *A Portrait of the Artist as a Young Man* and a first edition of the offending *Ulysses*, one of 750 copies on handmade paper, previously owned by her beloved friend Walter Berry [Ramsden 67]).

Hemingway could be equally, and publicly, damning, as witnessed in his Sherwood Anderson–bashing *The Torrents of Spring* (1926). In *A Moveable Feast* (1964), he looked back on his early years in Paris, when many of the cast of characters were long gone—both rivals and those who had been hugely helpful and instrumental in his career. Fitzgerald was presented as a man worried that he literally did not measure up; Zelda Fitzgerald as the crazy, jealous wife convinced that Al Jolson was greater than Jesus, alongside a somewhat sniffy depiction of Stein; while Wyndham Lewis was defined by the eyes "of an unsuccessful rapist." Both writers would pen memoirs, both proving masters of omission, gaps, and evasion, and the settling of real or imagined scores. In *A Backward Glance* (1934), Wharton herself often appeared curiously absent. The most valuable sections of both memoirs are those focused on their writing processes—Hemingway's determination to break down all his writing, to get rid of all facility, and try to make instead of describe, and Wharton's chapter "The Secret Garden" in which she opens up about the genesis of her ideas and her working practices, while complaining that 1930s critics deemed "only the man with the dinner pail" worthy of attention (206).

Omission in the work of both writers is a tangible presence. Hemingway is renowned for minimalism; Wharton is not. Edmund Wilson once wrote of her adopting "the practice of inventorying the contents of her characters' homes," yet the writer he calls the poet of interior decoration can also prove extraordinarily minimalist (Wilson 22, 23). In Wharton's hieroglyphic world, a "deaf-and-dumb asylum" as Newland Archer's son Dallas terms it in *The Age of Innocence,* a realm in which social rituals and behavior codes are prevalent, it is the gaps, the silences, that are often amplified the loudest on her page. And Wharton too engaged in modernism. She would never condone, let alone embrace its full experimentalism—and indeed Tyler's volume rightly points to Wharton's satire in the Vance Weston novels. Yet modernism was never a one size fits all. Look closely and what we would readily signal as modernism in any other writer is on display from the beginning of Wharton's career. An early, abandoned narrative, *Disintegration,* notably plays with multiple points of view, at times contradictory; in *The House of Mirth,* as Lily Bart's life spirals out of control, the narrative structure begins to unfurl, form enhancing theme as Lily falls through the social strata towards the "rubbish heap." *The Custom of the Country* is a remarkably disorienting narrative, where the narrator often denies the reader an assured vantage point on the text, while *Ethan Frome* leaves narrative veracity dangling by a very tenuous thread.

Neither are the writers' topics as divergent as one might expect. Certainly Wharton explored high society, privilege and affluence, but also prostitution, abortion, euthanasia, and incest, and much more of her work than she is credited for deals with lives lived lower down the social scale. "I was once called, you know, a 'revolutionary writer,'" Wharton suggested to a journalist the year before her death: "Critics then talked about my 'audacious treatment of unpleasant themes'" ("Edith Wharton in Profile"). And both writers were obsessed with money in their fiction. Transactions of many kinds pervade the page: a monetary exchange, an invitation, a trading of a title, a dinner investment, sex as a form of economic exchange whether as a prostitute on the streets of Paris or a young lady on the marriage market in the drawing rooms of New York society; money and attitudes to money mark character exposition as much as status. And both writers can prove remarkably open-ended in their "conclusions." Hemingway famously punctuates the final line of *The Sun Also Rises* with a question mark: "Isn't it pretty to think so?" Similarly Wharton refuses to shut down the end of *Ethan Frome*, or permit the characters a merciful release, whereas *The Custom of the Country* leaves the indefatigable Undine Spragg musing over the future role for which she was really made.

At times there can be a reluctance to offer comparative studies of male and female modernists. Stein, as so often, can prove an exception, but male modernists are more likely to be paired. We have seen multiple comparative studies of Hemingway and Fitzgerald—though in 2007 Faith Pullin offered a rare counter-proposition that Fitzgerald's narrative concerns "in fact align him more closely with female modernists of the period" (177). With this volume Tyler and her contributors offer exciting new avenues of exploration. Like her subjects, she wisely resists convenient closure. The collection opens up and continues dialogue, Tyler's introduction suggesting arenas for further research. In a letter to Charles Scribner on 10 December 1923, Wharton countered: "I do not write 'jazz-books' and never expected to be a best-seller. . . . I believe my books have a certain staying power which . . . I would far rather think they possess than the qualities requisite at present for a sensational sale" (qtd. in Lee 606). Both Hemingway and Wharton have proved their exceptional "staying power," and this collection offers welcome new comparative ways of looking at careers Wharton aptly labeled in her reminiscences "Adventures with Books."

—LAURA RATTRAY

WORKS CITED

Benstock, Shari. "Landscapes of Desire: Edith Wharton and Europe." *Wretched Exotic: Essays on Edith Wharton in Europe*. Ed. Katherine Joslin and Alan Price. New York: Peter Lang, 1993. 19–42. Print.

———. *No Gifts from Chance: A Biography of Edith Wharton*. London: Hamish Hamilton, 1994. Print.

"Edith Wharton in Profile." *New York Herald Tribune*, Paris ed. 16 Nov. 1936. Print.

"Edith Wharton Tells of German Trail of Ruin." *New York Sun*. 6 Apr. 1917. Print.

Lee, Hermione. *Edith Wharton*. New York: Knopf, 2007. Print.

Lewis, R. W. B., and Nancy Lewis, eds. *The Letters of Edith Wharton*. New York: Collier Books, 1989. Print.

Martin, Robert A., and Linda Wagner-Martin. "The Salons of Wharton's Fiction." *Wretched Exotic: Essays on Edith Wharton in Europe*. Ed. Katherine Joslin and Alan Price. New York: Peter Lang, 1993. 97–110. Print.

"Mrs. Wharton's Nativity: The Clever and Subtle Disciple of Henry James a Native of the American Metropolis." *Munsey's Magazine* 25 (June 1901): 435–36. Rpt. in *Edith Wharton: The Contemporary Reviews*. Ed. James W. Tutteton, Kristin O. Lauer, and Margaret P. Murray. Cambridge: Cambridge UP, 1992. 43. Print.

Pullin, Faith. "Gender Anxiety: The Unresolved Dialectic of Fitzgerald's Writing." *Twenty-First-Century Readings of "Tender Is the Night."* Ed. William Blazek and Laura Rattray. Liverpool: Liverpool UP. 2007. 177–91. Print.

Ramsden, George, comp. *Edith Wharton's Library: A Catalogue*. Settrington, York: Stone Trough Books, 1999. Print.

Wharton, Edith. *A Backward Glance*. New York: Appleton-Century, 1934. Print.

Wilson, Edmund. "Justice to Edith Wharton." *Edith Wharton: A Collection of Critical Essays*. Ed. Irving Howe. Englewood Cliffs, NJ: Prentice Hall, 1962. 19–31. Print.

ACKNOWLEDGMENTS

I am profoundly grateful to all of the people who said yes to this project along the way: Hilary Justice, Laura Rattray, and Gail Sinclair, who all agreed to participate in a Hemingway-Wharton roundtable at the International Hemingway Society in Venice in June 2014; Mark Cirino and Mark Ott, co–program directors of that conference, who quickly accepted our proposed roundtable for the program and gave us a coveted midday time slot; Parley Ann Boswell, Dustin Faulstick, Jennifer Haytock, Cecilia Macheski, Noreen O'Connor, and Milena Radeva-Costello, who joined me in two different panels at the Wharton in Washington conference in June 2016; Wharton in Washington conference codirectors Melanie Dawson and Jennifer Haytock, who gave us two full panels in gorgeously lovely rooms; and Susan F. Beegel and Linda Wagner-Martin, wise mentors who advised and encouraged me (and talked me down from ledges).

Thanks to Margaret Lovecraft and James W. Long, acquisitions editors for Louisiana State University Press, for their patience and professionalism in shepherding this book through the review process. I am also grateful to the Press's anonymous reviewer for insightful recommendations that improved the final work.

Finally I would like to thank Jim Tyler, who has always encouraged me and has made my life better in so many ways, and Rose Tyler, who keeps me grounded and gives me joy.

WHARTON, HEMINGWAY, *and the* ADVENT OF MODERNISM

Introduction

LISA TYLER

Although they never met, Edith Wharton and Ernest Hemingway had a great deal in common. Both lived as expatriates in Paris. Both wrote in an astonishingly wide range of genres, including novels, short fiction, poetry, drama, travel writing, and magazine journalism, and they shared a publisher, Scribner's. Both spent time in Italy and Africa—the latter at a time when relatively few Americans traveled there—and wrote about those experiences in their fiction and nonfiction. Both volunteered for humanitarian medical work during World War I. Both wrote critically acclaimed literary novels that became best sellers, and both won the Pulitzer Prize. Wharton and Hemingway are now routinely taught in high-school and college courses, and their short stories are widely anthologized.

Notably, Wharton and Hemingway had several mutual acquaintances. Hemingway's close friend F. Scott Fitzgerald sent Wharton a copy of *The Great Gatsby,* and Wharton, who liked the novel, invited Fitzgerald to her home, Pavillon Colombe. Drunk and nervous, he related a lewd anecdote about a bordello, and Wharton asked for more information (Bruccoli 231). She later summarized the awkward visit in her diary: "To tea, Teddy Chanler and Scott Fitzgerald, the novelist. Horrible" (Lewis and Lewis 481–82).[1] Louis Bromfield, who most likely met Hemingway in 1925 (Hemingway, *Letters* 2: 428), was close enough to Hemingway to read *Torrents of Spring* before publication (*Letters* 2: 434); Bromfield later met Wharton, probably in 1931 (Bratton xiii n1), and became such a trusted friend that she wrote him asking for advice on how to handle a problem with a magazine editor (Loesch 47).

But perhaps the most startling connection between the two writers is Harry Crosby, the cousin (actually, the first cousin once removed) of Walter Van Rensselaer Berry, Wharton's literary mentor. After Walter Berry's death, Wharton called Berry "The Love of all my life" in her diary (qtd. in Lee 655). Crosby first met Wharton on 17 June 1926 when he and his wife, Polly (who later renamed herself Caresse), had tea at Berry's home in Paris (Wolff 124). Harry and Caresse met Hemingway skiing at Gstaad in December 1926 (Hemingway, *Letters* 3: 561; Wolff 319), and he and Hemingway "were together for the running of the bulls in Pamplona in July, 1927" (Wolff 182). Ernest introduced Harry to James Joyce in 1928 (Mellow 351). In October 1929, Harry went to the races at Auteuil with Ernest and his wife Pauline (Wolff 151). Berry must have thought highly of his protégé, for he named Crosby his residual legatee in his will. After Berry's death on 12 October 1927, Wharton asked for his cremated ashes, and Crosby delivered them to her door, followed closely by the French police, officiously eager to make sure the ashes were not scattered but buried in accordance with national law (Wolff 129). Conflicting codicils to Berry's will resulted in Wharton and Crosby quarreling over who should inherit his books; Wharton took seventy-three books or sets of books, and Crosby took the remaining eight thousand or so—only to turn around and give them away randomly, often to complete strangers (Wolff 131–32). After Berry's death, Wharton wrote a friend, "Walter's young cousin Crosby turns out to be a sort of half-crazy cad" (qtd. in Wolff 131). While perhaps uncharitable, Wharton's comment turned out to be amazingly accurate; after a long history of substance abuse and mental instability, Crosby shot himself and his lover on 10 December 1929 in a murder-suicide that resulted in lurid international newspaper coverage. Hemingway wrote a letter to Fitzgerald after learning the news, asking Scott if he had known Crosby: "He was a hell of a good boy and I feel awfully bad today about him" (Hemingway, *Selected Letters* 314).

Other, presumably less terrifying mutual acquaintances included Sinclair Lewis and Bernard Berenson. There is at least a suggestion that Wharton and Hemingway might have had one more direct point of contact. Adeline Tintner speculates that Wharton might have written Hemingway to send him a copy of Vivienne de Watteville's 1935 memoir, *Speak to the Earth: Wanderings and Reflections among Elephants and Mountains*, in hopes that he might review it: "Wharton, knowing that Hemingway's *Green Hills of Africa* had appeared in 1934 with its theme of East African safaris, may well have decided the book would interest him at the same time she would be promoting a book by a young writer she admired and with whom she had worked closely" (Tintner 136). Hemingway did own a copy of *Speak to the Earth* and from it selected an epigraph—later omitted before publication, apparently on the advice of editor Arnold Gingrich (Baker 617–19)—to the manuscript of his short story "The Snows of Kilimanjaro," first published in *Esquire* in 1936 (Brasch and Sigman 125; Tintner 134).

Given their large number of mutual acquaintances, the fact that they never met can almost certainly be attributed to a deliberate choice on Wharton's part, for in the 1920s the opportunistic young Ernest willingly met with anyone he thought might be able to further his career. Hemingway was part of Gertrude Stein's literary circle; Robert Martin and Linda Wagner-Martin speculate that Stein's identity as a lesbian and a Jew might have deterred Wharton from wishing to make her acquaintance.

Hemingway was nevertheless familiar with Edith Wharton's writings from an early age. His sister Marcelline recalls in her memoir that *Scribner's* was among the magazines "we grabbed the minute they arrived" (Sanford 134). From 1910 to 1920, when Hemingway would have been eleven to twenty years old, *Scribner's Magazine* serialized Wharton's novels *Ethan Frome, The Custom of the Country,* and *The Bunner Sisters* and her nonfiction book *In Morocco.* During that time the magazine also published more than half a dozen of her nonfiction articles about France as well as her short stories "The Legend," "The Eyes," "Xingu," "Pomegranate Seed," "The Triumph of Night," and "Kerfol."

Hemingway's 1955 inventory of his library at Key West included three Wharton novels—*The Age of Innocence, The House of Mirth,* and *Ethan Frome*—and her memoir *A Backward Glance,* a volume that both his correspondence with Maxwell Perkins and a publisher's bill at Scribner's confirm he ordered personally (Reynolds, *Hemingway's Reading* 200). All four books were present in his library at Finca Vigía, his home in Cuba, along with two additions: *The Best Short Stories of Edith Wharton* and *French Ways and Their Meaning* (Brasch and Sigman 373). He owned more books by Wharton than he did by Sherwood Anderson, Joseph Conrad, Herman Melville, or Theodore Roosevelt, all of whom have been recognized by Hemingway scholars as important influences upon his work.[2]

It is perhaps not coincidental that for the title of his first novel, *The Sun*

Also Rises, he turned to the same book of the Bible—Ecclesiastes—from which Wharton chose her title *The House of Mirth* (Ecclesiastes 1:5 and 7:4, respectively). Indirect evidence suggests that Hemingway thought highly enough of Wharton to disparage her, always the highest compliment Ernest could pay to a worthy contemporary writer. In "The Friend of Spain: A Spanish Letter" (published in *Esquire* in 1934), in what some might consider a catty aside, Hemingway writes:

> My old friend had written an article entitled Mister Hemingway, Friend of Spain. Now when you become known as A Friend of France it usually means that you are dead, the French would not commit themselves that far if you were alive, and that you have either spent much money for France, obtained much money for France, or simply sucked after certain people long enough to get the Legion of Honor. In the last case they call you a Friend of France in much smaller type. (Hemingway, *By-Line* 126)

This nasty and otherwise gratuitous comment seems like a clever roundabout way to insult Wharton, who in March 1916 had been made a Chevalier of the Legion of Honor—the highest order bestowed by the French government—for her tireless efforts on behalf of French and Belgian refugees (Lewis 386; Price 205–6n51). Ironically, one of her signal accomplishments was raising $100,000 to fund ambulances for the French Red Cross (Lewis 385)—and it was as an ambulance driver for the American Red Cross that Hemingway was injured in Italy in 1918.[3]

Wharton might have been part of the reason Hemingway was so eager to have the prestigious Scribner's as his publisher that he deliberately sabotaged his relationship with Boni and Liveright by parodying its star author, Sherwood Anderson, in *Torrents of Spring.* Yet Hemingway later hesitated when offered $3,000 to serialize *A Farewell to Arms* in *Scribner's Magazine.* Maxwell Perkins responded by hiking his offer to $10,000—"the going rate that Scribner's paid Edith Wharton . . . for serialization. In the end, Hemingway received $16,000" (Mellow 364–650). There is at least a suggestion that he regarded Wharton as the standard of literary success to which he aspired.

During the 1920s, which one biographer termed her "Age of Acclaim"

(Benstock, *No Gifts* 385), Wharton was arguably the most distinguished American writer in the world. She was certainly astonishingly productive: From 1920 through 1930, she published seven novels, two short-story collections, four novellas, a travel book, a book on writing fiction, and a volume of poetry (469). She became the first woman to win a Pulitzer Prize when she received the honor in 1921 for her novel *The Age of Innocence.* In 1923 she became the first woman to be awarded an honorary doctorate of letters by Yale University (381). In January 1925, the National Institute of Arts and Letters awarded her its gold medal in literature (385–86). She was also nominated for the Nobel Prize for Literature in 1927, although Henri Bergson received the prize that year (386).

No wonder, then, that "Wharton was an easy target of modernist irony—and jealousy," as Shari Benstock suggests ("Landscapes" 32). Kristin Olson Lauer further contends that the modernists' animosity toward Wharton had resulted from her attitude regarding World War I, which Wharton saw as a conflict between German barbarians and French civilization: "To see the war in terms of the salvation of French culture was, in the twenties, to be old-fashioned, even reactionary" (Lauer 88). Hemingway contemporary Kay Boyle recalled—in her 1984 afterword to Robert McAlmon's *Being Geniuses Together, 1920–1930*—the rallying cry of the expatriate writers in 1920s Paris: "Down with Henry James! Down with Edith Wharton! Down with the sterility of 'The Wasteland!'" (336). As Boyle explains, "There was no grandly experimental, furiously disrespectful school of writing in America, and we were going to create it" (336).[4] The Lost Generation expatriates therefore rebelled against Wharton and everything she represented. In his memoir, *That Summer in Paris: Memories of Tangled Friendships with Hemingway, Fitzgerald, and Some Others*, Canadian author Morley Callaghan recalls categorizing Wharton with "popular writers of the day" like James Branch Cabell, Hugh Walpole, and H. G. Wells as "showoff writers; writers intent on proving to their readers that they could be clever and had some education" (15). Fitzgerald mocked Wharton's fiction (as well as that of other well-known American writers) in a humorous sketch in *Vanity Fair* in December 1920 (Bruccoli and Bryer 227–30). Hemingway's friend Donald Ogden Stewart (one of two men—along with Bill Smith—that Ernest used in creating the composite character Bill Gorton in *The Sun Also Rises*) wittily parodied Wharton's work in "Custer's Last Stand in the Manner of Edith Wharton," chapter 8 of his 1921 book *A Parody Outline of History* (181–89).

The disrespect was mutual. Wharton was never anything but disparaging about Hemingway in her private writings, as a comment from a letter to Sinclair Lewis makes clear: "I hope your Americans in Europe . . . will really be in Europe and not in little continental Americas like the café du Dôme and kindred haunts. Do let them forget America for a while and become aware of Europe, for current fiction has had too many of the other kind lately, and it would be an exciting change to have [a] young American in Paris become even faintly aware that he was not in Broadway" (qtd. in Lee 625).[5] In an unpublished 1930 letter to Bernard Berenson, Wharton wrote, "Have you read the ridiculous article in 'Life & Letters,' saying that Americans should no longer write English, & that Hemingway is evolving a new language for our use? Such drivel makes me despair."[6]

She was even harsher in a letter she wrote to Minnie Cadwalader Jones, her sister-in-law, on 2 November 1934: "What a country! With Faulkner & Hemingway acclaimed as the greatest American novelists, & magazine editors still taking the view they did when I began to write! Brains & culture seem non-existent from one end of the social scale to the other, & half the morons yell for filth, & the other half continue to put pants on the piano legs" (qtd. in Bauer 33). Hemingway was evidently one of the cultureless morons clamoring for filth, in Wharton's estimation.

Mary Suzanne Schriber suggests Wharton satirized American novelists of the 1920s broadly and Hemingway specifically in two related novels, *Hudson River Bracketed* (1929) and *The Gods Arrive* (1932): "Perhaps quite significantly, Wharton sets Vance Weston to writing a novel set in Spain, reminiscent of Hemingway, and she includes in *The Gods Arrive* two minor characters, Jane and Kate, who operate a bookstore in Paris that brings to mind Shakespeare and Company, Sylvia Beach, and perhaps Gertrude Stein and Alice B. Toklas" (179).

But there is much more substantial evidence than that to support the case for Wharton's satirizing Hemingway in *Hudson River Bracketed* and its sequel, *The Gods Arrive*.[7] Like Hemingway, Vance Weston is from small-town Illinois. He has "a passionate taste" for "a rough life in the open" (Wharton, *Hudson* 43) and much later in that novel goes "on a long tramp, to a wonderful swampy wood" that recalls the swamp of Hemingway's short story "Big Two-Hearted River" (*Hudson* 513). Like Jake Barnes in *The Sun Also Rises,* Vance later enjoys trout fishing with his friends (Hemingway, *The Sun Also Rises* 112–25; Wharton, *The Gods Arrive* 79).

Vance Weston rapidly becomes "the literary hero of the hour" (*Hudson* 384). He frequents the literary cafés in Montparnasse and has a flat near the Luxembourg Gardens (*The Gods Arrive* 74, 73). Like Hemingway, Vance Weston briefly contemplates suicide (30–31). Wharton writes, "He liked the idea of a heroine who could be called *Pilar*" (*The Gods Arrive* 64). "Pilar" was Hemingway's nickname for Pauline Pfeiffer during their 1926–27 affair and was to have been the name of their daughter, if they had had one. Much later, in 1934, Hemingway used the name for his fishing boat, and he eventually used the name for an important character in *For Whom the Bell Tolls* (Reynolds, *The 1930s* 169). Wharton even refers to the sentimental painting of Christ known as *The Light of the World,* which gave Hemingway the title for one of his short stories (*Hudson* 196).

Halo Spear, who leaves her husband for Vance, worries that she is only "a peg to hang a book on" (*The Gods Arrive*), and Hemingway has often been criticized for needing a new wife for each novel, a theory first propounded by Fitzgerald (Callaghan 157; see Clancy Sigal's discussion of the "helpmate" syndrome [84] for a recent example). Halo also observes that "by pouring his suffering into a story he had been able to cleanse his soul of it" (*The Gods Arrive* 323), anticipating the later claim by Hemingway's semi-autobiographical protagonist Nick Adams that "If he wrote it he could get rid of it. He had gotten rid of many things by writing them" (*Complete Short Stories* 371). Halo is later concerned about Vance's drinking (*The Gods Arrive* 332), and Hemingway's alcoholism is widely known.

Although Vance initially aspires to become a journalist and poet (*Hudson* 25), he instead elects to write autobiographical fiction about his own experiences: "He would set them down just as they had befallen him in all their cruel veracity, but as if he were relating the tragedy of someone else" (32). He writes "blunt prose, almost telegraphic in its harsh directness" (194). Wharton describes her protagonist as "hard-boiled" (200) and given to thinking "big manly thoughts" (21). In what certainly sounds like an acerbic dismissal of the vaunted Hemingway style, Wharton notes of her protagonist, "He was quick at picking up tricks of language and technique," particularly "brilliant verbal gymnastics—or the staccato enumeration of a series of physical aspects and situations" (335).

Yet very little attention has been paid to the aesthetic connections between these two American authors. There are presently no comparative collections or monographs on Hemingway and Wharton. By comparison, there are at least eight works on Hemingway and Fitzgerald and nine on Hemingway and Faulkner (who have considerably less in common). Only a handful of articles linking Wharton and Hemingway have been published, most notably those by Adeline Tintner and Linda Wagner-Martin (the latter is a contributor to this collection). *Wharton, Hemingway, and the Advent of Modernism* begins to remedy that deficit.

The first section of this collection, "Wharton, Hemingway, and the Modernist Canon," offers opposing perspectives on Wharton's relationship to the modernist canon. Peter Hays identifies in Wharton's *Ethan Frome* modernist characteristics that a younger generation of writers are usually credited with initiating and argues that Wharton was herself a modernist writer. Ellen Andrews Knodt proposes Wharton's *The House of Mirth* as a transitional work between nineteenth-century realism and the twentieth-century modernism of Hemingway, F. Scott Fitzgerald, and William Faulkner.

In the second section, "The Great War," two scholars offer perspectives on the war that traditionally marks the advent of modernism. Arguing that the injured tend to disappear from war stories, Jennifer Haytock analyzes the presentation of the injured in the short fiction of Wharton and Hemingway, encompassing not only the physical wounds sustained on the battlefield but also the psychic injuries of shell shock and rape. She contends that the medical system restricted the agency of its injured patients as much as the military restricted the agency of individual soldiers.

Milena Radeva-Costello examines in Wharton's and Hemingway's war fiction the idea of the gift, as theorized by Jacques Derrida. For Wharton, wartime philanthropy enables her women characters to take on liberatory public roles that would otherwise be unavailable to them and thus transform their lives. For Hemingway, however, the trauma and abjection associated with death as the ultimate gift, one that (as Derrida reminds us) can neither be given nor taken away, open up the possibility for identification with the other.

In "Geographies," the third section, Cecilia Macheski documents both authors' undisputed love of Italy and their enthusiastic appreciation of its beauty. Drawing on their fiction and nonfiction, she argues that they critique modern tourism while condemning the fascism that makes Italy a contested landscape and threatens what they most love about the country. Sirpa Salenius explores how Wharton and Hemingway use space as a literary device in the novella "False Dawn" and the short story "A Very Short Story," respectively, contrasting men's experiences with passion and mobility in the liberating spaces of Italy with their defeat and decline in the repressive and claustrophobic enclosures of their native United States.

The fourth section, "Gender and Modernity," includes discussions of gender roles, literary tropes, and transportation technologies. Comparing Anna Leath of *The Reef* with Brett Ashley of *The Sun Also Rises*, Linda Wagner-Martin argues that Wharton portrayed the sexually free "New Woman" much more effectively than Hemingway did. In my own article in this collection, I argue that the tropes of architecture and interior decoration function in Wharton's and Hemingway's writings as a site of contested gender politics in the creation of literary modernism.

In her travel memoir *A Motor-Flight through France*, Wharton writes of the automobile as a vehicle that offers women agency and opportunities for adventure, exploration, and discovery, Anna Green contends. In contrast, Green notes that Hemingway, who prefers walking the streets of Paris as an urban flâneur, writes in his own memoir of the automobile's tendency to strip away human agency, especially masculine agency. Green suggests that both writers use the travel memoir to negotiate gender politics, the opportunities and psychic costs of evolving transportation technologies, and even changing modes of aesthetic perceptions.

In the fifth and final section, three essays address intertextualities with respect to the Bible, *Scribner's Magazine*, and film. Both *The House of Mirth* and *The Sun Also Rises* take their titles from the biblical book of Ecclesiastes, and Dustin Faulstick explores how both Wharton and Hemingway draw on the joy and skepticism of Ecclesiastes to define the good life and critique modern society. He aptly notes, "Both Wharton and Hemingway were fascinated by religion, but wanted a more demanding, complex, and realistic experience than the religion offered to them in childhood."

Caroline Chamberlin Hellman contrasts the ways in which *Scribner's* presented the serialized versions of Wharton's *A Son at the Front* and Hemingway's *A Farewell to Arms* just seven years apart in the 1920s: "Reading these works in their original contexts illustrates shifts in both readership and literary culture, in addition to the evolving role that *Scribner's* played, first as a protector of cultural conservatism and later as a simultaneous guardian of genteel tradition and purveyor of modernism."

In the final essay, Parley Ann Boswell traces a literary and cinematic tradition of *noir* from Wharton, who she argues anticipates *noir*, through Hemingway, two of whose works became classic *noir* films, to Patricia Highsmith, "the most articulate and elegant of the mid-century *noir* writers." She argues that all three of these master storytellers push readers to recognize that "the lines between victim and victimizer, right and wrong, good and evil, are constantly shifting."

Together, these essays prove conclusively that comparative study of the works of Wharton and Hemingway helps us better understand not just the two authors' writings but also the transition from realism to modernism, the ways in which that transition was inflected by gender, and the relationships between modernist texts and modernist and postmodernist culture.

Although this collection begins the work of examining the aesthetic connections between these two canonical twentieth-century American authors, much work remains to be done. Areas deserving attention include Wharton's and Hemingway's memoirs (which elide as much as they reveal), both writers' inadvertent involvement with the byzantine politics of the Pulitzer Prize, and their very different visions of modern masculinity. Given their long writing careers, it would be interesting to examine their bleak views about aging as reflected in such fiction as Wharton's "Mrs. Manstey's View" and Hemingway's "A Clean, Well-Lighted Place." The two novelists' casual anti-Semitism and their disparaged and sometimes stereotypical Jewish characters (most notably, Simon Rosedale and Robert Cohn) certainly deserve further scrutiny. Their mutual love of Spain and their fascination with Santiago de Compostela merit attention, as do their writings about their travels in colonial Africa. With these dozen essays, the contributors and I are together launching a lively, thought-provoking conversation that we hope our readers will help us continue.

NOTES

1. Matthew J. Bruccoli (231) debunks the amusing (but probably entirely apocryphal) story that, after the encounter with Wharton, Fitzgerald "put his head on his arms and began to pound the table with his fists," crying, "They beat me. They beat me. They *beat* me!" (Mizener 185).

There is also a possibly apocryphal story that Fitzgerald first met Wharton at Charles Scribner's office and fell to his knees before her in a dramatic gesture of obeisance, exclaiming, "Could I let the author of *Ethan Frome* pass through New York without paying my respects?" (Bruccoli 229). Ironically, although uncredited, Fitzgerald had contributed to the script of the 1923 silent-film version of Wharton's novel *Glimpses of the Moon* (Lee 594–95).

Robert A. Martin and Linda Wagner-Martin have argued that literary history and comparative textual analysis prove that the real nature of the relationship between Wharton and Fitzgerald was much more complicated and richer than the anecdote about their unsuccessful tea together might suggest.

2. For a discussion of Sherwood Anderson's influence on Hemingway, see "Hemingway v. Anderson: The Final Rounds," by Judy Jo Small and Michael Reynolds. See "Conrad and Hemingway," by Peter L. Hays (misspelled "Hayes" in the journal), and "Conrad's Influence on Modern Writers," by Jeffrey Meyers, on Conrad's influence. See Nathaniel Philbrick and Albert Gerard for discussions of Melville's influence on Hemingway; see also "Hemingway's Bartlebys" by Peter Hays for a discussion of the two writers' intertextualities. Suzanne Clark and Edward Whitley both discuss Roosevelt's influence on Hemingway.

3. Alan Price notes that the American Red Cross "became the official designated charity of the United States government and the specified relief agency of the American Expeditionary Force" (158). Initially welcoming, Wharton later turned against the American Red Cross because of its high-handedness and cultural insensitivity: "The Red Cross has been & is still—a perfect night-mare to me! I am sick to think of the mischief they have done, & the impression they are giving everywhere of incompetence and arrogance combined" (qtd. in Price 137). She was particularly bitter about what she saw as the Red Cross's mishandling of the charity she had founded: "The extent to which our organization has broken down since the Red Cross have taken it in hand is so humiliating and heart-breaking to me, and I receive such daily evidence of neglect and indifference, and of complete misunderstanding of the moral problem to be dealt with, that I do not wish to have my name associated with any work run on such principles" (qtd. in Price 142). For detailed information on Hemingway's involvement with the Red Cross, see Stephen Florczyk.

4. Robert McAlmon was a bit more charitable in his memoir, writing, "Edith Wharton's *Ethan Frome* is worth more than all [Sinclair] Lewis has written" (33).

5. Wharton had a valid point. The expatriates did not assimilate well: "When William Carlos Williams asked Robert McAlmon, who was at the dead center of life in the American village of Montparnasse, to introduce him to some French poets, McAlmon could not,

because after years in Paris he knew none. Fitzgerald never learned French; Hemingway learned it, but preferred the speech and company of Americans" (Wolff 116).

Hemingway's French was profoundly limited, as Roger Asselineau pointedly explains:

> Hemingway used to boast of his linguistic ability. Indeed, he felt at home in France, as well as in Spain and Italy, but all he knew was restaurant French. He could talk with waiters and concierges, but he was unable to sustain a real conversation or exchange ideas with another writer. Ramon Guthrie, who taught French at Dartmouth and published some excellent collections of poems, told me that he once called on the French poet Robert Desnos in the company of Hemingway. Jean-Louis Barrault was there, too, and they discussed Stendhal with Desnos, but Hemingway could not join in. He had to keep silent. On the contrary, Edith Wharton . . . could write to André Gide on equal terms and be friends with [major French novelist] Paul Bourget. . . . she was thus perfectly integrated in French literary life and regarded as a *confrère* by all the French writers she met. (Asselineau 358)

Even had Wharton chosen to invite Hemingway to join her literary coterie, his French language skills were so weak he would not have been able to participate.

6. I am grateful to Wharton scholar Laura Rattray for drawing my attention to this comment.

7. Although *Hudson River Bracketed* and *The Gods Arrive* are not generally reckoned among Wharton's best work, it's interesting to note that Wharton herself said they were among her top five favorite novels she had written (qtd. in Haytock 160).

WORKS CITED

Asselineau, Roger. "Edith Wharton—She Thought in French and Wrote in English." *Wretched Exotic: Essays on Edith Wharton in Europe*. Ed. Katherine Joslin and Alan Price. New York: Peter Lang, 1993. 355–63. Print.

Baker, Carlos. *Ernest Hemingway: A Life Story*. New York: Scribner's, 1969. Print.

Bauer, Dale M. *Edith Wharton's Brave New Politics*. Madison: U of Wisconsin P, 1994. Print.

Benstock, Shari. "Landscapes of Desire: Edith Wharton and Europe." *Wretched Exotic: Essays on Edith Wharton in Europe*. Ed. Katherine Joslin and Alan Price. New York: Peter Lang, 1993. 19–42. Print.

———. *No Gifts from Chance: A Biography of Edith Wharton*. New York: Scribner's, 1994. Print.

Boyle, Kay. "Afterword." *Being Geniuses Together, 1920–1930*. Rev. ed. Ed. Kay Boyle. Baltimore: Johns Hopkins UP, 1984. Print.

Brasch, James D., and Joseph Sigman. *Hemingway's Library: A Composite Record.*

New York: Garland, 1981. John F. Kennedy Presidential Library. Web. Accessed 27 May 2015.

Bratton, Daniel, ed. *Yrs. Ever Affly: The Correspondence of Edith Wharton and Louis Bromfield.* East Lansing: Michigan State UP, 2000. Print.

Bruccoli, Matthew J. *Some Sort of Epic Grandeur: The Life of F. Scott Fitzgerald.* New York: Harcourt Brace and Jovanovich, 1981. Print.

Bruccoli, Matthew J., and Jackson R. Bryer, eds. *F. Scott Fitzgerald in His Own Time: A Miscellany.* New York: Popular Library, 1971. Print.

Callaghan, Morley. *That Summer in Paris: Memories of Tangled Friendships with Hemingway, Fitzgerald, and Some Others.* New York: Dell, 1963. Print.

Clark, Suzanne. "Roosevelt and Hemingway: Natural History, Manliness, and the Rhetoric of the Strenuous Life." *Hemingway and the Natural World.* Ed. Robert P. Fleming. Moscow: U of Idaho P, 1999. 55–67. Print.

Florczyk, Stephen. *Hemingway, the Red Cross, and the Great War.* Kent, OH: Kent State UP, 2014. Print.

Gerard, Albert. "Romanticism and Stoicism in the American Novel: From Melville to Hemingway, and After." Trans. Elaine P. Halperin. *Diogenes* 23 (1958): 95–110.

Hays, Peter L. "Conrad and Hemingway." *American Notes and Queries* 14 (1976): 87–88. Print.

———. "Hemingway's Bartlebys." *North Dakota Quarterly* 68.2–3 (Spring–Summer 2001): 85–90. Print. Rpt. in *Fifty Years of Hemingway Criticism.* Blue Ridge Summit, PA: Scarecrow P, 2013. 161–65. ProQuest. Web. 13 Jan. 2016.

Haytock, Jennifer. *Edith Wharton and the Conversation of Literary Modernism.* New York: Palgrave Macmillan, 2008. Print.

Hemingway, Ernest. *By-Line: Ernest Hemingway.* Ed. William White. New York: Bantam, 1967. Print.

———. *The Letters of Ernest Hemingway.* Vol. 2: *1923–1925.* Ed. Sandra Spanier, Albert J. DeFazio III, and Robert W. Trogdon. Cambridge: Cambridge UP, 2013. Print.

———. *The Letters of Ernest Hemingway,* Vol. 3: *1926–1929.* Ed. Rena Sanderson, Sandra Spanier, and Robert W. Trogdon. Cambridge: Cambridge UP, 2015. Print.

———. *The Sun Also Rises.* New York: Scribner's, 1926. Print.

———. *Ernest Hemingway: Selected Letters, 1917–1961.* Ed. Carlos Baker. New York: Scribner's, 1981. Print.

Lauer, Kristin Olson. "Can France Survive This Defender? Contemporary American Reaction to Wharton's Expatriation." *Wretched Exotic: Essays on Edith Wharton in Europe.* Ed. Katherine Joslin and Alan Price. New York: Peter Lang, 1993. 77–95. Print.

Lee, Hermione. *Edith Wharton.* New York: Knopf, 2007. Print.

Lewis, R. W. B. *Edith Wharton: A Biography.* New York: Harper & Row, 1975. Print.

Lewis, R. W. B., and Nancy Lewis, eds. *The Letters of Edith Wharton.* New York: Scribner's, 1988. Print.

Loesch, Harold G. "A Study of the Life of Louis Bromfield from 1925–1939 with Emphasis on His Association with Edith Wharton." MA thesis, Kent State University, 1964.

Martin, Robert A., and Linda Wagner-Martin. "The Salons of Wharton's Fiction." *Wretched Exotic: Essays on Edith Wharton in Europe.* Ed. Katherine Joslin and Alan Price. New York: Peter Lang, 1993. 97–110. Print.

McAlmon, Robert. *Being Geniuses Together, 1920–1930.* Rev. ed. Ed. Kay Boyle. Baltimore: Johns Hopkins UP, 1984. Print.

Mellow, James R. *Hemingway: A Life without Consequences.* Reading, MA: Addison-Wesley, 1992. Print.

Meyers, Jeffrey. "Conrad's Influence on Modern Writers." *Twentieth-Century Literature* 36.2 (Summer 1990): 186–206. *Academic Search Complete.* Web. 13 Jan. 2016.

Mizener, Arthur. *The Far Side of Paradise: A Biography of F. Scott Fitzgerald.* Boston: Houghton Mifflin, 1951.

Philbrick, Nathaniel. "A Window on the Prey: The Hunter Sees a Human Face in Hemingway's 'After the Storm' and Melville's 'The Grand Armada.'" *Hemingway Review* 14.1 (Fall 1994): 25–35. Print.

Price, Alan. *The End of the Age of Innocence: Edith Wharton and the First World War.* New York: St. Martin's Press, 1996. Print.

Reynolds, Michael. *Hemingway: The 1930s.* New York: Norton, 1997. Print.

———. *Hemingway's Reading, 1910–1940: An Inventory.* Princeton, NJ: Princeton UP, 1981. John F. Kennedy Presidential Library. Web. Accessed 27 May 2015.

Sanford, Marcelline Hemingway. *At the Hemingways, with Fifty Years of Correspondence between Ernest and Marcelline Hemingway.* Centennial ed. Moscow: U of Idaho P, 1999. Print.

Schriber, Mary Suzanne. *Gender and the Writer's Imagination: From Cooper to Wharton.* Lexington: UP of Kentucky, 1987. Print.

Sigal, Clancy. *Hemingway Lives! Why Reading Hemingway Matters Today.* New York: OR Books, 2013. Print.

Small, Judy Jo, and Michael Reynolds. "Hemingway v. Andersen: The Final Rounds." *Hemingway Review* 14.2 (Spring 1995): 1–17. Print.

Stewart, Donald Ogden. *A Parody Outline of History.* New York: Doran, 1921. Print.

Tintner, Adeline R. *Edith Wharton in Context: Essays on Intertextuality.* Tuscaloosa: U of Alabama P, 1999. 134–38. Print.

Wharton, Edith. *The Gods Arrive.* New York: Scribner's, 1932. Print.

———. *Hudson River Bracketed.* New York: Scribner's, 1929. Print.

———. Letter to Bernard Berenson. 18 June 1930. MS. Biblioteca Berenson. I Tatti—The Harvard University Center for Italian Renaissance Studies, Florence, Italy.

Whitley, Edward. "Race and Modernity in Theodore Roosevelt's and Ernest Hemingway's African Travel Writing." *Issues in Travel Writing: Empire, Spectacle, and Displacement.* Ed. Kristi Siegel. New York: Peter Lang, 2002. 13–17. Print.

Wolff, Geoffrey. *Black Sun: The Brief Transit and Violent Eclipse of Harry Crosby.* New York: Vintage, 1977. Print.

I

WHARTON, HEMINGWAY, AND THE MODERNIST CANON

Hemingway and Wharton

Both Modernists

PETER HAYS

Ernest Hemingway has long been recognized as a modernist, but Edith Wharton, who also deserves the title, has not. Hemingway's prose changed the way fiction was written. His short, bare, precise sentences changed American prose from the long, carefully modulated sentences of Henry James with their multiple imbedded modifiers. Both, through their styles, forced reader attention and involvement—with James, to figure the precise meaning of the convoluted prose; with Hemingway, to weigh what was said and what was omitted. Hemingway made reader involvement even more necessary by eliminating many of the "he saids" and "she saids," forcing readers to know the characters speaking well enough to attribute speeches correctly to their authors.

But style alone does not make a modernist. Hemingway was a distinct anti-romantic, an extreme realist, presenting subject matter heretofore not published: date rape, overt promiscuity and homosexuality, and post-traumatic stress disorder, among other topics. He eschewed editorial comment, the "dear gentle reader" of the Victorians. And in his stories, virtue is not always rewarded, wickedness not punished. Unlike William Ernest Henley in his poem "Invictus," Hemingway's protagonists may struggle to be captains of their souls (842), but they are almost never masters of their fate, a fate which, in Hemingway, is frequently malignant. Hemingway's world is not one where "God's in his Heaven / All's right with the world!" (Browning, "Pippa Passes," part 1, 11227–28). Hemingway's *The Sun Also Rises*, to quote from Lorin Stein, editor of the *Paris Review*, in Leslie Blume's recent *Everybody Behaves Badly*, "was modern literature fully arrived for a grand public" (Blume x). Charles Scribner III says of their firm's author that Hemingway "was inventing a whole new idiom and tonality. . . . [H]e was completely twentieth century" (Blume x–xi).

For class I once made a list of modernist traits; Eliot's *The Waste Land* would be a paradigmatic example of them:

Experimental
Transgressive, changing previous ways of expressing the same genre
Multiple points of view
Fragmented
Featuring alienation
Not sentimental
Anti-romantic
Brings background into foreground, sometimes confusing as to who the protagonist is
Insists on reader participation
Foregrounds method
Not eminently salable.

I won't defend *The Waste Land* as meeting these criteria; that's for another time and venue, but the applicability of the list to *The Waste Land* should be apparent. For *The Sun Also Rises*, all but multiple points of view and salability are applicable: Jake is the sole narrator—although he presents us with enough information that we can determine others' points of view—and Hemingway desperately wanted sales of this novel, however unusual it was in form and content, winning praise from early reviewers for its vigorous style, but condemnation for its sorry content. His letters to editor Maxwell Perkins about sales of his stories to *Scribner's Magazine* (the same one Wharton published in) and of his novels show his need for money (as well as fame). He questioned his editor, Maxwell Perkins, about the sales of *Torrents of Spring* (*Letters*, 88), asked about the reviews in a letter to Perkins where he said he had a bet on the sales of *The Sun Also Rises* (101), and boasted to Ezra Pound when the novel went into its fifth printing (202).

To go briefly through the list, Hemingway's style was experimental for readers of the time: short, clipped sentences, with little direct clue as to the narrator's feelings, except for such passages as where Jake declares his love for Brett (*The Sun Also Rises* 21–22), cries himself to sleep (26), feels jealous of Cohn (80), feels uncomfortable having set Brett up with Romero (149), and is angry with himself to have to rescue Brett one more time (192). Other times, we have to infer his jealousy of both Michael and Cohn, his uncomfortableness being with the woman he loves and her two current lovers. When Bill says "Must be swell being a steer" (107), how does the emasculated Jake feel? He doesn't tell us, but the remark must cut. When Mike asks Jake to tell Robert to leave (115), Jake's "it would be nice for me to tell him" is loaded with bitter irony, although Hemingway does not say so explicitly. Jake's heavy drinking at Botin's at novel's end is an indication that, however much he is willing to recognize that Brett will never be his life partner, the awareness still causes him great pain.

The novel was transgressive in style, as reviewers noted, but also in content, detailing the lives of drunken, promiscuous expatriates, and asking the readers to care for these characters, at least for the emasculated narrator, a very unusual protagonist in any novel of the time, and especially in a novel about love affairs. It was fragmented, consisting of Jake's incomplete accounts of events in Paris, Pamplona, Burguete, Pamplona, San Sebastian, and Madrid. Unlike most novels, it did not provide descriptions of the characters. Is Brett a blonde or brunette? How tall is she? What does Jake look like? We do not know. *The Sun Also Rises* most definitely dealt with alienation, giving its epigraph of the Lost Generation to those who had fought in the First World War and who had come home disillusioned, their values shattered.

The Sun Also Rises is not sentimental. When Brett says to Jake, "Good night, darling," Jake even responds, "Don't be sentimental" (28). For the most part, feelings are repressed, and love does not conquer, as both Jake and Cohn find out. It is anti-romantic in its harsh depiction of those who endured the war: Jake, Brett, and Mike. The comparison with Marshal Ney (24), whose loyalty to Napoleon cost him his life, in contrast to the promiscuous Brett, underscores the destruction of prewar values. The novel begins with a portrait of Robert Cohn beguiling the reader into thinking he will be the protagonist; a manuscript version began, "This is a novel about a lady. Her name is Lady Ashley and when the story begins she is living in Paris" (273). Only gradually does the reader realize that Jake is not just narrator, but also the antihero of this anti-romantic novel. And several times Jake breaks the third-person point of view to address the reader directly—"You understand me" (8); "Somehow I feel I have not shown Robert Cohn clearly" (37)—calling attention to his role as narrator, foregrounding his method. And finally, the novel insists on reader participation, not just to fill in Jake's feelings when he does not announce them, but also to judge the novel. Is it the tale of a love misplaced, a tragic story; is it the story of a man seeking self-control in a destructive world, learning to come to live with the fact that he can never have the woman he loves, and thereby somewhat optimistic? For all these reasons *The Sun Also Rises* is clearly a modernist novel.

Blume, in her praise for Hemingway, juxtaposed him to those who wrote with the "more florid, verbose approaches of Henry James and Edith Wharton" (x–xi), condemning both to the dustbin of the past. Hemingway, by the way, did not agree with her. His library contained six volumes of Wharton: *Age of Innocence, A Backward Glance,* a collection of short stories, *French Ways and Their Meaning, House of Mirth,* and *Ethan Frome* (Brasch and Sigman 397). I've already suggested that James's style, especially the late style, necessitated the same reader involvement as Hemingway's did. James was also less interested in what was done than why it was done, revelation of character, in the same way as many modernists. But Edith Wharton deserves special scrutiny because, judging by my list of criteria, she was very much a modernist writer. To make that claim, I'll examine one novella in particular, *Ethan Frome* (1911, fifteen years before *The Sun Also Rises*).

First, there are the multiple regressive flashbacks in the tale proper, unusual for Wharton. Then, most readers focus on the lamentable tale of Ethan, Mattie, and Zeena, not registering that the story is a frame tale, told us by an unnamed engineer-narrator. The verifiable facts in the story are few: Ethan Frome married his cousin Zenobia after his mother's death; his farm is poor; Zeena's cousin Mattie came to stay with them and help Zeena; Ethan and Mattie were seriously injured in a sledding "accident," leaving Mattie a quadriplegic and Ethan seriously hampered. Everything else, beyond a few words from Harmon Gow and Ruth Varnum Hale, comes from the engineer's imagination. No one else confirms the validity of his making Ethan into a ruined Greek hero, or his romantic speculations between Mattie and Ethan, least of all his belief—if there had been feeling between Mattie and Ethan—that Ethan was too repressed to act on them. Thus the novella is as much about the engineer's character, repressed and romantic, as it is about the inhabitants of the Frome household.

To go back to my checklist: the novel was experimental, both for Wharton and for the reading public. Never before had she used an unreliable first-person narrator, rather than an omniscient third-person one, to tell a tale, and the public, for the most part, still does not realize that an unreliable narrator is telling the story. In using this technique, Wharton is being transgressive, shattering a complacent audience's trust that what it is being told actually happened. Not until Ford Madox Ford's *The Good Soldier* four years later in 1915 do we have such another modernist fiction of unreliability (had he read *Frome*?). The multiple points of view are Harmon Gow's, Ruth Varnum Hale's, Ethan's few words, Mattie and Zeena's, if either of them expressed personal information the night the engineer stays at the Fromes—which is highly unlikely—and that of the narrator. Wharton announces her technique in her introduction, referring the reader to other assembled tales told by interested and involved narrators in Balzac's "La Grande Bretèche" and Browning's *The Ring and the Book*. More particularly, she signals the nature of the narrator's personal and idiosyncratic account when she, with her always deliberate and accurate word choice, has him say that what he presents to us is his "vision" (25), clearly a loaded term.

The tale is fragmented by its frame-tale format, dividing the story into three parts, as well as by the intermittent encounters the narrator has with Frome. Most certainly the story involves alienation: the Fromes isolated from their community, Ethan from any hope of an engineering career (if that conversational piece of information ever actually occurred), and the inhabitants of the Frome household from each other: they tolerate each other and endure—there's nothing more than duty between them.

It is not sentimental, although, in the narrator's mind, both Ethan and Mattie are: Ethan imagining "her pies and biscuits [would] become the pride of the county" (36), an amazingly unerotic romantic fantasy, she confessing that she had thought of running off with him "summer nights, when the moon was so bright I couldn't sleep" (158). That is, Ethan and Mattie may or may not be sentimental, but the narrator most assuredly is, putting these thoughts and words into their heads, all the while identifying with Ethan, "the most striking figure in Starkfield" (3), "his brown seamed profile, under the helmet-like peak of his cap, . . . like the bronze image of a hero" (14). The romantic visions the engineer conjures up for Ethan are remarkably chaste and constrained, appropriate perhaps for the descendants of Puritans that the Fromes are, yet as Hester Prynne has shown us, not all Puritans acted puritanically. Would a man, despising his wife and enamored of a pretty girl in his household, only kiss the hem of her sewing material when they are alone together overnight? It bespeaks either high morals, severe psychological repression, or very low testosterone. Yet so would the narrator have us believe. Finally, at face value, the tale is tragic, three lives wasted, enduring pain until death takes them, and Harmon tells us that Ethan has more to endure: "But the Fromes are tough. Ethan'll likely touch a hundred" (6).

Most assuredly the tale is anti-romantic, the thwarted romance (if there was one) between Mattie and Ethan, the Sartrean no exit of the three continuing to live together in poverty and pain: young Ethan not confessing his feelings, hampered by the remnants of a Puritan upbringing and introversion, Mattie not confessing hers because "nice" girls did not speak first, and Zeena complaining, rightfully, that Ethan married her for company and then ignores her. Perhaps the most tellingly ironic anti-romantic event occurs at the suicide attempt (if that is indeed what it was). Ethan and Mattie decide to kill themselves by sledding into a tree. Sleds are more easily controlled from the rear, giving the steersman the length of the sled as leverage. At the last instant Ethan changes position with Mattie, moving to the front of the sled, saying that he wants to feel her arms about him. In actuality, he wants to protect her—to save her from death in their suicide attempt—and as a result his stronger body absorbs much of the force and, instead of at least her dying, both end up crippled. Romanticism here, chivalry, pays a dreadful bodily cost.

As to who the protagonist is, there are two: Ethan in the engineer-narrator's imagined tragic story, what he might have become under different circumstances; and the narrator himself, presumed scientist, yet very much a romantic. One can read the central story unencumbered by the significance of the frame tale, reading it as a tragic love story, but then one has to also ignore Wharton's sarcastic remarks about the proscriptions of Puritan repressiveness and the utter foolishness of Ethan's chivalry. The more astute reader recognizes the narrator's unreliability and has two stories to enjoy. By foregrounding her method in her introduction, telling us of Balzac and Browning, Wharton invites knowledgeable reader participation. And like Hemingway (and unlike Eliot with his very difficult poem), Wharton expected this novella to sell, and it did.

An interesting narrative use of the second person links Wharton and Hemingway. In *Frome,* the narrator begins his story saying, "If you know Starkfield, Massachusetts, you know the post office. If you know the post office you must have seen Ethan Frome" (3). Hemingway opens *To Have and Have Not* with "You know how it is there early in the morning in Havana" (3), and Jake-as-narrator directly addresses the reader, leaving behind the third-person point of view, just as Wharton's narrator does.

Two Wharton scholars, however, deny her the claim to be a modernist. Stephanie Lewis Thompson writes that "Wharton esteemed something other than the alienated, fragmented and egoistic personae of emerging writers like James Joyce" (8–9). *Ethan Frome* most definitely does deal with alienation, and the engineer/narrator does impose, egoistically, his interpretation onto the events, describing them in accordance to his romantic vision. Thompson never gives a clear definition of the modernism that Wharton fails to achieve, but seemingly Wharton's lack of stream of consciousness—something also not present in Hemingway's earliest fiction such as *The Sun Also Rises*—is why Thompson believes she is not a modernist. Interestingly though, Thompson sees Wharton's reverence for the past, tradition, and history as similar to that of T. S. Eliot in "Tradition and the Individual Talent," particularly Eliot's statement that tradition

> involves, in the first place, the historical sense . . . ; and the historical sense involves a perception, not only of the pastness of the past, but of its presence; the historical sense compels a man to write not merely with his own generation in his bones, but with a feeling that the whole of literature of Europe from Homer and within it the whole of the literature from his own country has a simultaneous existence and composes a simultaneous order. This historical sense, which is a sense of the timeless as well as of the temporal and of the timeless and temporal together, is what makes a writer traditional. (38)

Eliot's sexism aside, ascribing authorship only to males, this was a tradition he believed in and championed. He, like Pound, knew much of the history of Western poetry, and the two poets incorporated that history into their own verses, yet no one seriously challenges their claim to being modernists.

Wharton was equally well read, also from Homer to Proust, Joyce, and Gide. She spoke English, French, Italian, and German, even translating a German play for production. And if her experiments in fiction were not as genre-bending as theirs in poetry, it also has to be acknowledged that she, unlike Pound and Eliot, never received a formal education, was largely self-taught, and as a woman whose writing exploits were initially seen by those of her upper class as déclassé, slumming of a sort, her fiction depicted the restrictions on women that shared the territory of Kate Chopin and Charlotte Perkins Gilman, but with a wider public readership, one that got Wharton the first Pulitzer Prize awarded to a woman, and the first honorary doctorate from Yale awarded to a woman. She also discussed euthanasia, prostitution, and abortion in her fiction, at a time when even male writers did not.

The second scholar who feels that Wharton has not written a modernist novel is Robin Peel, who writes of Wharton that the "conservative discourses which surrounded her from childhood and were questioned by her but never rejected, led her to esteem duty and *the power of society above the individual*" (11; my emphasis). Criticizing the patriarchy, as Wharton does, and the coercive power of society, may be realism or even naturalism, but, for Peel, it is not modernism. He does concede, however, that "*Ethan Frome* . . . stands on the verge of modernism" (15).

Peel defines "modernism [as] an expression of a particular political view that argues that societies should be shaped by a recognition that artistic perception is in the vanguard of the development of civilization" (18). Such a statement echoes Shelley's "A Defence of Poetry," which concludes that "Poets are the unacknowledged legislators of the world" (535), a highly Romantic view, and one that would not be agreed to by all modernists, certainly not Hemingway. Again, would Eliot, who said of himself that he was a "classicist in literature, royalist in politics, and anglo-catholic in religion" (18–19), describe art as being in the vanguard of civilization, and not religion; would Virginia Woolf, whom many saw as much a privileged upper-class snob as Wharton, make the same claim?

Peel continues: "Wharton's apparent disregard for the experiments of modernism can be explained by her rejection of its perceived solipsism and lack of social commitment" (24). For the woman who wrote feverishly to get America into World War I in order to defend Europe, who won France's Chevalier of the Legion of Honor for her work with refugees during the war, there seems to be no "lack of social commitment"; she even financially adopted several of the orphan refugees as well as financially supporting her sister-in-law. Peel seems to shift his criteria. First, Wharton was not modern because she was not politically engaged. Then she is not because she does not play with language as Gertrude Stein did (126; again, did Woolf so experiment?). He acknowledges the narrator of *Frome* as a "speculative, unreliable narrator' (125), but he takes the narrator's account unquestioningly and never deeply engages his motives for constructing the "vision" as he does, even though, on the same page, he writes, "It is recognized that *Ethan Frome* can be read as a narrative about narrating, a quality that would seem to qualify it for the label 'modernist,' or even 'postmodernist'" (125). In short, Peel is all over the place, denying Wharton the right to be a modernist, and then acknowledging that she was.

Both critics, Thompson and Peel, pick an element of Wharton's writing that in their estimation denies to Wharton the mantel of modernist: for Thompson, it is lack of stream of consciousness; for Peel it is lack of a social commitment that recognizes that "artistic perception is in the vanguard of the development of civilization." He also faults Wharton for failing to engage in the wordplay that characterized Stein, and I would add e. e. cummings. I would argue that such narrow distinctions would eliminate many other modernists as well. Modernism is a broad category, going back to Ibsen and Strindberg in drama, Stravinsky in music, Frank Lloyd Wright in architecture, and—again, depending on one's definition—Cézanne and Brâncuşi in art. To deny someone because he or she fails to meet all criteria is to ask the artist to lie on the critic's Procrustean bed.

Those readers, like Blume, who consign Edith Wharton to an antiquated past because many of her novels deal with the intricacies of New York's shifting societal mores in the 1870s and 1880s neglect how she showed the subjugation of women, the repression that social custom forced upon women, offering those in the upper class no other choice than to be well-dressed ornaments, educated to please a man and decorate his house, and no more. They neglect her wide-ranging social criticism, her broad range of publications in many genres, her facility in a number of languages (like Pound and Eliot), her interest in anthropology, evolution, and science; they see the grande dame in corseted gown and feathered hat and ignore the professional author who negotiated her own contracts and left Scribner's when she thought she could do better. And they ignore that, fifteen years before Hemingway, Wharton had penned a very modernist novel.

WORKS CITED

Balzac, Honoré de. "La Grande Bretèche." *Great French Short Stories.* Selected by Germain Brée. New York: Dell, 1960. 111–34. Print.

Blume, Lesley M. M. *Everyone Behaves Badly: The True Story behind Hemingway's Masterpiece "The Sun Also Rises."* Boston: Houghton Mifflin Harcourt, 2016. Print.

Brasch, James D., and Joseph Sigman. *Hemingway's Library: A Composite Record.* New York: Garland, 1981. Print.

Browning, Robert. "Pippa Passes." *The Complete Works of Robert Browning.* Vol. 3. Ed. Roma A. King Jr. et al. Athens: Ohio UP, 1971. Print.

———. *The Ring and the Book.* In *The Works of Robert Browning.* Vol. 5. New York: AMS Press, 1966. Print.

Eliot, T. S. *Selected Prose.* Ed. Frank Kermode. London: Faber and Faber, 1975. Print.

Hemingway, Ernest. *The Letters of Ernest Hemingway.* Vol. 3: *1926–1929.* Ed. Rena Sanderson, Sandra Spanier, and Robert W. Trogdon. Cambridge: Cambridge UP, 2015. Print.

———. *The Sun Also Rises.* Hemingway Library Edition. New York: Scribner's, 1926, 2014. Print.

———. *To Have and Have Not.* New York: Scribner's, 1937, 1996. Print.

Henley, William Ernest. "Invictus," *The Oxford Book of English Verse, 1250–1900.* Ed. Arthur Quiller-Couch. Oxford: Oxford UP, 1919. Print.

Peel, Robin. *Apart from Modernism: Edith Wharton, Politics, and Fiction before World War I.* Madison, NJ: Fairleigh Dickinson UP, 2005. Print.

Shelley, Percy Bysshe, *Shelley's Poetry and Prose.* Ed. Donald H. Reiman and Neal Freistat. New York: Norton, 2002. Print.

Thompson, Stephanie Lewis. *Influencing America's Tastes: Realism in the Works of Wharton, Cather, and Hurst.* Gainesville: UP of Florida, 2002. Print.

Wharton, Edith. *Ethan Frome.* New York: Scribner's, 1911, 1939. Print.

From Wharton to Hemingway

The Evolution of Modernism

ELLEN ANDREWS KNODT

The evolution of modernism in America may have begun with Edith Wharton's *The House of Mirth* (1905), which might at first seem an odd choice, given that the First World War is the oft-used defining moment of modernism. But Wharton's novel helps one to understand how modernist literature did not just suddenly appear full-fledged from the pens of Fitzgerald, Hemingway, and Faulkner but was evolving before the catalyst of the war made its mark. Recently, moreover, literary scholars "no longer perceive modernism simply as a reaction to the devastation of the First World War and the constraining morality of the nineteenth century but, also, as a response to changing economics and gender relationships" (Haytock, "Marriage and Modernism" 216). With this redefinition, even Edith Wharton's early work looks quite transitional. How does *The House of Mirth* provide evidence of this response to change? And why choose Hemingway as the modernist author to provide degrees of comparison?

On the surface, these authors could not be more different: Wharton was a wealthy, well-connected New York and European socialite, whereas Hemingway was a middle-class midwesterner, more used to the campsite than the drawing room. And Wharton's first major success as a novelist with the serialization and publication of *The House of Mirth* came when Hemingway was a six-year-old. Yet, the two authors were destined to be contemporaries. Both served as volunteers in and wrote about World War I. Wharton, living in Paris, supported the French, raising funds, helping refugees, and even visiting the front, for which service the French president awarded her the Chevalier of the Legion of Honor in 1916. Wharton wrote two World War I novels, *The Marne* (1918) and *A Son at the Front* (1923). Hemingway, an eighteen-year-old Red Cross volunteer, was wounded on the Italian front, inspiring several short stories and *A Farewell to Arms* (1929) set largely in wartime Italy. Although both authors lived in Paris after World War I, they did not know each other and had harsh judgments, generally, of their styles of writing. While Hemingway doesn't name Wharton in comments on writing in *Death in the Afternoon* (1932), he seems, nevertheless, to be criticizing her style: "Prose is architecture, not interior decoration, and the Baroque is over" (191). And Wharton objected to "the apparent indifference to the past and lack of principles in the work of the new generation of writers" (Haytock, "Modernism" 364). Few reading *The House of Mirth* and *The Sun Also Rises* would view the novels as artifacts of the same era. And yet, as different stylistically as these novels are, one can see similar elements despite surface differences.

The biggest difference between these two authors is the change in literary style. One can compare Wharton's writing style to the dress of a society woman in 1905 as "upholstered," full length with many folds of elegant material, whereas Hemingway's writing could be said to reflect the bare minimum flapper's dress that hardly covers the figure—or the novel's intent. Wharton herself acknowledged these differences in a 1925 letter to F. Scott Fitzgerald: "I feel to your generation, which has taken a flying leap into the future, I must represent the literary equivalent of tufted furniture and gas chandeliers" (*Letters* 481). For an example of this style, note the longer sentences, more "literary" vocabulary, and a certain delicacy describing a woman's physical appeal in the following description by Lawrence Selden of Lily Bart at the beginning of *The House of Mirth:* "As she moved beside him, with her long light step, Selden was conscious of taking a luxurious pleasure in her nearness: in the modeling of her little ear, the crisp upward wave of her hair—was it so ever so slightly brightened by art?—the thick planting of her straight black lashes. Everything about her was at once vigorous and exquisite, at once strong and fine" (27). Readers immediately recognize that Selden is drawn to Lily, but the reticence of his noticing the shape of her ear, her hair, and eyelashes (even with the sly question of coloring her hair) marks the style as what some would call "Victorian."

In contrast, note the shorter, more direct sentences and the earthier vocabulary in Jake Barnes's introduction of Brett Ashley in *The Sun Also Rises* (1925): "Brett was damned good-looking. She wore a slipover jersey sweater and a tweed skirt, and her hair was brushed back like a boy's. She started all that. She was built with curves like the hull of the racing yacht, and you missed none of it with that wool jersey" (22). In more explicit language, Hemingway describes Brett's charms ("built with curves") and her trend-setting boyish haircut. These descriptions—both by male characters—of the main female characters in the novels reflect a difference in literary style—and yet a similar emphasis on women's external beauty in both novels.

Both Lily and Brett are given a backstory that provides a sympathetic context for their behavior, but the ways in which the authors reveal their characters' pasts illustrate the more linear style of 1905 and the more fragmented, almost "Cubist," style of 1925. Lily's being raised in a wealthy family followed by the family's bankruptcy is revealed in an extensive chapter 3 flashback and helps explain her lack of any useful skills and subsequent dependence on marrying for money. In contrast, Brett's history of two marriages emerges superficially in early dialogue between Jake and Robert Cohn (38–39) and more completely in much later dialogue between Jake and Mike Campbell (203). Only in Mike's account do we understand that Brett has been traumatized by the death of her first husband from "dysentery" during the war and her victimization by her second husband, who threatened to kill her and "slept with a loaded service revolver" as a result of his post-traumatic stress disorder (203). Readers may have picked up on Brett's trauma by references throughout the novel to her nervousness, need to "bathe," and often frenetic activity. However, Mike's later story provides explicit information about Brett's past.

Other differences in style are evident as modernist writers moved from a narration that "tells" readers what a character is thinking or feeling to one that "shows" thoughts through dialogue between characters or by a character's physical actions. One can see the "older" style of Wharton and the "newer" style of Hemingway illustrated in the passages below. In *The House of Mirth*, Wharton's narrator satirically characterizes one of New York's society women: "Mrs. Fisher's latest hobby was municipal reform. It had been preceded by an equal zeal for socialism, which in turn replaced an energetic advocacy of Christian Science. Mrs. Fisher was small, fiery and dramatic; and her hands and eyes were admirable instruments in the service of whatever cause she happened to espouse. She had, however, the fault common to enthusiasts of ignoring any slackness of response on the part of her hearers" (63). Wharton *tells* the reader that Mrs. Fisher's cause is her "latest hobby" after two others, casting doubt on her real dedication to reform, and that Mrs. Fisher is "admirable" in her advocacy but has a "fault" in that she does not notice the reaction of her listeners.

Now compare Hemingway's Jake Barnes satiric description of a group of young men about to enter a dance hall in Paris: "Two taxis were coming down the steep street. They both stopped in front of the Bal. A crowd of young men, some in jerseys and some in shirt sleeves, got out. I could see their hands and newly washed, wavy hair in the light from the door. The policeman standing by the door looked at me and smiled. They came in. As they went in, under the light I saw white hands, wavy hair, white faces, grimacing, gesturing, talking" (20). Hemingway *shows* how Jake characterizes these young men by objective description and indirect suggestion. First, Jake objectively describes the appearance of the young men without any stated opinion, mentioning wavy hair (twice), white hands and faces, and the way they talk. Second, what one might notice as a "crystallizing detail" is the line between Jake's two objective descriptions: "The policeman standing by the door looked at me and smiled." Again, the interpretation is not given—why would the policeman smile? Why does he look at Jake and smile? The juxtaposition of the policeman's reaction to the group with Jake's description can mean much to a reader, especially one tuned into sexual stereotypes—young gay men dress in a certain way; the policeman, who is not gay, finds young gay men somehow comical, and shares his viewpoint with a man he determines not to be gay by smiling in Jake's direction. That's a lot to unpack based on one sentence. As Robert Paul Lamb summarizes in his excellent analysis of Hemingway's craft *Art Matters,* "How, then, does judgment take place in the Hemingway story? Most of the time, *it occurs in the reader's mind* as the characters reveal themselves through their thoughts, words and actions, and as they judge each other" (27; emphasis mine).

This difference in style is the very heart of modernism and serves to distinguish Wharton's "baroque" or "upholstered" prose from Hemingway's minimalism. Some readers find both styles problematic—too much detail on the one hand and too little direction on the other. Wharton's longer sentences and more formal vocabulary often obscure her humor and biting satire. And, as the above unpacking of one sentence illustrates, Hemingway's style asks much of his readers. Hemingway's stripped-down prose means that one can "finish" reading *The Sun Also Rises* in a flash but perhaps won't realize fully the novel's intent and may dismiss the novel as just a bunch of characters drinking too much and enjoying the torturing and killing of animals in bullfights. Readers may overlook the conflicts in values and loyalties that Jake experiences, as well as the decisions he and the novel's other characters must make about their lives.

If this difference in style separates Edith Wharton and Ernest Hemingway, what can we say links them together? What qualities in *The House of Mirth* as early as 1905 presage the development of modernism a bit later in the twentieth century? Wharton, despite her reputation as a chronicler of "Old New York" aristocracy, belongs with other transitional authors like Stephen Crane, Joseph Conrad, Theodore Dreiser, and Sherwood Anderson who influenced the development of modernist literature. What we discover in *The House of Mirth* is just how transitional an author Edith Wharton is. If we compare her early novel with Hemingway's first novel, *The Sun Also Rises*, we see, despite the stylistic differences, three main links: insider-outsider status, the exploration of previously taboo subjects, and the increasing role of ambiguity.

Insider-Outsider Status

Edith Jones Wharton is perfectly situated to be on the cusp of modernism because of the contradictions she represents in her life story. Born into an "Old New York" family, Edith Jones never felt she really belonged: her mother may have resented her rather late-in-life pregnancy or perhaps the rumors that her daughter was the product of an illegitimate affair (Benstock 10). And then Edith displayed her imagination and interest in writing, deemed not suitable for a socialite of the time. So Edith Wharton was both an insider and an outsider, a keen observer of society but not totally of the society she inhabited. Lily Bart, her protagonist in *The House of Mirth*, shares this insider-outsider status, having been born and raised in a wealthy family which loses its money through business losses and the death of the father/breadwinner. Lily, like the young Edith Jones, is made to understand that only a marriage to a man of wealth and suitable societal position will enable her to maintain respectability in this materialistic society. The author, rejected by a fiancé's mother, ostensibly because she was too "intellectual," eventually marries Teddy Wharton, a marriage of convenience that ends in divorce. Lily Bart, having no skills beyond a beautiful face and figure and a taste for fashion, struggles throughout the novel to reconcile her absolute need for a society marriage with her personal revulsion against a marriage that is not based on love and mutual respect. Wharton's rendering of the problems Lily faces because of economic conditions and gender expectations in her society mark her as an author ahead of her time. As Linda Wagner-Martin comments, "*The House of Mirth,* in the past thirty years, has been read very differently, and [is] a testament to what Wharton knew early on about the character of both men and women" (247).

Hemingway originally focused *The Sun Also Rises* on a woman: "Her name was Lady Ashley and she was living in Paris" (Baker 153). But Hemingway settled on his first-person narrator Jake Barnes, who is also both an insider and an outsider in his society, but based on different circumstances than Lily Bart's. Jake Barnes is part of a group of American and British expatriates in France and can view them "close-up" from the inside, much as Wharton depicts Lily Bart's society. However, Jake differs from his fellow expatriates in significant ways, which endows him also with an outsider's perspective. First, unlike many of his friends, he is not independently wealthy but works for a living as a journalist. Several early scenes in the novel refer to his going to the office, or adding up his bank balance. This insider-outsider status is not clear as the novel opens but is gradually revealed, which can be confusing to readers. Readers may be mystified by the voice of the narrator at the beginning of the novel and his portrayal of his "tennis friend" Robert Cohn. Jake emphasizes that Cohn comes from a wealthy family, and "read many books, played bridge, played tennis, and boxed at a local gymnasium" (*The Sun Also Rises* 6). These pursuits seem to mark Cohn as a dilettante in Jake's eyes. Several others in Jake's circle of expatriates are or were wealthy and do not work (especially Lady Brett Ashley and Mike Campbell), and the disparity between their views of money and Jake's is a thread that figures prominently in the novel (almost as much as it does in Lily Bart's society).

A second source of Jake's outsider status is even more hidden than his different economic circumstances and is even more likely to provoke confusion and curiosity. In an early conversation with Robert Cohn, Jake says that he has "had plenty to worry about one time or another" (11), although his reasons are left unexplained. Nothing at the opening of the novel suggests that Jake had been wounded in World War I and still suffers the effects of that wound until, in chapter 3, Jake mentions to Georgette, a prostitute that he has picked up that "I got hurt in the war" (17). In chapter 4, the devastating effects of the wound which prevents a sexual relationship between Jake and Brett, along with Jake's emotional reaction to his condition, deepen his outsider status.

The stance that both Wharton and Hemingway take with characters that are part of their societies, yet are not wholly of their societies, illuminates their respective cultures. Hemingway is just as critical of the expatriate society he depicts (and that Jake Barnes finds himself corrupted by) as Wharton is of her destructive, materialistic culture. The insider-outsider stance also allows their narrators to reveal characters' behaviors that violate conventional norms.

The Exploration of Taboo Subjects

Jake's condition (a war wound to his genitals that leaves him incapable of sexual intercourse but not immune to sexual feelings), though not explicitly explained, breaks conventional Victorian taboos, as do the many sexual liaisons portrayed in the novel, but then so did Wharton's society characters some twenty years before.

Though both Lily Bart and Brett Ashley wish to live on their own terms, Lily (like Henry James's Daisy Miller) is shunned by polite society for daring to appear with men alone, no matter the innocent circumstances, and Brett takes Robert Cohn, Mike Campbell, and Pedro Romero as serial lovers. Today's readers find Lily's desperate dilemma of needing to find a wealthy husband while at the same time recoiling from spending her life with someone she doesn't love as quaint, questioning why she can't marry Lawrence Selden or maybe just get a job. And yet, Wharton explores the difficulties of being female in this society with other female characters who illustrate bleak paths for single women in 1905 that help readers to see why Lily is so conflicted: Gerty Farish lives simply and unfashionably on a fixed inheritance spending dreary days in charity work, and Nettie Struther, a woman whose fiancé left her pregnant and alone, is presented as one step from homelessness and ruin before being befriended by Lily and eventually married. Married women don't fare much better in Wharton's portrayal, tolerating bores as Judy Trenor does, or having affairs as does Bertha Dorset. Though Lily's life at first is not as gritty as Stephen Crane's Maggie (1893) or Theodore Dreiser's Sister Carrie (1900), Wharton's society protagonist Lily Bart discovers that her depressed economic circumstances and society's conservative expectations for her behavior have devastating consequences. Though Lily is judged harshly even by her own relatives, Wharton reveals the hypocrisy of Lily's "soul mate" Lawrence Selden's affair with the married Bertha Dorset, who in turn dallied with the younger Ned Silverton. Added to those discoveries is the treachery of Gus Trenor, who expects sexual favors from Lily for the favor he did her by "investing" her money in the market. Lily's downward spiral from her social position to loss of respectability and resultant poverty stems from vicious gossip based on deliberate misrepresentation of Lily's actions. Although Wharton herself and other early twentieth-century writers might not have deemed her a modernist (Haytock, "Modernism" 372), Wharton unconventionally breaks ranks with her social class and depicts the moral and ethical lapses in her contemporary New York society.

Shari Benstock reports that mixed critical reception of *The House of Mirth* (in contrast to its enormously popular public reception, resulting in over 140,000 copies being sold in its first year) varied from dislike of its characters, to questioning of its view of society, to praise for its "psychological and sociological realism" (312–13). In a generally positive 1906 review of the novel in *The Atlantic Monthly*, Mary Moss is still critical: "*The House of Mirth* has a certain shallowness; it is thin. . . . Indeed, after the somewhat arid glitter of *The House of Mirth*, you turn with a sense of comfortable repose to the seasoned solidity of the average English novel" (52–53). Compared with other novels by other popular writers of Wharton's day, Hermione Lee concludes, "The modernity and ruthlessness of *The House of Mirth* is astounding" (15).

Hemingway's *The Sun Also Rises* engenders similar criticism as a novel about dissolute characters that drink to excess and that ends without any real resolution or "uplifting message." One reviewer objected to the "extreme moral sordidness" of the characters that "defeated Hemingway's artistic purpose" (Baker 179). Hemingway's own staid suburban Oak Park,

Illinois, mother criticized *The Sun Also Rises* as "one of the filthiest books of the year," and his father urged him to apply "his wonderful ability" to "a different subject matter" (*Letters* 3: 201). Hemingway's depiction of Lady Brett Ashley's ever-changing lovers and several other characters that slide in and out of sexual relationships without much societal opprobrium is certainly more explicit than Wharton's. Hemingway's language ("damned" in the earlier passage) would not have been acceptable in 1905, and indeed Hemingway had to argue with his editor, Maxwell Perkins, to keep any of his more profane words even in 1925.

Other taboos that both authors violate offend contemporary readers. Edith Wharton depicts Simon Rosedale as a social climber hampered by being Jewish in Lily's otherwise wealthy Christian New York society, but Hemingway's Jake Barnes's comments on Robert Cohn's Jewish background are far more negative. (The fact that Jake and Robert are both in love with Brett can account for some of Jake's jealous comments, but the emphasis on Cohn's Jewish identity is offensive to many readers.) In addition to Cohn, Jake also makes casual slurs about gay men (20), a black jazz drummer (62ff.) and a black boxer (71ff.). These violations of readers' sensibilities require an understanding of the context of both the societies represented in the novels and changing standards of what is acceptable. Of course, it is interesting that the cited criticism directed at Hemingway's novel focused on sexual issues and not prejudicial ones, a choice that today's society would likely reverse.

AMBIGUITY

Critics generally agree that modernist literature emphasizes the uncertainty that people felt following the First World War, the so-called "War to End All Wars." However, as early as 1905, Edith Wharton's *The House of Mirth* employs ambiguity from the very beginning of the novel. Lily Bart is "of two minds" in her pursuit of a suitably rich husband and at the same time in her revulsion at what that pursuit would mean for her life as a society wife: "She had been bored all the afternoon by Percy Gryce—the mere thought seemed to awaken an echo of his droning voice—but . . . she must follow up on her success, must submit to more boredom . . . and all on the bare chance that he might ultimately decide to do her the honor of boring her for life" (44). Lily attracts rich suitors with her beauty and ingratiating manner but then destroys her chances to marry by her own actions (missing church, playing bridge for money), which cause them to doubt her. Her waffling, while maddening to some readers, underlines the ambiguity of her situation and is a hallmark of modernism—an uncertainty, a denial of absolutes. Wharton's ending of the novel, with Lily's death by an accidental sleeping-draught overdose or suicide, emphasizes the ambiguous nature of the novel. Shari Benstock explains that Wharton "struggled over the ending . . . and finally decided on a closing to the novel that does not figure either-or choices, either for Lily or the society which she inhabits" (19). As Lily drifts off to her final sleep, she thinks "that there was something she might tell Selden, some *word* she had found that would make life clear between them (300; my emphasis). Lily can't bring the word to consciousness, but her last thoughts of Selden and the "word" presage his almost telepathic appearance at her room in the final chapter.

Wharton's ending leaves ambiguous not only Lily's final act of taking the sleeping potion but also the nature of the relationship between Lily Bart and Lawrence Selden. Their relationship begins the novel with Selden's seeing Lily at Grand Central Station. As his comment above about Lily's beauty attests, he is attracted to her. He also admires her independent spirit, as her agreeing to have tea with him alone, smoking cigarettes, and talking frankly of her need to marry a wealthy man indicate. As Lily and Selden talk about marriage, the restrictions on Lily and the freedom for Selden are clearly defined. Marriage is optional for men. As Lily says, "a girl must [marry], a man may if he chooses" (33). Throughout the novel, Selden appears at parties and often steals Lily away from dreary events, one time ruining her chance to marry Percy Gryce (86) and on another occasion even kissing her (141). Selden seems to be a trusted friend, but when he sees Lily leaving Gus Trenor's house at night (161), he deserts her when she sends for him (173). At the ending of the novel, it is not only Lily's death that is ambiguous, but also Selden's assessment of Lily. He needs the assurance of her "innocence" that she paid her debt to Gus Trenor before realizing that he has failed Lily, a "realization of his cowardice" (304). As he kneels by Lilly's deathbed, "penitent and reconciled," Selden's final action in the novel is as ambiguous as Lily's taking of the sleeping potion: "He knelt by the bed and bent over her, draining their last moment to the lees, and in the silence there passed between them the word which made all clear" (305). Many readers feel that the "word" Lily struggles to voice and that Selden silently conveys is "love." James Gargano, noting Lily's personal sacrifice of burning Bertha Dorset's letters to Lawrence Selden and repaying Gus Trenor with her entire inheritance, cites Wharton's recurring use of the word "faith" in the final chapters. Faith, for Wharton, is "an almost mystical assurance that only moral action" can save humanity from the "abyss" (Gargano 141). Lily avoids losing her soul at the price of her life. Selden discovers her sacrifice too late but takes some comfort from "the kiss . . . left upon his forehead" as absolution (305). Discussion of the ending continues to today, showing the power of ambiguity and another hallmark of Wharton's move toward modernism.

The Sun Also Rises employs an ambiguous ending to the unrequited love story of Jake and Brett that has long intrigued readers. After Jake has introduced Brett to Pedro Romero, the young bullfighter, and they have gone off together, Jake is shunned by the bullfighting aficionado Montoya for potentially corrupting the future of such a promising bullfighting talent. Jake is also knocked out in a fight with Robert Cohn, the collegiate boxing champion (3), who has had a brief fling with Brett and blames Jake for setting her up with Romero. But, of course, the novel doesn't end in Pamplona with Brett's departure. Readers are generally intrigued by what will happen to Jake and follow his travel to San Sebastian where he spends time alone contemplating the events in Pamplona and perhaps coming to a decision about his future (Knodt). Then Brett's telegram comes from Madrid, and "that meant San Sebastian all shot to hell" (*The Sun Also Rises* 239). After Jake has spent the summer suffering from his doomed love for Brett and becoming involved with her various affairs, readers wonder what Jake's "rescue" of Brett in Madrid means, going forward. Has their relationship changed, or does Jake reestablish the same association the two had at the beginning of the novel? Hemingway gives clues to Jake's decision when Jake says, after he sends his reply telegram to Brett in Madrid, "That seemed to handle it. That was it. Send a girl off with one man. Introduce her to another to go off with him. Now go and bring her back. And sign the wire with love" (239). But reading such comments depends on getting the sarcastic tone just right. When Brett and Jake meet in Madrid, Jake's actions are ambiguous. Jake drinks heavily at a bar and at lunch at the end of the novel. Does his drinking mean that Jake, despite his better judgment, is going to rekindle his doomed pursuit of Brett? Do we see a difference in his behavior between the taxi ride with Brett at the beginning of the novel and the one in the final scene? How should one interpret the famous final line of the story: "Isn't it pretty to think so?" (247). Readers and critics must read between the lines to discern Jake's course of action with Brett.

Both authors tantalize their readers with multiple interpretations of their characters' outcomes. Of course, Lily Bart does die, but the manner of her death, her motivation under her straitened circumstances, raises the question: Is her death a tragedy that a few alternative actions on her part or others' intervention might have averted or a capitulation to a weakness in her character? Lily's struggles in the latter part of the novel to come to terms with herself are echoed in Jake Barnes's and Brett Ashley's struggles, albeit not as tragic, to find meaning in their lives. Whether characters in either novel find peace is left an open question.

Though stylistically Edith Wharton's *The House of Mirth* is truly representative of its turn-of-the-century character, Wharton presages the changes in literary culture that were to evolve after World War I into the genre known as modernism. As Laura Rattray comments, "Wharton was a writer whose fiction often captured the very moment of social transition," noting the author's chronicling "the erosion of traditional values" (4). Wharton depicts the traps that Lily Bart's society sets for single women with its insistence on marriage as the only really acceptable path and ruin as the price a woman pays for any transgression of social mores. Hemingway's Brett Ashley shows how far the "erosion of traditional values" went after World War I. Stylistically different, both novels challenge the conventions of their societies, a hallmark of emerging modernism.

WORKS CITED

Baker, Carlos. *Ernest Hemingway: A Life Story.* New York: Scribner's, 1969. Print.

Benstock, Shari. "A Critical History of *The House of Mirth.*" Wharton, *The House of Mirth: Case Studies in Contemporary Criticism.* Ed. Benstock. 309–25.

———. "Introduction: Biographical and Historical Contexts." Wharton, *The House of Mirth: Case Studies in Contemporary Criticism.* Ed. Benstock. 3–23.

Gargano, James W. "*The House of Mirth:* Social Futility and Faith." *American Literature* 44.1 (1972): 137–43. Print.

Haytock, Jennifer. "Marriage and Modernism in Edith Wharton's *Twilight Sleep.*" *Legacy* 19.2 (2002): 216–29. Print.

———. "Modernism." *Edith Wharton in Context.* Ed. Laura Rattray. Cambridge: Cambridge UP, 2012: 364–74. Print.

Hemingway, Ernest. *Death in the Afternoon.* New York: Scribner's, 1932. Print.

———. *The Letters of Ernest Hemingway.* Vol. 3: *1926–1929.* Ed. Rena Sanderson, Sandra Spanier, and Robert Trogdon. Cambridge: Cambridge UP, 2015. Print.

———. *The Sun Also Rises.* New York: Scribner's, 1926. Print.

Knodt, Ellen. "Diving Deep: Jake's Moment of Truth at San Sebastian." *Hemingway Review* 17.1 (Fall 1997): 28–37. Print.

Lamb, Robert Paul. *Art Matters: Hemingway, Craft, and the Creation of the Modern Short Story.* Baton Rouge: Louisiana State UP, 2010. Print.

Lee, Hermione. "The Republic of Letters: Edith Wharton at the Start of Her Career." *Yale Review* 95.2 (Apr. 2007): 1–37. Print.

Moss, Mary. "Notes on New Novels: *The House of Mirth.*" *Atlantic Monthly* 97.2 (January 1906): 52–53. Print.

Rattray, Laura. "Edith Wharton: Contextual Revisions." *Edith Wharton in Context.* Ed. Laura Rattray. Cambridge: Cambridge UP, 2012. 3–21. Print.

Wagner-Martin. Linda. "Wharton and Gender." *Edith Wharton in Context.* Ed. Laura Rattray. Cambridge: Cambridge UP, 2012. 243–50. Print.

Wharton, Edith. *The House of Mirth: Case Studies in Contemporary Criticism.* Ed. Shari Benstock. Boston: Bedford/St. Martin's, 1994.

———. *The Letters of Edith Wharton.* Ed. R. W. B. Lewis and Nancy Lewis. New York: Scribner's, 1988. Print.

II

THE GREAT WAR

Sewing Up the Tears

Medical Systems and the Great War in Wharton's and Hemingway's Short Fiction

JENNIFER HAYTOCK

> The rapid progress made in the treatment of war wounds through clinical observation, but more especially by the active research work at the front, as well as at base hospitals and laboratories in England, France, and the United States, has been such that this edition is almost a new book, so largely has it been rewritten.
>
> —W. W. KEENE, "Prefatory Note" to second edition of *The Treatment of War Wounds*

> It is arranged that men should be broken and that they should be mended. Just as you send your clothes to the laundry and mend them when they come back, so we send our men to the trenches and mend them when they come back again. You send your socks and your shirts again and again to the laundry, and you sew up the tears and clip the ravelled edges again and again, just as many times as they will stand it. And then you throw them away. And we send our men to the war again and again, just as long as they will stand it; just until they are dead, and then we throw them into the ground.
>
> —MARY BORDEN, *The Forbidden Zone*

War stories can be grand adventure tales, coming-of-age stories, and narratives of physical and ideological loss. Plots of combat, however, often elide stories of the injured. After the attack, not everyone dies or charges into the next battle, yet the wounded tend to disappear from history and the literary imagination. Recently, historians of World War I have attended to this gap, and in their short fiction Edith Wharton and Ernest Hemingway explore the nature and effect of medical systems and technologies in a war that created new wounds, both physical and psychological. These stories suggest what it might mean for an individual to be incorporated into the wartime medical system, as injured or healer. In "Coming Home," Wharton mines the mobility of ambulance corps members in contrast to the more limited possibilities of soldiers to explore how individuals could access and exert agency in a mechanized war. Her "Writing a War Story," set in a Paris hospital full of wounded British soldiers, examines the erasure of the injured body as the healthy insist on looking away to other concerns. Writing with more temporal distance from the war, Hemingway interrogates the relationship between the body and the mechanical in "In Another Country," as the narrator and his fellow wounded soldiers suffer enforced passivity as part of the healing process. Finally, "A Way You'll Never Be" represents an individual case of shell shock, controversies about how this condition was treated, and, more broadly, its cultural meaning. All of these stories extend the trope of the passive Great War soldier into the post-combat experiences of the injured and suggest how the demands of wartime medical care constrain them in a system that restricts their agency as much as mechanized trench warfare does.

The First World War saw the implementation of new weaponry, resulting in new kinds of violence to the body. The machine gun, the breech-loading rifle, chemical weapons, and quick-firing artillery all produced wounds of greater magnitude on human flesh than previously seen.[1] In a letter home, Dr. William W. van Dolsen described shrapnel injuries as "queer things. . . . Just small holes here and there but you see they have great power of penetration and go way down deep and are apt to carry lots of clothing and gas forming bacillus. You have to cut down deep and open them wide taking out all of the damaged tissue" (qtd. in Farwell 45). Men injured in the damp agricultural fields of France were at particular risk from gangrene. Further, trench warfare created a ripe environment for diseases like trench foot, typhus, and trench fever. Working prior to the discovery of antibiotics, French and British medical professionals had to find ways to minimize infection; the adoption of the new antiseptic Dichloramin-T alone meant many more injuries were survivable (Keene 111–17).[2] In order to treat the wounded, however, doctors and nurses had to have access to them, so military units set up systems of transporting the wounded from the battlefield: first by stretcher-bearer, then by horse-drawn or motor ambulance to field stations, then again by ambulance to base hospitals far back of the combat lines, and then possibly by train and boat out of the country. As Emily Mayhew notes in her recent history *Wounded*, in 1914 French and British doctors discovered that by the time injured soldiers reached a base hospital, it was often too late to help them, so by early 1915, when the trench system was established, staff and equipment had moved forward to field stations, thus making expert care available to the wounded as soon as possible (5–6). Stretcher-bearers received advanced training so that they could provide treatment, such as stopping hemorrhaging, right on the battlefield (6). During the Great War, wounded soldiers received treatment at a variety of locations, with care and transportation governed by a set of bureaucratic protocols that were both medical and military. With new wounds came new systems, with distinct purposes.

Saving the wounded was not just a humanitarian gesture. As the British *Times History of the War* explained in 1915, the injured "began to have a potential value when new recruits were difficult to obtain in large numbers . . . and when the campaign was likely to be of long duration" (qtd. in Harrison 10). While many people seemed at first to think that the war would be brief, by early 1915 it became clear that this would not be the case. In a war of attrition, no nation could afford to write off the injured, so soldiers needed to be treated and sent back to the lines as quickly as possible. The injured body was valuable. Thus the wounded soldier found himself incorporated into a new bureaucracy, a medical system that took control of his life much as the military had. In *Healing the Nation*, historian Jeffrey Reznick argues that "this [medical] culture represented to many men a continuation of the war machine at play in their lives, an extension of the combined rationalization-anarchy-madness they had experienced at the front" (3). Wharton's and Hemingway's fiction shows both soldiers and medical staff experiencing the medical system as an extension of the "war machine" with its bureaucratic process and its own interests that provoked resistances and submissions of the patients and personnel.

Both Wharton and Hemingway had firsthand experience with the injuries and medical system created by the Great War. In Paris, Wharton began charity work almost immediately after the outbreak of hostilities, including establishing sewing rooms for out-of-work seamstresses, hostels for refugees, and sanatoriums for tuberculosis patients.[3] Driven partly by her vast curiosity as well as a desire to prod the apparently indifferent United States, she also traveled to the front, often bringing medical supplies. She saw physical devastation of the land and towns and encountered wounded soldiers. After visiting a makeshift hospital, she relates how "with admirable ingenuity, [the chief medical officer] had managed to create out of next to nothing the indispensable requirements of a second-line ambulance: sterilizing and disinfecting appliances, a bandage-room, a pharmacy, a well-filled wood-shed, and a clean kitchen in which 'tisanes' were brewing over a cheerful fire" (*Fighting France* 67). She also described the patients: "In almost every [cot] lay a soldier—the doctor's 'worst cases'—few of the wounded, the greater number stricken with fever, bronchitis, frost-bite, pleurisy, or some other form of trench-sickness" (68). In a 28 February 1915 letter to Henry James, Wharton reports that, during just one of her trips to the front, she saw combat between French and German troops, an ambulance station, and a hospital with wounded (Lewis and Lewis 348–50)—almost the full range of treatment centers an injured soldier could experience. She also knew many young men who participated in the war, including her cousin's son, Newbold Rhinelander, who joined the American Ambulance Corps in 1916 and later died as a member of the US Army Corps (Lee 455). Her friend Ronald Simmons assisted Wharton in her charity work and later became part of an intelligence branch for the US Army; he died of illness in 1918, and Wharton greatly grieved his loss.

Hemingway experienced the medical systems of the war as ambulance driver, patient, and witness. While the facts of his wounding vary, in part because Hemingway gave different versions of events, medical and military records indicate that he suffered injuries from both shrapnel and a machine gun on 8 July 1918 while delivering chocolate and other amenities to troops in a trench outside Fossalata di Piave. He was treated at two dressing stations, a field hospital, and the Milan base hospital, where he underwent surgery and physical therapy (Villard and Nagel 176–77). He met other patients and medical professionals, including the nurse Agnes von Kurowsky, with whom he fell in love. As his biographers and scholars note, Hemingway's experience being wounded and treated informed much of his fiction of the late 1920s, including *A Farewell to Arms* and several short stories.

The son of a doctor, Hemingway had significant medical knowledge from a young age (Reynolds, "Doctors" 113), and his letters from the Milan Red Cross Hospital show great interest in the wounds he sustained and the care he received.[4]

For Wharton and Hemingway, war writing inevitably included aspects of medical care, and they both published war novels that might also be considered hospital novels. Wharton's *A Son at the Front* (1923) includes characters who perform charity work in hospitals in Paris during the war and partially takes place within the wartime medical system, from the forward aid station where John Campton and Anderson Brant find Campton's wounded son George to the base hospital in Paris where George dies. The son of another character, a surgeon, dies in the first months of the war because he can't get medical care before gangrene sets in (120). By the time George is wounded a few months later, medical systems have changed to situate doctors and medical theaters close to the front (278). In other words, Wharton understood the issues facing the medical profession during the war and knew how the system changed its practices. A substantive portion of Hemingway's *A Farewell to Arms* (1929) is set in the Milan hospital where Frederic Henry is sent for surgery and recovery and where his relationship with Catherine Barkley becomes serious.[5] Unlike many other war writers, Wharton and Hemingway intertwined the wounds of war with what happened after: the soldier's incorporation into the wartime medical system.

Amid working on behalf of charities, visiting the front, producing reportage, and coping with her own ill health, Wharton wrote "Coming Home" for *Scribner's*, published in December 1915. Of the stories discussed in this essay, "Coming Home" is most concrete in its representation of bodies, healthy and injured. Wharton prepares the way for this emphasis at the beginning of the story, as the narrator connects storytelling to bodily injury and healing: "such fragments of experience as one got were torn from their setting like bits of flesh scattered by shrapnel. Now things that seemed disjointed are beginning to link themselves together, and the broken bones of history are rising from the battle-fields" (26). While the frame narrator receives no physical representation, H. Macy Greer, who relates the action, is described particularly as "a small hard-muscled youth, with pleasant manners, a sallow face, straight hemp-coloured hair and grey eyes" (26).

As Elsa Nettels notes, Wharton frequently employed educated white male narrators to lend authority and credibility to her short fiction, a distancing act that also opens a space for irony and question. In "Coming Home," the contrast between the disembodied narrator and the physically present Greer establishes an interest in bodies and what can happen to them.

In addition to being white, male, and educated, H. Macy Greer has other characteristics that make him a particularly useful narrator. According to the frame narrator, Greer "has the gift of making the thing told seem as true as if one had seen it" (26). Further, as a member of the ambulance corps, he is a mobile participant in a war in which so many individuals remain stationary: he travels among the soldiers stuck in trenches, the wounded and medical staff at aid stations and hospitals, and civilians behind the lines. He can carry information across these spaces, and the frame narrator is not the only character to appreciate the advantages of his mobility. Greer's story opens with a surgeon asking him to talk with a French soldier who is desperate for information about his family, whose town is now behind enemy lines. While Greer has no news to share, his position allows him to pursue the question.

In "Coming Home," knowledge and bodies both circulate within the medical system. While Greer carries stories to the rear, other characters have opportunities to gather information through the unlikely connections that the medical system creates. Jean de Réchamp first learns of the villain Oberst von Scharlach from wounded German soldiers in the hospital where they're all being treated, the hospital serving as a neutral space where both sides trade information (32–33). In fact, the passivity of the hospital experience fuels a need for communication: Jean was "not talkative before the war, but his long weeks in hospital, starving for news, had unstrung him" (31). Amid the chaos of war, Jean values firsthand oral reports more highly than written sources. Official stories are outdated, such as Jean's first news of Réchamp (27–28), and he distrusts letters from his family, who he assumes would keep bad news from him (31–32). Throughout the story, the most valued information comes from within the medical system, including gossip from other soldiers in the hospital, the information Jean wants from Greer, and the confirmation of von Scharlach's identity at the end of the story.

Greer's role in the medical system heavily informs his perspective: he has an eye for bodies and their degree of health. The protagonist of Greer's story, Jean de Réchamp, receives a physical description, "trim and slim," with "a leg smashed" (27), an injury that crucially leaves Jean "dead lame" for the rest of the story (56). Greer describes most of the other characters in physical terms: the Réchamp family consists of "a grey-haired lady knitting with stiff fingers, an old gentleman with a high nose and a weak chin . . . ; a pretty girl at his feet, with a dog's head in her lap" (43), and the grandmother who can "bring on a valvular heart-attack by just sitting still and holding her breath" (36). The story pays attention to bodies as a medical professional would, highlighting what can fail or be damaged.

Jean's fiancée Yvonne Malo, however, receives a different kind of physical description, suggesting a distinct kind of damage to bodies. Jean "remembered her as an ugly little girl" (33) who "shed her chrysalis" as a young woman (34). On first meeting her, Greer attempts to describe her, focusing on her eyes and her voice, but his narration interrupts itself with disclaimers about adjectives and an inability to capture her, marked by ellipses and dashes (44). The next day, Greer finds her "less effective. . . . She looked older for one thing; her face was pinched, and a little sallow and for the first time I noticed that her cheek-bones were too high" (49). Before he hears that Yvonne saved Réchamp, she appears indescribably attractive; once he begins to guess *how* she saved Réchamp, he finds flaws. In other words, his descriptions of Yvonne focus on her appearance and are informed by his assumptions about her sexual behavior. Yet his later description includes more details about her, as Greer recognizes her humanity. Critics agree that the unspoken secret of the story is Yvonne's use of her body to protect her fiancé's family and home. Wharton registers this sexual bartering symbolically, the "breach in the wall," which is "the only scratch the place has got" (48). By linking the sexual trade to a "breach" and a "scratch," Wharton makes clear that Yvonne's actions, despite her apparently voluntary participation, are a wound. This injury, however, cannot be seen, like Jean's limp, and it can't be articulated by any of the characters. Because of prohibitions of even speaking about sexual behavior, the medical system offers no place for Yvonne, even as she functions as a nurse within it.

While the medical system fails to recognize sexual injury, it accommodates another crime, in part because bodies and their state of health dictate action. When Greer is asked to take "a German with an abdominal wound who was in a bad way, but might be saved by an operation if he could be got back to the base before midnight," he does so without question or comment, as "there is only one answer to such requests" (55). On this journey, Jean apparently manages to kill the patient without Greer's awareness, much to Greer's bewilderment. For one thing, he can't figure out how Jean could have caused the leak in the gas tank without his knowledge; for another, Greer has no idea how Jean even knows who the patient is, as his unopened identification papers remain secure in Greer's pocket.

Wharton offers a significant clue to at least one of these mysteries. Throughout the story, von Scharlach's facial scar "that drew up the left corner of his mouth" (40) recurs as his distinguishing facial characteristic. Tellingly, while Greer examines the patient's face several times and notices a forehead injury and expressions of pain, he never mentions a scar. The story only works as a tale of murder if Greer is unobservant, which the frame narrator's faith in Greer's descriptive powers indicates he is not, or because Greer is who he is: a medical professional who sees a stomach wound, a patient's suffering, and a short time frame in which to provide care. A scar marks an old injury, one that requires nothing of a medical system committed to saving life. Jean—angry, hurt, and vengeful—looks for the tell-tale scar as a sign of identity; Greer—interested but not invested in the Réchamp story—looks for more recent and treatable bodily damage. Further, Greer's faith in the medical system restores his shaken opinion of Jean: "For, after all, I *knew* there wasn't a paper of any sort on that man when he was lifted into my ambulance the night before: the French officials attend to their business too carefully for me not to have been sure of that" (58; emphasis in original). Thus "Coming Home" illuminates how the medical system of the Great War facilitated a flow of bodies and information in an otherwise stationary war, as well as what can be considered an injury and how training and perspective shape what is seen and therefore known.

Whereas "Coming Home" focuses on the mobile aspects of the Great War and what bodies mean within that system, Wharton's later "Writing a War Story" takes a different approach to representing the medical system: it draws attention to the erasure of injured bodies from the public consciousness. This story, published in 1919, focuses on a young woman's failure to write a story that conveys truth to the experience of war, a fear that some critics speculate that Wharton may have shared. Yet Julie Olin-Ammentorp convincingly points out that by the time Wharton wrote this story she had developed strategies for avoiding the pitfalls that Ivy Spang stumbles into (110–11) and that Wharton carefully shows how Ivy has been set up to fail by a male editor who doesn't understand war experience either (105–6). Set partly in a hospital, the story lends itself to a reading of how injured bodies were regarded and represented. In contrast to "Coming Home," which is full of physical descriptions, "Writing a War Story" notably lacks bodies: that is, few characters receive physical descriptions and have bodily experiences. Even though Ivy's hospital ward is "full at the time" (255), the story makes no reference to suffering, cries of pain, blood, or other bodily matters, which Wharton certainly knew about.

In *A Son at the Front*, she portrays hospitals much more realistically: the forward hospital where John Campton finds his son is full of "bloody linen," "a smell of disinfectants," "a sickening odor" of gangrene, overworked nurses, "a nauseating scream in a queer bleached voice that might have been man, woman or monkey's," wooden pallets for beds, flies, overcrowding, and death (276–78). Although the situation at Ivy's base hospital in Paris would be less dire, as most patients who made it this far would be in stable condition, the lack of signs of physical suffering is striking. The soldiers exist almost entirely as voices that call to Ivy for copies of her photograph, and they are metonymized at one point as "the long line of beds" (257). Even the famed writer-turned-soldier Harold Harbard, who winds up in this hospital and thus is presumably injured, is referred to merely as being "rather down on his luck" (256); Wharton describes only his "brown, ugly, tumultuous-locked head" (258).

The sanitized representation of the hospital may be considered part of Wharton's strategy. Within the layers of the story is one wounded soldier, whom Ivy never meets. Emile Durand appears only in the journal of Ivy's former governess: "Military Hospital No. 13. November, 1914. Long talk with the Chasseur Alpin Emile Durand, wounded through the knee and the left lung at the Hautes Chaumes" (253).[6] The governess, Ivy, and the novelist-critic all recognize in these lines an important "subject," and their competing views of literature demonstrate the struggle to find a writing strategy that will bring Durand's injured body to the foreground and provide a context for the reader to understand what that body means. Wharton's own strategy in "Writing a War Story" is silence: Durand's body appears briefly as he passes through the hospital; then he moves on to the next center of treatment—to be healed or to die, to be sent home or back to the front. The glimpse that Ivy and the reader receive of him through the governess's writing lends insight into the medical system that copes with the aftermath of combat and very little of Durand himself: What was he like? What did he say in his "long talk"? What did he feel about his experience of war and wounding? The answers to these questions are what Ivy fails to imagine, and the individual is lost amid the bureaucracies of war and medical care.

Ironically, the most visible body in this story is Ivy's, a description of which appears shortly after the sketch of the wounded Emile Durand. This description is of her photograph rather than her actual body: "she saw herself, exceedingly long, narrow and sinuous, robed in white and monastically veiled, holding out a refreshing beverage to an invisible sufferer with a gesture half way between Mélisande lowering her braid over the balcony and Florence Nightingale advancing with the lamp" (253). In this photograph, the injured bodies are "invisible," as they are in "Writing a War Story" itself. Unlike Emile Durand's body, Ivy's is mediated through images and allusions. While Durand's body is concrete yet lacks commentary to give it meaning, Ivy's, in contrast, abounds with imagery that imposes meaning and history upon it, the very history and meaning that make up the civilization that supposedly justifies the war. At the hospital, Ivy's patients beg for a signed copy of this photograph, suggesting that bodies that can be understood through existing systems of meaning displace those whose significance seems to question the civilization built on those systems. Although Wharton wrote openly in support of the defense of Western civilization, "Writing a War Story" suggests that she found placing that civilization next to injured bodies to be unnerving.

Perhaps, then, it's not surprising that the body apparently most in danger in the story is Ivy's. During the conversation with the famous author, she responds physically to his criticism. When she sees that he's been reading her story, "her heart gave an apprehensive twitch" (258); when he offers his first comments, "she sat before him with her head drooping, and the blood running back from her cheeks" (259). Her flush of embarrassment prompts the only mention of blood in this wartime hospital, highlighting again the sanitization of the actual injured bodies. Further, "to save her life she could not conceal her disappointment" (259), as if Ivy's comeuppance is on par with the danger soldiers face. Thus the story points out the ways in which authorities shift attention away from the wounded soldiers; the "invisible sufferer" in Ivy's portrait and the story itself eliminate the injured body from view, just as, as Elaine Scarry argues, official discourse hides these bodies through language.

One other bodiless soldier calls attention to injury much as Emile Durand does: at the end of the story, Ivy learns that Harold Harbard is in the same room as a patient she already knows, a polo-player. When she arrives at the room, "the polo-player's bed was empty," a fact reported to the reader but apparently barely registered by Ivy (258). An empty bed has meaning for the body that occupied it: where is the polo-player? Recovered and out for some exercise? Discharged? Shipped back to a British hospital? Dead? Ivy never asks, and the story never tells. He's simply replaced by the writer, just as one soldier's body replaces another on the front lines, however famous a novelist he may be. In "Writing a War Story," Wharton points out how military and medical systems repeatedly shunt aside bodies injured in war in favor of more comfortably addressed issues.

Like Wharton's short fiction about the Great War, Hemingway's stories seldom render the moment of wounding, instead focusing on how medical systems take over the lives of injured soldiers. "In Another Country," first published in *Scribner's* in 1927, then collected in *Men Without Women*, portrays the emotional impact of wartime medical treatment for the wounded. Much as soldiers experienced combat as a conflict between technology and the body, the story opens by portraying the healing process in the same way: "My knee did not bend and the leg dropped straight from the knee to the ankle without a calf, and the machine was to bend the knee and make it move as in riding a tricycle. But it did not bend yet, and instead the machine lurched when it came to the bending part" (206). In this story, Hemingway points out that the technological advances that made the war so devastating also include widespread use of machinery intended to undo the damage of the weaponry. Although what we now know as physical therapy began before the Great War, the number of soldiers who survived physical trauma, rather than dying from those wounds on the battlefield or undergoing amputation, meant that the medical establishment had opportunities for devising methods to restore the use of damaged limbs. As Reynolds points out about Frederic Henry, "Had [he] been wounded sixty years earlier in the American Civil War, his medical treatment would have been quick and final: At the field hospital, his leg would have been taken off at the knee, the stump cauterized, and he would have been sent away on crutches" ("Doctors" 118). For Frederic, the narrator of "In Another Country," and Hemingway himself, disinfectants, advanced surgical techniques, and physical therapy offered the possibility of saving the leg.

By reframing the war as machine against machine, "In Another Country" reiterates the trope of passivity in literature of the Great War and in doing so shows how soldiers' emotional suffering becomes invisible. The passivity of physical therapy replicates the passivity that marked the war as a whole, as soldiers waited out weeks or months in the trenches. The protagonist notes that "we all knew that being wounded, after all, was really an accident" (208)—something that happened to them, not something they did or earned. Further, the narrator reports that "the machines were new then and it was we who were to prove them" (208–9). Just as many soldiers of the Great War were disappointed to find that battle was not a proving ground for masculinity and courage, in this story the injured exist to validate the machines, not the other way around. This passive physical therapy erodes individuals' sense of agency: the patients' bodies are acted upon by the machines, light, and massage therapists. The doctor shows a patient a picture of "a hand that had been withered almost as small as the major's, before it had taken a machine course" (207). This photograph fragments the body into parts, similarly to how weaponry would shatter a body. Tellingly, the narrator indicates that the hand—"it"—has received treatment, not that the person to whom it belongs took the course of therapy. In this story, the medical system reduces injured soldiers to body parts fitted into machines for an unclear outcome.

Yet the story also portrays the patients' resistance to the passivity of physical therapy. The second paragraph establishes the centrality of medical treatment to the narrator's daily routine—"We were all at the hospital every afternoon"—even as the narrator asserts a degree of control over his life through choosing how he gets to the hospital: "there were different ways of walking across the town through the dusk to the hospital" (206). Even though "always . . . you crossed a bridge across a canal to enter the hospital," the narrator emphasizes that he has "a choice of three bridges"; some choice, it seems, is better than none. The major, too, who openly calls the machines "nonsense" and "idiotic" (208–9) and who stops coming for three days after the death of his wife, nevertheless returns. The major chooses not to look at the inspirational photographs that the medical staff posts, but he still returns for therapy.

Despite the optimism of the medical staff, the patients' despair permeates the story. The narrator remarks that "there was a time when none of us believed in the machines" (208), as if belief in machines has replaced belief in God.[7] Richard Irwin points out that "the *kind* of treatment [the machines] provide is inappropriate to the internal, psychological 'wounds' the major has sustained" (29; emphasis in original). Like many critics, Irwin reads the story primarily as about the major; focusing on the narrator, I suggest, is also illuminating. The narrator, too, feels "a little detached" (207), and while the major articulates the disbelief in the machines, the narrator reports that "none of us," presumably including himself, "believe" in the machines. The narrator's retrospective narration implies that there is another time when they, or some of them, do come to believe in the machines. He similarly indicates, in regard to the man without a nose: "this was a long time ago, and then we did not any of us know how it was going to be afterward" (207). The bleakness of the story contrasts with the suggested future, in which the narrator recovers. Ironically, his body's eventual submission to the machine restores his physical agency if not his emotional health.

Part of the bleakness may be cynicism about the medical profession as well as despair caused by the war. Even while the efficacy of the machines is unknown, the narrator sees the doctor as hypocritical and dishonest. When the major returns after his outburst, the staff have posted before-and-after photographs of wounds treated by the machines: "I do not know where the doctor got them. I always understood we were the first to use the machines" (210). Either the doctor has lied that these patients are the first, or the photographs are misrepresentations. While the doctor's motives in either case seem to be kind and inspirational, the narrator and the major fail to respond to them, possibly because, no matter how close the doctor and medical staff are to the injured bodies of war, they are not close enough. The narrator notes that his bond with the other wounded soldiers comes from "there being something that happened that they, the people who disliked us, did not understand" (208), even as he believes the other soldiers, the "hunting-hawks" (208), possess a bravery that he does not. The narrator registers degrees to which others have claim to authority and status, claims that rest on performance and bravery in combat and from which the medical personnel are excluded.

The story suggests that, ultimately, whether patients believe in the machines and the medical staff makes no difference. As the bodies sit passively under treatment, the retrospective voice implies that they do heal, even if imperfectly, like the soldier whose face had to be "rebuilt," although "they could never get the nose exactly right" (307). The wounded soldiers have no need of belief. The mechanistic world triumphs over the spiritual world: the machines do not need to be believed in in order to produce their salvation. Thus the story indicates that, for injured soldiers, the medical system as much as the war undermines their sense of a meaningful and ordered world.

Stories about psychological trauma are another way in which Hemingway approached the postwar loss of meaning, a loss that is literally also an injury. Shell-shock victims often felt disengaged from the world, among other symptoms, and medical practitioners found themselves having to help patients with a new and categorically problematic condition. Hemingway's "A Way You'll Never Be," published in 1933 as part of *Winner Take Nothing*, illuminates how shell shock was treated, including the significant debates about the condition, and how both injury and treatment pervade military culture. In this story, Hemingway portrays Nick Adams at the point of physical but not psychological healing after being wounded. He can't focus, can't sleep without a light, suffers from hallucinations, and ultimately uncovers the buried memory of being shot that the intrusive memory of the yellow house by a river covers. While scholars such as Kenneth G. Johnston and Frank Scafella have recognized Nick as a shell-shock victim and more recently Ronald Smith has diagnosed Nick with PTSD,[8] here I find it useful to look closely at how the complicated and contested diagnosis and treatment of shell shock inform Nick's sense of despair in "A Way You'll Never Be."

Considering shell shock within its historical context allows for understanding the particular suffering of and treatment possibilities for those patients and how such a label positioned a victim culturally in ways that a general diagnosis such as trauma, or an anachronistic diagnosis of PTSD, do not permit. I follow the lead of historian Tracey Loughran, who usefully considers shell shock to be "a collection of ideas about illness rather than . . . an illness" (100). Peter Leese also approaches shell shock as a historical construction: "Shell shock is modern because surrounding it are scientific and bureaucratic procedures designed to manage human emotions and behavior and direct them towards mass, state-controlled activity, in this instance, making war." Further, he explores how "both patients and doctors made shell shock after their own image, sometimes negotiating common meanings, sometimes resisting the soldierly and disciplinary medical roles they were expected to play" (4). Recognizing shell shock as a historically specific diagnosis rather than a transhistorical kind of suffering places Nick Adams, Captain Paravicini, and the Italian soldiers within particular medical and military bureaucracies and systems of meaning.

During and after the Great War, medical practitioners focused much attention on investigating the causes of shell shock. Frederick Mott's *War Neuroses and Shell Shock* (1919) devotes approximately 265 pages to the causes and symptoms of war-related psychological disorders and fewer than 50 pages to treatment. An article in the *Lancet*, published on 5 February 1916, reports on a conference held by the Royal Society of Medicine the previous month, during which

> Dr. Henry Head was not even content to allow the separate existence of the subject under discussion, holding it to be a heterogeneous collection of different nervous affections from concussion to sheer funk, which have merely this much in common that nervous control has at last given way. To him it would be just as reasonable to sweep up the various fruits which fall from the trees in a strong wind and then to discuss them without first stating that some fell from an apple and some from a pear tree. ("A Discussion" 306)

In other words, anyone trying to understand the cause of Nick's shell shock wades into a hotly contested territory among medical professionals and laypeople. According to Reynolds, Hemingway read extensively about shell shock and neurasthenia on his return from Milan and thus was likely aware not only of these conditions but also of the medical debates surrounding them (*Young Hemingway* 47).

One article that Hemingway may have come across is Francis X. Dercum's "So-Called 'Shell Shock': The Remedy," which, as its title suggests, resists the diagnosis of shell shock itself. Dercum argues that victims of shell shock, like those of hysteria, suffer from an innate flaw: "They lack endurance, lack persistence, lack fixity of purpose, lack those staying qualities which are necessary to bear the strain of life, to meet the exigencies of existence" (67). Nick's reluctance to talk about his past performance in the war—"Let's not talk about how I am. . . . It's a subject I know too much about to want to think about it any more" (309)—may refer to the psychotherapy he has undergone as well as to the specific discoveries that he may have made, that is, that he is unable "to bear the strain of life." If this flaw is congenital, as Dercum argues, then there's nothing Nick can do about it.

This understanding of shell shock affects how Nick relates to others. Dercum notes that, among the "many causes other than fright which may induce excessive emotional reaction in hysterical persons, are, as we all know, annoyance, disappointment, mortification, fancied slights, wrongs or insults, grief, shame, the shock of sexual experiences, the worry over sexual peccadilloes and kindred matters" (67). In his stream-of-consciousness reflections, Nick focuses on moments of fear during bombings, memories of nights in Paris with Gaby Delys and his girl, who "sometimes . . . was with some one else and he could not understand that," and a "fear that they might take the same driver twice" (310–11); in his memory he links the fear that arises in war with "worry over sexual peccadilloes." When Nick assures the Italian soldiers that the soon-to-arrive Americans are "twice as large as myself, healthy, with clean hearts, sleep at night, never been wounded, never been blown up, never had their heads caved in, never been scared, don't drink, faithful to the girls they left behind them, many of them never had crabs, wonderful chaps" (311), he's saying not only that these soldiers are not like him, they are not predisposed to become like him and suffer shell shock.

Unable to agree on the causes of shell shock, medical professionals were similarly divided on treatment methods. Leese, following Eric Leed, divides the British methods into the disciplinary and the analytic, the former relying on electric shock therapy, bromides, and massage, the latter characterized by psychological therapy, although some practitioners employed both methods.[9] British attitudes toward shell shock differed from the French: according to Leese, even the term "shell shock," used by the British, indicates their greater likelihood to regard the condition as having at least some physical component, while the French medical system, which was also more uniform, tended to consider psychological cases as malingerers (34–35). In one medical manual, *Shell Shock and Its Lessons* (1917), G. Elliot Smith and T. H. Pear emphasize the importance of addressing each case on its own merits: "the essence of the mentally afflicted patient's trouble is in some particular form of anxiety or worry which is *individual and personal.* The aim of the diagnosis, therefore, should be not merely to determine the appropriate generic label for the affliction, but rather to discover the particular circumstances which have given rise to the present state" (48; emphasis in original).[10] This fluid and contingent approach to treating shell-shock sufferers, though perhaps positive in its attention to individual needs, may also have contributed to the perception that shell shock was not a real malady and, even if it was, had uncertain treatment methods and outcomes. Unlike a bullet wound, shell shock remained invisible to the observer and lacked a clear treatment protocol.

"A Way You'll Never Be" exposes the effect of dissension, however legitimate, among medical professionals about shell shock on patients. Is Nick a malingerer, the unfortunate product of bad heredity, a coward, or a victim of a head wound? There's no secret answer hidden in the pages of the story; the point is that Nick and his doctors don't know and might not agree, and any of the answers influences how Nick thinks about himself, as does the fact of dissent. Nick Adams may be regarded as caught within a publically contested medical diagnosis that affects how he is treated by others and how he regards himself. Scafella argues that Nick chooses to undertake the journey to the front with the "conscious intention" of searching out the origins of his visions of the yellow house (183). Johnston argues that Nick has been sent back to the front on the pretext of displaying the new American uniform and that, in fact, the trip is actually meant to be "therapeutic: that is, to boost Nick's morale and restore his self-confidence," specifically, to "exorcise some of his fear and self-doubt" (430). The difference in these readings is one of agency: is Nick in charge of his treatment, or is he subject to medical and/or military authority? How Nick perceives himself may be greatly influenced by how his psychological and physical symptoms have been treated.

In any case, it seems likely that Nick's trip to the front is at least approved by his doctors, if not suggested by them. Nick's reference to the "they" who have authority over him seems to shift between military and medical bureaucracies: "they've put me in [the American uniform]" (308); "they said to circulate around anyway" without chocolate and cigarettes (309); "they thought it was better to have it absorb" (310); "It's a hell of a nuisance once they've had you certified as nutty" (310). One of Nick's last "theys" conflates medical and military: "Why don't they bury the dead?" (314). This flow between medical and military authority reflects the intertwining of the systems and their goals. Medical personnel had the task of restoring soldiers' bodies and minds, often for the purpose of sending them back to the front. Thus Nick's trip to the front may be a therapeutic quest for a cause of his shell shock, or it may be a sign that the authorities consider him well enough to take up work.[11]

Understanding the ways in which shell shock was pathologized and treated also illuminates Nick's friend Captain Paravicini. Paravicini exhibits genuine concern for Nick, some of which takes the shape of medical advice. As he himself admits, he's "no doctor," but, as an officer, he's responsible for the physical and psychological well-being of the men he commands. In a previous battle, he treated his soldiers' "hysterics" by having Nick walk them around outside during a bombing (310), a "treatment" that may have caused further deterioration in the psychological state of all his soldiers. He has definite opinions about how Nick's head wound should have been treated, weighing in on the medical debate about trepanation.[12] This debate includes how shell shock could be treated, as Mott indicates that draining the brain can help, showing again that shell shock was approached as both a physical and a psychological wound. Paravacini also treats Nick's shell shock by advising him to take a nap. While this advice may be a way to get Nick away from the soldiers he seems to be frightening, rest was also an accepted treatment. Paravacini enacts the qualities of a strong leader, showing concern for the men under him, including Nick, spiced with a good bit of medical knowledge. Paravacini's advice, however, directly contradicts the treatment Nick's doctor has prescribed, if we accept the notion that Nick's trip to the front is a therapeutically aimed journey to the scene of his trauma. Nick, regardless of whether he's aware of the different approaches to treating shell shock, finds himself subject to differing philosophies of treatment and hence possibly as confused by his treatment as by the trauma itself.

Together, Wharton's and Hemingway's stories portray a wartime medical system that brings individuals to its service, making bodies "useful" in a Foucauldian sense, as any bureaucracy does: in this way, wartime resembles peacetime. These systems have a profound impact on the individuals who serve them and are treated by them. Given that many individuals regarded this war as the crucible that changed meaning—that created modernity—how one fit into a medical system that affected so many mattered. Both Wharton's and Hemingway's characters are swept along by the medical system, much as they are swept into war and able to assert agency only in limited capacity.

NOTES

Many thanks to Laura Dumuhosky for her invaluable research assistance.

1. See Farwell, chap. 3, for a discussion of these weapons.

2. Not only was Dichloramin-T effective in preventing infection, it lasted for twenty-four hours, so dressings could be changed less often, saving on gauze and, more importantly, the time of doctors and nurses (Keene 115).

3. See Lee 463–78.

4. See Villard and Nagel, chap. 4, for these letters.

5. See Michael Reynolds's "Doctors in the House of Love" for more on the medical treatments that Hemingway included in *A Farewell to Arms.*

6. Both Olin-Ammentorp (138–39) and Lee (494) point out that Wharton anticipates Frederic Henry's famous monologue against empty idealistic words in a speech by Paul Dastry in *A Son at the Front.* In "Writing a War Story," Wharton actually embeds a story that consists only of names, places, dates, and injured body parts within the larger story.

7. The narrator's experience of physical therapy does not seem to have been Hemingway's. In his 11 November 1918 letter to his parents, he reported that the machines "do wonders" (Villard and Nagel 189). On 28 November he wrote that they are "very good" (194).

8. See also Hays, chap. 8, for a discussion of whether Hemingway himself suffered from shell shock.

9. See Leese, chap. 5.

10. Teasing through how Nick Adams would be treated involves considering how the

Italians regarded shell shock, except the story indicates that he's under the authority of Americans in Italy. Further, Hemingway would have been more likely to know British and American attitudes toward shell shock, as by the time he himself was in Italy, the United States had established its own medical presence there, and he later learned about the condition from British and American medical journals.

11. Knodt has recently shown that the Americans really did have soldiers circulate in the lines to raise Italian morale.

12. See Keene's *Treatment of War Wounds*, "Wounds of the Head," for example, for a contemporary discussion of how head wounds should be treated.

WORKS CITED

Borden, Mary. *The Forbidden Zone*. 1929. London: Hesperus P, 2008. Print.

Dercum, Francis X. "So-Called 'Shell Shock': The Remedy." *Archives of Neurology and Psychiatry* 1.1 (1919): 65–76. Print.

"A Discussion on Shell Shock." *Lancet* 187 (5 Feb. 1916): 306–7. Print.

Farwell, Byron. *Over There: The United States in the Great War, 1917–1918*. New York: W. W. Norton, 1999. Print.

Harrison, Mark. *The Medical War: British Military Medicine in the First World War*. New York: Oxford UP, 2010. Print.

Hays, Peter. *Fifty Decades of Hemingway Criticism*. Washington, DC: Scarecrow Press, 2013. Print.

Hemingway, Ernest. *A Farewell to Arms*. 1929. New York: Scribner's, 1959. Print.

———. "In Another Country." *The Complete Short Stories of Ernest Hemingway: The Finca Vigía Edition*. New York: Scribner's, 1987. 206–10. Print.

———. "A Way You'll Never Be." *The Complete Short Stories of Ernest Hemingway: The Finca Vigía Edition*. New York: Scribner's, 1987. 306–15. Print.

Irwin, Richard. "'Of War, Wounds, and Silly Machines': An Examination of Hemingway's 'In Another Country.'" *Serif* 5.2 (1938): 21–29. Print.

Johnston, Kenneth G. "'A Way You'll Never Be': A Mission of Morale." *Studies in Short Fiction* 23 (1986): 429–35. Print.

Keene, W. W. *The Treatment of War Wounds*. Philadelphia: W. B. Saunders and Co., 1918. Print.

Knodt, Ellen Andrews. "Towards a Better Understanding of Nicholas Adams in Hemingway's 'A Way You'll Never Be.'" *Hemingway Review* 35.2 (2016): 70–86. Print.

Lee, Hermione. *Edith Wharton*. New York: Knopf, 2007. Print.

Leese, Peter. *Shell Shock: Traumatic Neurosis and the British Soldiers of the First World War*. New York: Palgrave, 2002. Print.

Lewis, R. W. B., and Nancy Lewis, eds. *The Letters of Edith Wharton*. New York: Macmillan, 1988. Print.

Loughran, Tracey. "Shell Shock, Trauma, and the First World War: The Making of a Diagnosis and Its Histories." *Journal of the History of Medicine and Allied Sciences* 67.1 (2012): 94–119. Print.

Mayhew, Emily. *Wounded: A New History of the Western Front in World War I*. New York: Oxford UP, 2013. Print.

Mott, Frederick W. *War Neurosis and Shell Shock*. London: Hodder & Stoughton, 1919. Print.

Nettels, Elsa. "Gender and First-Person Narration in Edith Wharton's Short Fiction." *Edith Wharton: New Critical Essays*. Ed. Alfred Bendixen and Annette Zilversmit. New York: Garland, 1992. 245–60. Print.

Olin-Ammentorp, Julie. *Edith Wharton's Writings from the Great War*. Gainesville: UP of Florida, 2004. Print.

Reynolds, Michael. "*A Farewell to Arms:* Doctors in the House of Love." *The Cambridge Companion to Hemingway*. Ed. Scott Donaldson. Cambridge: Cambridge UP, 1996. 109–27. Print.

———. *The Young Hemingway*. New York: Blackwell, 1986. Print.

Reznick, Jeffrey S. *Healing the Nation: Soldiers and the Culture of Caregiving in Britain during the Great War*. Manchester, UK: Manchester UP, 2004. Print.

Scafella, Frank. "The Way It Never Was on the Piave." *Hemingway in Italy and Other Essays*. Ed. Robert W. Lewis. New York: Praeger, 1990. 180–88. Print.

Scarry, Elaine. *The Body in Pain: The Making and Unmaking of the World*. New York: Oxford UP, 1985. Print.

Smith, G. Elliot, and T. H. Pear. *Shell Shock and Its Lessons*. 2nd ed. Manchester, UK: Manchester UP, 1917. California Digital Library. Web. Accessed 15 June 2014.

Smith, Ronald. "Nick Adams and Post-Traumatic Stress Disorder." *War, Literature, and the Arts* 9.1 (1997): 39–48. Print.

Villard, Henry S., and James Nagel. *Hemingway in Love and War: The Lost Diary of Agnes von Kurowsky*. Boston: Northeastern UP, 1989. Print.

Wharton, Edith. "Coming Home." *Collected Stories, 1911–1937*. Ed. Maureen Howard. New York: Library of America, 2001. 26–58. Print.

———. *Fighting France, from Dunkerque to Belfort*. 1915. New York: Charles Scribner's Sons, 1919. Print.

———. *A Son at the Front*. New York: Scribner's, 1923. Print.

———. "Writing a War Story." *Collected Stories, 1911–1937*. Ed. Maureen Howard. New York: Library of America, 2001. 247–60. Print.

Gender, Philanthropy, and the Great War in the Works of Wharton and Hemingway

MILENA RADEVA-COSTELLO

In writing about the Great War, Edith Wharton and Ernest Hemingway engage with philanthropy and the gift, construing giving and questioning the possibility of the gift in the context of war relief. Even though both authors appear to doubt the authenticity of philanthropy, in the Derridean sense their characters strive after the (im)possibility of the gift.

Wharton's heroines are transformed as a result of their involvement in philanthropy: they take on masculine and public roles that are otherwise closed to them; they achieve sexually and personally fulfilling lives. Hemingway's masculine characters question the uses of philanthropy but affirm the encounter with trauma, abjection, and death as an ultimate gift. Whereas for Wharton's characters giving is desire, something toward which they always feel inclined, for Hemingway's shell-shocked soldiers giving is a productive facet of their suffering, insofar as their acts of giving originate in their own war trauma as something that "can't be given to me, so it can't be taken away from me" (as Derrida says in *The Gift of Death*, 44).

"SHE DOES GOOD WORKS WITHOUT SEEMING TO NOTICE IT": EDITH WHARTON AND WAR RELIEF

The major biographies of Edith Wharton, by Shari Benstock, R. W. B. Lewis, and Hermione Lee, point out her extensive involvement with philanthropic activities during her stay in France at the time of the First World War. According to Benstock, her fund-raising activities during the war years were "on a scale that in our time only corporations could undertake" (307). In addition to workrooms and the "American Hostel for Refugees," her activities included the "Children of Flanders Rescue Committee" and convalescent homes for tuberculosis patients ("Maisons Américaines de Convalescence" and Tuberculous War-Victims). Her charities "managed twenty-one houses in Paris and outlying regions" by June 1917 (331). "Mrs. Wharton's Charities" grew to become "the most diverse privately funded charity in France during the war, second in size only to the American Hospital at Neuilly" (303). For her dedicated work for France and Belgium, Wharton was awarded high distinction: the French made her Chevalier of the Legion of Honor, and King Albert of Belgium presented her with the Medal of Queen Elizabeth and named her Chevalier of the Order of Leopold (Lewis 387).

Privately, however, Wharton frequently portrayed herself as reluctantly drawn into charity work; "'I'm not used to philanthropy,' she wrote to Berenson in fatigued handwriting. The 'fluffy fuzzy' people, she said, had all left Paris; those who remained assisted in war relief" (Benstock 308). In *A Backward Glance*, her memoirs of the war years, Wharton speaks of her "innate distaste for anything like 'social service'" (348); and, even though she believes that "[m]any women . . . found their vocation in nursing the wounded, or in other philanthropic activities," which "turned them away forever from a life of discontented idling, and made them into happy people" (356), she herself "was already in the clutches of an inexorable calling, and . . . conscious of lukewarmness in regard to organized beneficence" (356). And in her letters to friends Wharton refers to her philanthropic work as "dull drudgery" (379). Moreover, she repeated "as a *bon mot* Percy Lubbock's quip that he could forgive her for her industry because she 'so visibly' hated what she was doing" (Benstock 311). Similarly, the French newspaper *Le Temps* remarked, "She does good works without seeming to notice it" (qtd. in Lewis 387). Her attitude to charity is complicated at best, and often straightforwardly critical.

Wharton's philanthropic activities between 1914 and 1918 were so engrossing that she barely found time for writing fiction, her "inexorable calling." As documented by Julie Olin-Ammentorp in *Edith Wharton's Writings from the Great War*, Wharton's only notable literary output from the war years was the novel *Summer* (1916), a short novel entitled *The Marne* (1918), and the short stories "Coming Home" (1915), "The Refugees" (1919), and "Writing a War Story" (1919). The major books that came out of her philanthropic and fundraising ventures at that time were not fictional; they included two publications, her first-hand impressions from the front, *Fighting France: From Dunkerque to Belfort* (1915), and her edition of poems, articles, drawings, and paintings by famous contributors donated to benefit the refugee cause, *The Book of the Homeless* (1915). Unsurprisingly, *The Marne*, "The Refugees," and even *Summer* examine the machinery of philanthropy and question its purpose, motives, consequences, and meaning.

"A Man like That Hasn't Got Much Use for Decorations": Philanthropy on the Marne

The Marne carries the subtitle "A Tale of the War," yet it portrays not the physical horror of war that emerged in World War I literature, but the moral challenges that the war presented for the ardent volunteer. Therefore, perhaps, it has been largely forgotten by critics who read it as a story about World War I,[1] but, as a commentary on Wharton's own experiences with war relief, the novel portrays and critiques the notion of the gift in a range of philanthropic attitudes and their evolution. It narrates the United States' involvement in World War I through the eyes of a naive American teenager named Troy who romanticizes combat and passionately wishes he could go to the front. Troy is inspired by his French tutor, Paul Gantier, who is drafted and killed early in the war in the battle of the Marne. If Paul and Troy's experience of combat is idealized and isolated, the story of the home front is anything but that. *The Marne* records the evolution of the American involvement in the war with a range of civilian characters: Troy's parents, the Belknaps; the women who run charitable bazaars and adopt long-distance orphans; and the volunteers with the Red Cross, the YMCA, and the ambulance service. Troy himself only joins the war as an ambulance driver.

As Alan Price and Julie Olin-Ammentorp have noted, Wharton sharply criticizes the smugness and superficiality[2] of the home front. For example, Wharton describes the fun-seeking philanthropic young women as "pretty ghouls who danced and picknicked on the ruins of the world" (*The Marne* 114). The passionate but introspective Troy, who prefers Sophie Wicks, with her "ironic eyes" (68), is "sickened by [the] blatancy" (65) of the "war-goddesses" (56). Troy boards a ship to France to join the ambulance service, and develops an aversion to the other volunteers "overflowing with zeal" and embroiled in "wrangles and rivalries" (63) over rank and uniform. Some of these "young Columbias" (64) go on to serve the refugees with the same insensitivity; Miss Batchford, for example, is a "strange young woman who snap[s] out questions like a machine" (74) at the people she is supposed to be helping, including Mrs. Gantier, who has lost her whole family (including her son, Troy's French tutor) in the war.

Olin-Ammentorp is correct when she points out that "the novel's portraits of men are generally more flattering" (67). I would add that Wharton's portraits of the objectionable volunteers are far more believable. The only major character who is a combatant, Paul Gantier, appears as a memory, a voice, and a ghost. Paul's apparition lifts a wounded Troy at the end of the novel and carries him to safety. When Wharton portrays him in the action of saving a wounded boy, he embodies the spirit of a collective Pieta, and genuine kindness. "[H]aggard and battle-worn, looking down at him" (*The Marne* 136), Paul whispers, "Mon petit—mon pauvre petit gars" (136).

The soldier's spirit is a more perfect embodiment of philanthropy than the flesh-and-bones volunteers in the novel. As in Derrida's description of the true gift, he disappears without looking for a reward or recognition. The doctor who is treating Troy comments, "Chances are that a man like that hasn't got much use for decorations" (137). A love so perfect implies an obligation; as an "emotional nurse" exclaims, "Well, you must just devote the rest of your life to trying to find him" (137). Troy resolves to do this "on the battlefields of France" (138).

The ending of *The Marne* presents a portrait of philanthropy that falls short of Wharton's satirical vision earlier in the novel. An authentic philanthropy, if it were possible, would exclude reciprocity, exchange, return, and debt. In *Given Time: I. Counterfeit Money,* Derrida explains, "For there to be a gift, there must be no reciprocity, return, exchange, countergift, or debt. If the other *gives* me *back* or *owes* me or has to give me back what I give him or her, there will not have been a gift, whether this restitution is immediate or whether it is programmed by complex calculation of a long-term deferral or difference" (12).

The Marne presents two conflicting visions of philanthropy. On the one hand, it documents, and even accepts, the impossibility and elusiveness of the gift. In *The Marne,* Wharton argues that "charity hides a multitude of sins," as Thoreau suggested in *Walden* (70). Even the novel's wiser, less self-centered characters, like Sophie Wicks, Troy, and Mr. Belknap, join the war effort accidentally or late. Hungry for romance and adventure, Troy staggers in the lines "awkwardly" (122), "like a mascot dog trotting after its company" (123). Sophie Wicks takes a nursing course secretly and joins the Red Cross, after professedly being bored with the war. Mr. Belknap has "caught the war fever late in life, and late in the war" and is uncomfortable with what he sees as "his son's flippancy" (79). To various extents these characters embody Paul Gantier's wisdom that "self-satisfaction is death" (68). Only by a continuous self-examination, concealment of motives, and ownership of their own flaws can these characters approach the high ethical standard of the volunteer service that Wharton envisions in *The Marne.*

Wharton does not entirely answer the question of the possibility of altruism convincingly in *The Marne.* If the ending of the novel does not ring true, perhaps this is because it portrays philanthropy on the battlefield in terms very different from those it uses to render philanthropy on the home front. The partial conversion of one of the "war-goddesses," the midwestern young woman Miss Hinda Warlick, encapsulates the human limitations and the elusiveness of true charity. Previously prey to cultural prejudice, Miss Warlick learns that the French are not inferior to Americans in efficiency, fighting spirit, or home values. In statements that may make the contemporary reader cringe, she declares, "I tell you, they are *white!* And they are fighting as only people can who feel that way about mothers and babies" (106). Miss Warlick's racist and nativist tropes and her continued emotional effusiveness undermine her conversion; however, her evolution is a much more realistic portrayal of philanthropy than Troy's or Sophie's quiet submission to loving kindness.

On the other hand, *The Marne* combines the idea of the difficulty and elusiveness of the gift with the more propagandistic or attainable "economy of sacrifice" in the Judeo-Christian tradition described by Derrida in *The Gift of Death.* For Derrida, Christian philanthropy represents "an economy, but it is an economy that integrates the renunciation of a calculable remuneration, renunciation of merchandise or bargaining [*merchandage*], of economy in the sense of a retribution that can be measured and made symmetrical." This "profitability" (or measurement) is possible because it is "one that creatures cannot calculate and must leave to the appreciation of *the father as he who sees in secret*" (107; emphasis in original). And Wharton thus passes back and forth from impossibility to possibility.

In accordance with the tradition of Judeo-Christian altruism, Wharton casts Sophie Wicks, now a Red Cross nurse, as Ruth: "France [. . .] had drawn her with an irresistible pressure 'Whither thou goest will I go, thy people shall be my people . . . ' Yes, France was the Naomi-country that had but to beckon and her children rose and came" (*The Marne* 114). The ending of the story with Troy's miraculous rescue reasserts this idea that sacrifice ultimately counts, and that volunteerism is a repayment of debt, contrary to Derrida's idea of the genuine or (im)possible gift. Wharton's next story about philanthropy, "The Refugees," however, takes a more ironic stance towards repayment and questions more radically the meaning of genuine philanthropy.

FORGETTING THE "GREAT ADVENTURE" IN WHARTON'S "THE REFUGEES"

In contrast with Henry James's vision of Wharton as a "great *generalissima*" (Benstock 311) of good works, the ironic 1919 short story "The Refugees" portrays philanthropy as a comedy of errors. Whereas *The Marne* views the home front through the eyes of the idealistic teenager Troy Belknap, "The Refugees" sees philanthropy with the eyes of Charlie Durant, a dazed, spectacled, middle-aged American professor of Romance languages, who at the start of the war happens to be on "a hard-earned Sabbatical holiday" in Belgium and Flanders (*Collected Stories* 570).

Durant feels swept on the tide of historical cataclysms, a sort of refugee himself. The beginning of the war leaves him with "shaken nerves[,]" and "the whole business . . . [is] so contrary to his conception of the universe . . . that he need[s] time to steady himself" (570). As the war starts, he relocates to Normandy, then sets out for London in the middle of a mass migration of refugees tended to by resolute volunteers. The story repeatedly refers to Professor Durant's fogged or "misty" spectacles that signal his emotional confusion, his inability to process the war, and even his shortsightedness about his own and the United States' neutrality.

Charlie Durant also (and more realistically) experiences the refugee crowd as threatening and their neediness as overwhelming. He sees the refugees as a dangerous, pitiful crowd; they are "an indistinguishable animal welter" (571), "herded creatures," and a powerful "eddy" (574). When he attempts to extricate himself, a refugee steps on his lame foot (Durant suffers from "a slight congenital lameness"), and the human current overpowers him. Arriving in London, Durant again is wary of the fugitive masses: "On the platform at Charing Cross he stood motionless, trying to protect his lame leg and yet to take up as little room as possible, while he waited for the tide to flow by and canalize itself" (571).

Like Durant, Wharton takes a similarly dim view of the refugee children in her 1923 essay "Christmas Tinsel"[3] where, during a Christmas celebration, dignitaries and charitable workers need to "double-bar the doors to the approaching army and [sit] down aghast among the ruins" (277). In this memoir, there is no satisfying the children's "greed" for Christmas presents; they are as insatiable as "cannibals" (277). Philanthropy in these stories appears an impossible pursuit.

"The Refugees," unlike *The Marne,* also questions the very possibility of individual giving and the degree to which it makes a difference. Durant contributes generously "to the various appeals for funds" and gives the refugees "his last available penny" (*Collected Stories* 571), but his contribution seems inadequate: "There was no way in which he could help the doomed wretches: he kept repeating that without its affording him the least relief" (571). The hunger for relief and the hunger to afford relief are perpetually unsatisfied, which brings to mind Derrida's comment that the gift is desire, the striving towards the impossible: "[d]esire and the desire to give would be the same thing, a sort of tautology" (*Given Time* 4–5). By the end of the story the United States joins the war, and Durant is shaken out of his "gentle egotism" (571) and returns to Boulogne once again, as a YMCA volunteer. He is conscious of the small role he has to play by minding a library, but he feels "very content" and filled with "perfect serenity because he and his country, for all they were individually worth, had a stake in the affair" (*Collected Stories* 591).

Even though Wharton satirizes philanthropy in "The Refugees" as always tending towards economy, she also recognizes that it can upset the balance of power and bring adventure into obscure and sequestered lives, especially women's lives. The charity workers are the active agents that "crisscross" the refugee waters in a flurry of activity. For them, refugee work has the appeal of fashion and of shopping: repeatedly, the refugees are identified with consumer goods, and, like consumer goods, they are objects of desire. Miss Rushworth compares the frantic pursuit of refugees by Lady Beausedge to shopping at Harrods; "looking as wild as she does on sales days at Harrods," Caroline "never can make up her mind between bargains, and rushes about like a madwoman till it's too late" (577). In the end, the refugees have so flooded the market that they have depreciated: "they've become rather a drug in the market, poor dears" (592). These references to market or exchange value immediately negate the gift in Derrida's sense.

Aunt Audrey and Charlie take each other for refugees by mistake and are drawn to philanthropy because it proves an adventure: for Charlie, it is "the adventure of England . . . and of a baronial hall" (589); for Audrey, an escape from the decorum of her cottage covered in clematis (the name of one species of clematis, the first imported into English gardens, is "virgin bower"). As Audrey's niece Clio says, "Nothing much ever happened to the unmarried women of her time. Most of them were just put away in cottages covered with clematis and forgotten. Aunt Audrey has always been forgotten—even the refugee Committee forgot her" (589). But after mistaking Professor Durant for a refugee and bringing him to her home, "[Miss Audrey's] cheeks are pink with triumph" (585). Four years later, she is engaged "to marry the Bishop of the Macaroon Islands next month" (593). She is confident and powerful—a colonel (perhaps in the Salvation Army) and an administrator in charge of thousands of lives.[4] As Clio remarks, "There's no danger of *her* being forgotten—it's she who does the forgetting now" (593). Even when it is impossible, philanthropy effects cataclysmic changes, particularly in women's lives in "The Refugees."

In "The Refugees," there is a sense that true giving is elusive and nearly impossible; impossible, in any case for any act of giving, as Derrida says, "where there is subject and object" (*Given Time* 24). For Wharton, true giving is impossible not just because it is not what it claims to be: "the light battalions of the benevolent [. . .][are] industriously adding, by all the means known to philanthropy, to the distress and bewilderment of their victims" (*Collected Stories* 572). Or simply because the motives of these society ladies are tainted: as Lord Beausedge says, "Damned bad taste, all that sort of thing" (586). Even the adventure and romance of benevolence are only momentary: indifference, isolation, and routine inevitably take their place. In the end, Charlie Durant realizes that he is no longer "[Audrey

Rushworth's] great Adventure" (592). In fact, Audrey has forgotten him, and in the conclusion Charlie is "aware of a distinct humiliation" (593). The fleeting philanthropic connection between Charlie Durant and Audrey Rushworth makes obvious the elusive nature of all human relationships.

ERNEST HEMINGWAY, WORLD WAR I, AND THE GIFT OF DEATH

Like Wharton's war stories, Hemingway's war fiction arose out of his experience as a volunteer in World War I. In contrast to Wharton's examination of the motives, purpose, and the very possibility of philanthropy and human relationships, Hemingway's writing focuses repeatedly on the shocking and transformative experience of bodily injury and death during the war. Stories like "A Way You'll Never Be" and "A Natural History of the Dead" as well as his novel *A Farewell to Arms* portray a wrenching sense of depersonalization and abjection through the experience of death and wounding on the battlefields of Italy, but this encounter with mechanized death may just be the jolt in conscious experience that makes the characters capable of achieving a sympathetic identification with the other as well as a new sense of individual commitment.

In *The Gift of Death,* Derrida argues that death, like the gift, is outside economy: "dying can never be taken, borrowed, transferred, delivered, promised, or transmitted. And just as it can't be given to me, so it can't be taken away from me" (44). Because death cannot be given, he argues, death enables the true gift as well as responsibility. Death is the origin of the gift: "It is only from the site of death as the place of my irreplaceability, that is, of my singularity, that I feel called to responsibility. In this sense only a mortal can be responsible" (41). Seen in this light, Hemingway's portrayal of trauma, abjection, and death challenges philanthropy and demonstrates giving and taking to be possible.

HEMINGWAY'S SOLDIERS AND MOTHERS: *A FAREWELL TO ARMS*

Like Troy Belknap in Wharton's novel *The Marne,* Ernest Hemingway joined the war effort as a volunteer with the American Red Cross.[5] According to his biographers Michael Reynolds and Carlos Baker, in the winter of 1917 Hemingway "volunteered, eager for the experience" to be an ambulance driver for the Red Cross (Reynolds 15), and by June 1918 Hemingway and his friend Ted Brumback arrived in Schio, "24 kilometers to the northwest in the foothills of the Dolomites" to join their ambulance unit—the ARC Section Four (Baker 41). A few weeks later, when the battlefield moved to the Piave River valley, Hemingway volunteered as "director of the still nonexistent emergency canteen" near Fossalta (Baker 43–44). "Around midnight on July 8" he rode his bicycle to the frontline trenches on the west bank of the Piave River, "carrying a supply of cigarettes, chocolate, and postcards for the soldiers" (Baker 44). While distributing these supplies, he was hit by fragments of a trench-mortar shell, an incident that he later described in *A Farewell to Arms.*

Michael Reynolds argues that, "in 1919, the age demanded heroes" (21), and "Hemingway, along with other Red Crossmen, began to invent a different war life for himself" in which "the Red Cross became an embarrassment that he simply eradicated" (23). His parents "immediately turned in to the local newspaper" in Oak Park his letter home in which he claimed he sustained 227 wounds but nevertheless carried a wounded Italian soldier on his back to safety (20). His friend Ted Brumback repeated the same story. An article in the *New York Sun* from 22 January 1919 included the same number of wounds but omitted the heroics. As Reynolds points out, the Italian government had its own reasons to perpetuate the heroic myth: "the Italians decorated him with two medals, but they had need of American heroes to honor, for they needed America's support for the war" (21). But what Hemingway deemphasized in his firsthand account of the incident, he more than amplified in his fiction. *A Farewell to Arms* narrates the war from the points of view of doctors, nurses, ambulance drivers, bartenders, and civilians.

The main plot of the novel follows Frederic Henry, a lieutenant of the ambulance corps, from his wounding to his hospital stay in Milan and his love affair with nurse's aide Catherine Barkley. After he returns to the front, Frederic feels married to Catherine. At the retreat at Caporetto he abandons his ambulances in the mud, attempts to kill two sergeants as deserters, loses an ambulance driver to friendly fire and another to desertion, and makes his "separate peace" (*Farewell* 243). But when he deserts the army, rejoins Catherine, and takes them away to Switzerland, futility and suffering persist in the tragic story of Catherine Barkley's death. It is precisely Catherine's death in childbirth and the death of the baby, choked by a tangled umbilical cord, which for many readers of the novel underscore the futility and inhumanity of modern warfare.

Readers, critics, and editors have struggled to find the connection between the love story in the novel and the war plot. In *The New Death: American Modernism and World War I,* Pearl James astutely suggests that *A Farewell to Arms* "falsely assimilates the violence of war into a conventionally tragic love story" and "relocates vulnerability, death, and the abject away from the battlefield and away from men" (121). While I agree that the narrative of the novel distances itself from the descriptions of war, the novel's refocusing on the suffering of noncombatants depends on philanthropic tropes that strongly connected mothers and soldiers at the turn of the twentieth century and resonated with Hemingway's experience as a Red Cross volunteer.

Since the late nineteenth century, soldiers and mothers had been two particularly honored categories in the American welfare state.[6] Before Social Security came into being, welfare policies were designed to protect deserving constituencies such as veteran soldiers and "good" single mothers. At the First International Congress in America on the Welfare of the Child, in 1908, Theodore Roosevelt emphasized the importance of honoring and protecting mothers, "the one supreme asset of national life" (20). He argued, "A good woman, who does her full duty [as a wife and mother], is sacred in our eyes; exactly as the brave and patriotic soldier is to be honored above all other men" (21). Hemingway's "own father, who specialized in obstetrics, had been fond of quoting a Dr. De Lee, who wrote that 'more women die and are wounded in confinement every year than men die and are wounded on the field of battle'" (qtd. in Beegel 48). Hemingway's awareness of the brutality of maternal suffering is also evident in his Nick Adams story "Indian Camp" (1924).

Moreover, World War I was the first "total warfare" that affected civilian populations in ways war had never affected them before.[7] Civilian casualties were common, and the influenza epidemic of 1918, which was facilitated by the war, extended the number of deaths far beyond the 9.2 million casualties on the battlefield.[8] Red Cross volunteers during the war saw their philanthropic mission as alleviating suffering both at the front and at home. In *The Story of the American Red Cross in Italy,* published in 1920, Charles

Bakewell drew a parallel between the wounds on the battlefield and the suffering of civilians:

> There are other wounds besides those made by enemy guns, wounds that reach the entire civilian population. And every soldier at the front is linked by ties of affection to those at home, his mother, his wife, his children. Their wounds are his wounds. If they are neglected his courage is sapped. In a word, this war has brought into prominence the importance of what the Italians call the "inner front" (*il fronte interno*). The army is the nation, not merely the men in the trenches, and the work of the Red Cross must be correspondingly extended. It is its task to heal the wounds on the "inner front." And here, as with the soldier, the wounds may be of the spirit as well as of the body. (36)

Like Bakewell's account of the role of the Red Cross on the inner front, *A Farewell to Arms* portrays the connection between combatants and civilians, and Catherine's experience of death mirrors that of the soldier on the front lines. In contrast with Bakewell's representation of the nurturing mission of the Red Cross, however, Hemingway's novel paints a world of suffering unmitigated by philanthropy either at home or on the battlefield. The world "kills the very good and the very gentle and the very brave impartially" (*Farewell* 249). In the novel, Aymo (Bartolomeo), who often takes on feminine and philanthropic tasks such as preparing pasta for his sleeping comrades or giving a ride to two scared girls, dies gratuitously by friendly fire. Catherine dies in childbirth, and her baby is choked by a tangled umbilical cord. Fatalistically, the only sure fact of life in the novel is death: "That is what you did. You died. You did not know what it was about. You never had any time to learn. They threw you in and told you the rules and the first time they caught you off base they killed you. Or they killed you gratuitously like Aymo. Or gave you the syphilis like Rinaldi. But they killed you in the end. You could count on that. Stay around and they would kill you" (327). As the sole indisputable biological fact of life, death does not discriminate between heroes and cowards, altruists and warriors, men and women: the dead lie in indistinguishable heaps. And their bodies give the lie to the ideal of valor and the ideal of philanthropy.

By invoking Victorian tropes about two quintessentially tragic and heroic experiences, the masculine experience of war and the feminine experience of childbirth, *A Farewell to Arms* challenges not only the wartime rhetoric of duty, sacrifice, and glory but also the maternalist rhetoric of philanthropy and the "glory of woman." In the opening scene of *A Farewell to Arms*, Hemingway explicitly connects the bodies of the marching soldiers to pregnant women's bodies in a twentieth-century leveling of mechanized death: "their rifles were wet and under their capes the two leather cartridge-boxes on the front of the belts, gray leather boxes heavy with the packs of clips of thin, long 6.5 mm. cartridges, bulged forward under their capes so that the men, passing on the road, marched as though they were six months gone with child" (4). With its inversion of the natural order, the image of men bearing mechanized death strikes at the heart of the sentimental tropes about glory and ushers the reader into a deterministic world of biological and man-made entrapment.

"I KNOW HOW I AM AND . . . I AM NOT ASHAMED OF IT": THE GIFT OF DEATH IN "A WAY YOU'LL NEVER BE"

If *A Farewell to Arms* undermines the rhetoric of protecting soldiers and mothers, Hemingway's short stories "In Another Country," "Now I Lay Me," "A Natural History of the Dead," and "A Way You'll Never Be" demonstrate that for Hemingway, as for Derrida, "War is a further experience of the gift of death [*le mort donée*]" (Derrida, *Gift of Death* 17). By insisting on the enduring and leveling quality of death, Hemingway's war fiction opens up the possibility for identification with the other: the madman, the enemy, the victim. Only through his encounter with death is Nicholas Adams in "A Way You'll Never Be" able to grasp a different truth about the war, a truth at odds with war propaganda, and to grasp the meaning of war experience. Even though death is beyond giving and taking, "it is only on the basis of death, and in its name, that giving and taking become possible" (*Gift of Death* 4).

If Wharton's story about philanthropy, "The Refugees," is a satire and Hemingway's *A Farewell to Arms* is a tragedy, the portrayal of relief in "A Way You'll Never Be" approaches a farce. In this story Nicholas (Nick Adams) is a wounded American soldier on the Italian front who suffers from shell shock. After his injury he is sent on his bicycle to distribute refreshments to the soldiers in the trenches, as Hemingway did himself. However, in the story the army gives Nick no supplies; he continually apologizes he does not have "pockets full of cigarettes and postal cards and . . . a musette full of chocolate" (309). Captain Paravicini fears that Nick's movement along the line during the day "invites shelling" (*Complete Short Stories* 313). Concerned about Nick, he eventually advises him to go back and says, "I won't have you circulating around to no purpose" (313). Nick's gift giving is continually postponed. Even though he says at the end of the story that he will come back with the supplies, this promise seems uncertain, and he leaves in a confused state, looking for his bicycle and striving not to "lose the way to Fornaci" (315).

As Nick "circulates around with no purpose," he shows the absence of a market-based economy, of a structure of exchange. Readers, soldiers, and protagonist are equally unsure what to take away from Nick's story, his empty musette, and his fake uniform. Nick thus haunts the soldiers, who at best recognize him uneasily, as the very impossibility of the gift.

The protagonist has "no purpose" and yet he dons the uniform of the relief worker all the same. He acknowledges his impossibility. His shell shock and madness keep him there in front of himself and all of them, and yet something about Nick demands a reply, recognition. As the very personification of the gift within the schema of war, of death, Nick and his madness, his shell shock, motivate something like a sympathetic, philanthropic response—if not in his fellow soldiers, then in the reader.[9]

However, a philanthropic response is precisely what Nick, like Derrida's gift, seems to prevent or at least to make difficult. Nick's failure to contribute to the war even as a relief worker and his continual presence at the trenches invite the consternation of readers and of fellow soldiers alike. It is just so hard to do anything but pity him.

Seemingly, Nick is an abject figure that fails to live up to the heroic ideal his fake American uniform represents. Even before his wounding, he drinks before every attack and "wear[s] his own chin strap tight across his mouth to keep his lips quiet" (310). After his head wound, he experiences flashbacks, anxiety attacks, and disorientation; he is suddenly "confused without reason" (311). A large body of work on shell shock, including criticism by Joanna Bourke, Doris Kaufmann, Paul Lerner, George L. Mosse, Sandra M.

Gilbert, and Elaine Showalter, documents how during World War I, when it was first diagnosed, shell shock was confused with effeminacy, cowardice, hysteria, and degeneracy. What is known today as PTSD "was understood by the military as a failure of masculinity: a failure of hardness, courage or willpower" (Higonnet 93). Victims of war trauma were also considered "soft-hearted," lacking in critical abilities, and more primitive and feminine (Bourke 59). The stories of shell-shocked soldiers, in the hands of contemporary readers, often provoked condemnation, and at best invited pity.

But Nick's acquiescence with his status as a coward and an outsider who has been "reformed out of the war" is not typical and further challenges the reader's ability to identify philanthropically with him. Young men of Hemingway's generation were inspired by Theodore Roosevelt, for whom war relief was suitable only for women or those men who were unfit to be drafted: "Let him, if a man of fighting age, do his utmost to get into the fighting line—Red Cross work, Y.M.C.A. work, driving ambulances, and the like, excellent though it all is, should be left to men not of military age or unfit for military service, and to women" (qtd. in Florczyk 27–28). Michael Reynolds points out that the uniform of the ambulance driver was ambiguous since "one could not tell from the uniform who had been a front-line ambulance driver and who had been a slacker" (23). The young Hemingway tailored his Red Cross uniform and purchased a Sam Browne belt so that he would look as though he had been in combat (Reynolds 17).

A Red Cross uniform was not as respectable as a military one, and when Nick in "A Way You'll Never Be" clearly advertises that his American combat uniform is a fake and tells everyone how "Spagnolini made it but it's not quite correct" (*Complete Short Stories* 311), his unusually candid statement must be bewildering to his listeners. Nick has reached a state of acceptance of his cowardice and panic. "I know how I am," he says, and "I am not ashamed of it" (309).

The conflicted feelings that Nick inspires, both philanthropic feelings and consternation, mirror his own fragmentation, a fragmentation that is connected to death. The story begins with and returns to images of dead humped bodies lying unburied on the battlefield where "the hot air ha[s] swollen them regardless of nationality" (307). They appear to have been robbed of valuables, and the contents of their pockets lie about them:

prayer books, smutty postcards, pictures, “and the letters, letters, letters” (307). In death the soldiers are robbed of meaning like the spilled papers from their pockets. Like Nick Adams, they cannot simply, or once and for all, give meaning even to their own deaths.

His return to the site of his wounding and to his old comrade, the flashbacks of his wounding, and the recurring nightmare of the yellow house are the gifts of death that he both seeks and does not wish to have. Yet the experience of death—the humped-over bodies, the scattered papers, and Nick’s incoherent dreams—tells the story of his suffering and of the suffering of civilians that accompanies the brutality of war. It brings out the discrepancy between propaganda and lived experience, between the “group postcards showing the machine-gun unit standing in ranked and ruddy cheerfulness as in a football picture for a college annual” and the bodies of the soldiers “humped and swollen in the grass,” between “propaganda postcards showing a soldier in Austrian uniform bending a woman backward over a bed” and “actual rape” (306).

Within the challenge of his fragmentation, within the one who occupies the position of the gift without actually becoming it, Nick does not simply draw meaning out of death once and for all. In fact, he half wishes he did not have to see the truth about death; as he parts from his friend Paravicini, he demands to know, “Why don’t they bury the dead? I’ve seen them now. I don’t care about seeing them again. They can bury them any time as far as I’m concerned and it would be much better for you” (314). Similarly, the narrator of “A Natural History of the Dead” wants “to see what inspiration we may derive from the dead” (*Complete Short Stories* 335), “only to conclude that “most men die like animals, not men” (338).

But perhaps by virtue of his spectral otherness, by virtue of his attributed “femininity,” it seems that Nick is in fact trying to give meaning to their deaths in the act of his storytelling. In contrast with his precarious emotional state and his fake uniform, he spins a tale about larger-than-life heroes who are coming from overseas: “Americans twice as large as [himself], healthy, with clean hearts, sleep at night, never been wounded, never been blown up, never had their heads caved in, never been scared, don’t drink, faithful to the girls they left behind them, many of them never had crabs, wonderful chaps” (311). But this idealized vision falls apart when he quickly switches to a story about locusts and fishing that implicitly compares the soldiers to bait and to a biblical plague: "soon you will see untold millions wearing this uniform swarming like locusts" (312).

By confusing fishing and military training, soldiers and bait, a savior army and locusts, Nick's mad ramblings subvert language and military discourse, and challenge military discipline. The conclusion to Nick's locust parable, "Gentlemen, either you must govern or you must be governed" (313), could be interpreted as an encouragement towards disobedience. Even though Nick cannot bring either meaning or relief to the wasteland of his war experience, he inadvertently gives a voice to the soldiers' lived experience of combat and gives meaning to their own fragmentation. It is the overwhelming nature of death that initiates the gift of this story, Nick's challenge to received ideals, to propaganda, and to military authority.

AMERICAN MODERNISM AND GENUINE PHILANTHROPY

On the one hand, Wharton's fiction astutely thematizes and questions the very possibility of the gift. On the other hand, Hemingway's writing, through a profoundly decentering experience of death, offers the philanthropic possibility of evading propaganda and seeing the war on one's own terms. Across the work of both authors, we can see a common demand for a new language to address the rhetoric of giving, of the heroic and the abject. In their fiction, we can see how activities and discourses of philanthropy permeate their descriptions of the Great War and how Wharton and Hemingway work together to reconstrue the boundaries between the feminine and the masculine at the time of the largest wartime carnage in history in his time.

Far from being a nineteenth-century preoccupation, philanthropy (and the notion of the gift as such) is a theme that illuminates many of the central texts of modernism that have to do with the Great War. Even though Hemingway and Wharton employ philanthropy to make a point about the hypocrisy of the governing class and the emptiness of traditional social ideals, they reaffirm, to various degrees, the protagonists' commitment to personal values, their consideration for the unique perspective of marginalized individuals, and the persistence of giving outside any economy or exchange. As James F. English argues in *Comic Transactions*, "One should not follow Raymond Williams in critiquing the politics of modernism on the grounds of an ostensible hostility or indifference to community, a lofty contempt for the social, an aesthetic of transcendent individualism" (24). Instead of closing the chapter on Victorian philanthropy, Hemingway's and Wharton's writings about the Great War are best understood as movements towards a better understanding of the gift.

NOTES

1. Critics have pointed out the shortcomings of this story. In "Compromising Realism to Idealize a War," John J. Murphy "agree[s] with almost every critic of Edith Wharton's fiction that *The Marne* is, as Cynthia Wolff echoes, 'inferior.'"

2. In *The End of the Age of Innocence*, Alan Price discusses *The Marne* as "[Wharton's] satire of those society women who become involved in relief agencies" (174). Julie Olin-Ammentorp argues that many of the women in the novel are "portrayed as self-satisfied and self-concerned" (67) and "less in touch with the 'real' things in life than men" (68).

3. Wharton's essay "Christmas Tinsel" was published in *The Delineator*, 1923, and reprinted in *Edith Wharton's Writings from the Great War*, edited by Olin-Ammentorp.

4. Olin-Ammentorp argues that "Audrey Rushworth is unsympathetic: she is portrayed as tyrannical and ruthlessly ambitious—a more military version of her socially competitive relatives" (103).

5. In his book *Hemingway, the Red Cross, and the Great War*, Steven Florczyk comments, "[Hemingway's] family . . . placed a high value on the type of humanitarian work accomplished at the front" and adds that his grandfather Anson Hemingway "founded the Chicago YMCA" (25).

6. Works such as Skocpol, *Protecting Soldiers and Mothers*, and Mink and Solinger, eds., *Welfare*, document these sentiments.

7. See, for example, Hochschild, *To End All Wars*, 95, 373.

8. See Beegel, "Love in the Time of Influenza." She states, "Before the 1918 flu burned itself out it had killed between fifty and one hundred million people worldwide, about two-thirds of them in a twenty-four-week period from mid-September to early December. The pandemic killed far more people than World War I, with its 9.2 million combat deaths, or World War II, with 15.9 million dead in battle" (36). While Hemingway was still recovering from his injuries, the American nurse with whom he fell in love, Agnes von Kurowsky, "went to Torre di Mosta to nurse civilians struck by the epidemic" (46).

9. Nearly all of Hemingway's war stories, such as "In Another Country," "Now I Lay Me," "Soldier's Home," and "A Way You'll Never Be," portray soldiers who suffer from

post-traumatic stress disorder. In "Now I Lay Me," the Nick Adams protagonist is afraid to sleep at night. In "A Way You'll Never Be," the "young second lieutenant with a stubble of beard and red-rimmed, very blood-shot eyes" (*Complete Short Stories* 307) who points a pistol at Nicholas Adams, appears even more tense than Nicholas himself; his voice "[does] not sound natural," "and his face "look[s] like the face of a man during a bombardment" (308). One of Nicolo's recurring memories is how "the hysterics during the bombardment before the attack" overcome the "platoon of the class of 1899, just out at the front" (310).

WORKS CITED

Baker, Carlos. *Ernest Hemingway: A Life Story.* New York: Charles Scribner's Sons, 1969. Print.

Bakewell, Charles M. *The Story of the American Red Cross in Italy.* New York: Macmillan Co., 1920. Print.

Beegel, Susan. "Love in the Time of Influenza: Hemingway and the 1918 Pandemic." In *War + Ink: New Perspectives on Ernest Hemingway's Early Life and Writings.* Ed. Steve Paul, Gail Sinclair, and Steven Trout. Kent, OH: Kent State UP, 2014. 36–52.

Benstock, Shari. *No Gifts from Chance: A Biography of Edith Wharton.* New York: Charles Scribner's Sons, 1994. Print.

Bourke, Joanna. "Effeminacy, Ethnicity, and the End of Trauma: The Suffering of 'Shell-Shocked' Men in Great Britain and Ireland, 1914–39." *Journal of Contemporary History* 35.1 (2000): 57–39. Print.

Derrida, Jacques. *The Gift of Death.* Trans. David Wills. Chicago: U of Chicago P, 1992. Print.

———. *Given Time: I. Counterfeit Money.* Chicago: U of Chicago P, 1992. Print.

English, James F. *Comic Transactions: Literature, Humor, and the Politics of Community in Twentieth-Century Britain.* Ithaca, NY: Cornell UP, 1994. Print.

Florczyk, Steven. *Hemingway, the Red Cross, and the Great War.* Kent, OH: Kent State UP, 2014. Print.

Gilbert, Sandra M. "Soldier's Heart: Literary Men, Literary Women, and the Great War." *Signs* 8.3 (1983): 422–50. Print.

Hemingway, Ernest. *The Complete Short Stories of Ernest Hemingway.* New York: Charles Scribner's Sons, 1987. Print.

———. *A Farewell to Arms.* New York: Scribner's, 1995. Print.

Higonnet, Margaret R. "Authenticity and Art in Trauma Narratives of World War." *Modernism/ Modernity* 9 (2002): 91–107. Print.

Hochschild, Adam. *To End All Wars: A Story of Loyalty and Rebellion, 1914–1918.* Boston: Houghton Mifflin Harcourt, 2012. Print.

James, Pearl. *The New Death: American Modernism and World War I.* Charlottesville: U of Virginia P, 2013. Print.

Kaufmann, Doris. "Science as Cultural Practice: Psychiatry in the First World War and Weimar Germany." *Journal of Contemporary History* 34 (1999): 125–44. Print.

Lerner, Paul. "Psychiatry and Casualties of War in Germany, 1914–18." *Journal of Contemporary History* 35 (2000): 13–28. Print.

Lewis, R. W. B. *Edith Wharton: A Biography.* Fromm International Publishing Corp., 1985. Print.

Mink, Gwendolyn, and Rickie Solinger, eds. *Welfare: A Documentary History of U.S. Policy and Politics.* New York: New York UP, 2003.

Mosse, George L. "Shell-Shock as a Social Disease." *Journal of Contemporary History* 35.1 (Jan. 2000): 101–8. Print.

Murphy, John J. "Compromising Realism to Idealize a War: Wharton's *The Marne* and Cather's *One of Ours.*" *American Literary Realism* 33.2 (2001): 157–67. Print.

Olin-Ammentorp, Julie. *Edith Wharton's Writings from the Great War,* Gainesville: UP of Florida, 2004. Print.

Paul, Steve, Gail Sinclair, and Steven Trout, eds. *War + Ink: New Perspectives on Ernest Hemingway's Early Life and Writings.* Kent, OH: Kent State UP; 2014. Print.

Price, Alan. *The End of the Age of Innocence: Edith Wharton and the First World War.* New York: St. Martin's Press, 1996. Print.

Reynolds, Michael. *The Young Hemingway.* Oxford: Basil Blackwell, 1986. Print.

Roosevelt, Theodore. "Address to the Delegates: First International Congress in America on the Welfare of the Child." In Mink and Solinger, eds., *Welfare.* 20–21. Print.

Sanderson, Rena. "Hemingway and Gender History." *The Cambridge Companion to Hemingway.* Ed. Scott Donaldson. Cambridge: Cambridge UP, 1996: 170–96. Print.

Showalter, Elaine. *The Female Malady.* New York: Random House, 1985. Print.

Skocpol, Theda. *Protecting Soldiers and Mothers: The Political Origins of Social Policy in the United States.* Cambridge, MA: Harvard UP, 1992. Print.

Thoreau, Henry David. Ed. Stephen Fender. *Walden; or, Life in the Woods* (1854). New York: Oxford UP, 1997. Print.

Wharton, Edith. *A Backward Glance.* New York: Appleton-Century, 1934. Print.

———. "Christmas Tinsel." Rpt. in *Edith Wharton's Writings from the Great War.* Ed. Julie Olin-Ammentorp. Gainesville: UP of Florida, 2004.

———. *The Collected Short Stories of Edith Wharton.* Vol. 2. Ed. R. W. B. Lewis. New York: Charles Scribner's Sons, 1968. Print.

———. *The Letters of Edith Wharton.* Ed. R. W. B Lewis and Nancy Lewis. New York: Charles Scribner's Sons, 1988. Print.

———. *The Marne: A Tale of the War.* London: Macmillan and Co., 1918. Web. archive.org.

———. "The War." In *A Backward Glance.* D. Appleton-Century Co., Inc., 1934. Print.

III

GEOGRAPHIES

Emancipated from Baedeker

Wharton and Hemingway in Italy

CECILIA MACHESKI

"Tut, Tut! Miss Lucy! I hope we shall emancipate you from Baedeker," E. M. Forster's Miss Lavish pronounces in *A Room with a View.* "He does but touch the surface of things. As to the true Italy—he does not even dream of it. The true Italy is only found in patient observation" (122). Published in 1908, Forster's novel, set in Florence, is at once a satire on the rigidity of Baedeker tour guides and a celebration of middle-class travel in the same decade Wharton was visiting Italy to research villas and gardens. The English characters are tourists who begin their Italian sojourn with downcast eyes and notions of the rules of behavior that are their heaviest luggage. They are part of the rapidly increasing number of Europeans and Americans who traveled abroad as faster and safer transport made an expedited and cheaper version of the Grand Tour possible to members of the middle class with increasing leisure time. Italy as a destination for Hemingway has received attention in three important essay collections: *Hemingway and Italy: Twenty-first Century Perspectives* (2017), edited by Mark Cirino and Mark Ott; *Hemingway's Italy: New Perspectives* (2006), edited by Rena Sanderson; and *Hemingway in Italy and Other Essays* (1990), edited by Robert W. Lewis. Scholarship on Wharton's Italian travel essays and fiction has focused on architecture, gardens, and her short stories, especially "Roman Fever," but not often on the broad Italian social context.[1] Taken together, Wharton's and Hemingway's Italian travel and fiction reveal fresh insight on American tourism, the rise of fascism after World War I, and the writers' responses to modernism.

Not long after Forster wrote of Miss Lavish offering her advice to Lucy, Filipo Tomasso Marinetti and the Futurists staged protests decrying Italy's unhealthy attachment to the past. In his 1910 manifesto "Against

Past-loving Venice," Marinetti renounced "the old Venice, enfeebled and undone by worldly luxury" and "the Venice of foreigners, market for counterfeiting antiquarians, magnet for snobbery and universal imbecility, bed unsprung by caravans of lovers, jewelled bathtub for cosmopolitan courtesans, *cloaca maxima* of passéism" (Flint 55). The Futurists advocated the destruction of the very antiquities that drew tourists, the primary content of Baedeker guides, in order to "prepare the birth of an industrial and military Venice that can dominate the Adriatic Sea" (55). This outrage was in part a response to the 1902 collapse of the Campanile in Venice's Piazza San Marco, which left a massive pile of rubble where the landmark once stood. World news headlines mourned the disaster ("Venice's Famous" 1). With the slogan *com'era, dov'era*, the city authorities chose to rebuild the bell tower and preserve the famous cityscape. In just ten years tourists could once again see the Piazza as it was, where it was. Marinetti wanted instead to use the opportunity of the tower's collapse to modernize and rebuild. He advocated the burning of gondolas ("rocking chairs for cretins") in favor of "the birth of an industrial and military Venice" (Flint 55). By the 1920s he was supporting the Fascists. Both Wharton and Hemingway were drawn to Italy by the visible past preserved in the very architecture and literature Marinetti attacked, and both writers became critically concerned about the vision of the country's future called for in emerging voices like Marinetti's and, soon, Mussolini's. Their Italian work taken together suggests new ways to understand each writer's relationship to modernism.

They are an unlikely couple, Edith and Ernest, and it is unlikely that they ever met. Wharton was almost forty years older than Hemingway. Differences are obvious, and correspondences evade easy detection. Yet their careers, especially when viewed through an Italian lens, contain conjunctions. Early nonfiction writing for magazines and newspapers, service in the First World War, a passion for Italy and pride in knowledge of the Italian language, fondness for cross-country tours in luxury motor cars, friendship with art historian Bernard Berenson, and appreciation of the visual arts are among their common territory. Italy provided an archive of the historical past as well as opportunities for health cures and recuperation. Both restless, each chose to live an expatriate life, but not in Italy, resisting the rising fascism to which each would have been attuned by their wartime experiences. Their letters and fictions from and about Italy present two travelers who assert their positions as independent, even defiant, explorers, contemptuous of commonplace tourism. As "patient observers" and recorders, both assert independence from conventional guidebooks and commonplace tourist paths. Yet each writer creates texts that serve better than Baedeker to draw visitors to Italy, especially to Milan and Venice. Even as they eschew the little red tourist bibles, Wharton and Hemingway write their own Italian travel guides, creating new models and purposes for travel by Americans in the early twentieth century.

Wharton's *Italian Villas and Their Gardens* and *Italian Backgrounds* supported educated, informed prewar travel that encouraged Americans to adapt Italian "garden magic" (*Italian Villas* 5) for their mansions in New York, New England, and elsewhere. Wharton failed to persuade her publisher, the *Century* magazine, to include detailed ground plans of the sites she presented in her essays (Wright 130). Had these maps and elevations been included, her intention to provide the formulas for exporting the Italian style to American landscapes would have been even more influential among landscape architects. While Wharton did not acknowledge him, Charles A. Platt published *Italian Gardens* in 1894, rich with photographs, but lacking extended narratives on each garden. Handbooks like *The Old Gardens of Italy: How to Visit Them* (1908) by Aubrey Le Blond and Sir George Sitwell's *On the Making of Gardens* (1909) acknowledged her lead and further inspired garden makers like Alfred DuPont to create his Italianate pleasure gardens at Winterthur and Charles Deering his Vizcaya in Miami.

Hemingway generated a kind of tourism more familiar today, aimed at his middle-class American reader eager to visit Europe after reading his novels. *A Farewell to Arms* (1929), *Death in the Afternoon* (1932), and *For Whom the Bell Tolls* (1940) romanticize Europe for readers curious to see the places because Hemingway himself saw them that way as much as for their intrinsic interest. Although Wharton advocated for the adoption of Italianate landscape design in the New World, Hemingway triggered celebrity tourism, drawing Americans across the Atlantic to Milan, Pamplona, and Paris, and later back home to Key West and Havana. Earlier travelers who carried Byron and Ruskin and sought the antiquities catalogued by Baedeker were gradually outnumbered by a generation inspired by Hemingway's own exploits and his characters' adventures.

Wharton's "Picturesque Milan" (1905) is the penultimate chapter of *Ital-*

ian Backgrounds. Here she disdains the Baedeker sites—neglecting the magnificent Galleria, the Cathedral, and Leonardo's *Last Supper*—and draws our attention instead to "the great cloister of the Ospedale Maggiore, one of the most glorious monuments that man ever erected to his fellows. . . . It is at least pleasant to think of the poor sick people sunning themselves in the beautiful loggia of the Ospedale Maggiore, or sitting . . . in the garden, while their blue-gowned and black-veiled nurses move quietly through the cloisters" (160–62). Eleanor Dwight reminds us that Wharton assembled her travel impressions in a series of pictures because "in making these trips Wharton felt she was seeing the real Italy . . . not what tourists saw." She "hyped the ordinary and avoided the celebrated tourist attractions" (79). The large ornate Ospedale was begun in 1456 as a free public hospital to meet the needs of the poor of the city and, a decade or so after Wharton admired it, Hemingway was brought by train and ambulance to the American Red Cross hospital in Milan. He was taken regularly to the Ospedale for therapy and exercise, to sit in the sun, just as Wharton envisioned (Baker 50). The war provided Hemingway with his first experience of Europe, intense but remarkably brief: he left the United States in May 1918, was stationed in the Veneto, where he was wounded while supplying cigarettes and chocolate to the soldiers, was hospitalized on 8 July as the result of a leg-shattering shrapnel wound, and returned to the United States in January 1919, not yet twenty years old. In *A Farewell to Arms* Tenente Henry comes to Milan and meets Catherine Barkley, shadowing Hemingway's own arrival in the city. Henry is taken for X-rays to the Ospedale, where it is not the garden that is so pleasing but a nurse "more beautiful than Cleopatra" (82), and he is recommended by the hospital's surgeon to have six months of bed rest and then "take the sun cure" (85). While Wharton offers the grand Renaissance building as a suitable, even superior, destination to the conventional Baedeker sites, Henry and Catherine Barkley escape its confines to go out on the town, and with them we enter the world of the tourist guidebook: "dinner at Biffi's or the Gran Italia . . . we looked at the people, and the great galleria in the dusk" (97). Wharton observes that Milan "abounds in vivid effects, in suggestive juxtapositions of different centuries and styles—in all those incidental contrasts and surprises which linger in the mind after the catalogued 'sights' have faded" (*Italian Back-*

grounds 158). For Henry, seeing the sights of Milan with Catherine is, in contrast, a Baedeker chapter. Some of the alternate titles for Hemingway's novel emphasize the importance of Italy and tourism as the setting and highlight the touristic appeal of the work: "The Italian Journey," "The Italian Chronicle," "The Italian Experience," "Love in Italy," and "The Retreat from Italy" (*Farewell*, appendix 3: 323).

Wharton encountered Italy visiting as a child, from 1866 to 1872. She returned frequently during her married life with Teddy for health cures at spas like Salsomaggiore and later to visit Berenson annually in Florence at his villa, I Tatti. A letter to Ogden Codman in 1896 radiates Wharton's joy in Italy and Italian travel: "We left Paris eight days ago, and came to Italy by way of Milan—From there we went to Parma, Modena, then to Bologna and Ferrara and yesterday we came here—tomorrow we are going to Rimini, Urbino, Ancona, and Loreto, and by the end of the month we expect to be in Venice" (qtd. in Dwight 77). She later writes to him, "The fact is that Italy spoils me for everything else" (qtd. in Dwight 78; see also Benstock 81).

Hemingway shares Wharton's enthusiasm and echoes her word-map technique. In a passage later redacted from *Death in the Afternoon*, he mirrors Wharton's exuberance: "But from Milan to Brescia, to Verona, to Vicenza, not from Vicenza to Padova, I hated Padova, but from Padova to Mestre, up to Treviso, all around the Venetian plain and then up to Barca di Cadore . . . I loved Northern Italy like a fool, truly, the way I had northern Michigan" (qtd. in Junkins 120). Hemingway's route went from west to east across the country in almost a straight line from Milan to Venice. He was retracing in reverse the route on which he was shipped as a casualty after being wounded at Fossalta and taken to a field hospital near Treviso. Carlos Baker summarizes the wartime journey:

> [After five days in Treviso,] a slow hospital train pulled away for Milano. Outside Mestre the cars stood for hours on a siding in the thick heat of mid-July. From where they lay they could not see the magical city of Venice stretching out into the Adriatic. The boy in the berth did not care. Flies coursed through the open windows to settle on his bandages. . . . There were further waits at Vicenza and Verona.

> He did not see the Lago di Garda nor did he know when they had reached Brescia. They had been two full days in transit by the time the train pulled into the freight yards of Milano. (45–46)

The reversal of the wartime journey in his big blue Buick thirty years later recreates the trip as a touristic adventure rather than a wartime nightmare, suggesting intimacy with the cities and towns he once passed through blindly (Mary Welsh Hemingway, *How It Was* 256). Echoing Wharton's remark to Codman, in his far more vernacular style, Hemingway writes to Grace Quinlan in August 1929: "I hate buzzing all over Europe when there is so much of my own country I haven't seen. But the Wopland gets in the blood and kind of ruins you for anything else" (*Selected Letters* 37). A decade after the anti-tourist wartime journey, he is writing a personal guidebook.

Wharton wrote her article on Milan a decade before the war, and her sun-drenched patients are ghosts from the past centuries rather than glimpses of future residents. But, like Hemingway, Wharton experienced the war firsthand, though she did so in France, setting up workrooms and administering hostels, clinics, schools, and nurseries. She visited the Front several times with Walter Berry and raised funds with her pen, making extensive use of her social network to publish *The Book of the Homeless.* Despite these exhausting years, she could nevertheless write, "Once within the military zone *every* moment is interesting" (*Letters* 351). Surely Hemingway would have agreed. The combination of war and foreign travel was intoxicating, creating for both a variant on Baedeker and trench tourism.

Intimacy with Italy and advocacy for international aid depended upon knowledge of the language. Wharton had begun to absorb Italian as a girl when her family lived in Rome after the Civil War: "the new language came to me as naturally as breathing" (*A Backward Glance* 30). Early in her career, in 1898, she published three translations of Italian stories for Burlingame; Gianfranca Balestra labels the translations as "generally accurate and highly readable" (209). Wharton's library contained well-read copies of Dante (Ramsden 31), and she was well versed in the literary language of the *Commedia*, but, as a child in Rome and later as a woman motoring across the country, Wharton would surely have also developed her knowledge of colloquial Italian. In contrast, Hemingway's Italian was limited. Rosella Mamoli Zorzi and Gianni Moriani describe it as "precarious and incorrect" (17). Gail Sinclair suggests that Hemingway picked up his Italian by reading newspapers while hospitalized (50). Rena Sanderson, in "Hemingway's Italy: Paradise Lost," describes the young soldier's socializing at Christmas in 1918 with the wealthy Bellia family, among others, in Turin: "As the result of such hobnobbing, his Italian was no longer restricted to 'Italian of the front—all the language of the trenches and camp,' he declared, but now included the 'polite Sassiety' of his aristocratic friends and of the Italian officers he had befriended during this three months in Milan" (6). In an article he wrote in 1922 for the *Toronto Daily Star,* "Fascisti Party Half-Million," Hemingway recounts a meeting he has had with Mussolini. He describes the leader as "Talking slowly in Italian and choosing his words in order that he might be sure that I understood everything he said" (White 172).

If he sometimes claimed perhaps more fluency in Italian than was justified, Hemingway was likewise inclined to claim more familiarity with the landscape, geography, and culture than his experience supported. Michael Reynolds has noticed that, while Hemingway satirized Baedeker tourists, "at one point in *A Farewell to Arms* he found the Baedeker guide very useful, for a comparison of Hemingway's description of Udine (which he had not seen in 1928) and the Baedeker guide forces one to conclude that he either used this travel guide or one similar to it" (144).

The importance of landscape, maps, and a sense of place is further evident when Hemingway is writing to Bernard Berenson in 1949. He says: "I do not care for Firenze (you do not mind a heretic I hope) and am an old Veneto boy myself. I love it and know it quite well. Not as well as you but in a different, disorderly way. Mr. Kipling, who when he wrote well, wrote properly, wrote, 'A man has only one virginity to lose and there his heart will ever be'" (*Selected Letters* 666). Berenson had lived in Italy for decades, and it is hard to imagine that Hemingway's knowledge was a match for that of the art historian. To his Spanish translator Ferninanda Piviano, Hemingway once wrote that writing in Venice where "'Mr. Byron, Mr. Browning . . . and Mr. D'Annunzio . . . all wrote'" made "'Mr. Papa feel as if he had finally arrived at his proper estate'" (qtd. in Zorzi and Moriani 12). So possessive was he of this insider knowledge that in 1949, as he was working on *Across the River and Into the Trees,* he complained to Charles Scribner that his ex-wife Martha Gellhorn was competing with him to publish a book on Venice: "If Miss Martha publishes a book about Venice, the Island of Torcello, the Veneto, Mt. Grappa, Pasubio or the defense of the lower Piave before you publish my book I give you straight word that I will turn in my suit." He continues, "Two god-damned ex-wives in Venice now queering my pitch. . . . But doubt if they can do me much harm in that town. That is pretty much my town; or it was" (*Selected Letters* 669). Hemingway continues quite shamelessly to assert his *italianissimo* as he writes to Bernard Berenson through the 1950s. Hemingway never actually met Berenson, but began corresponding as a result of fourth wife Mary's meeting with the then eighty-three-year-old art connoisseur. Wharton, in contrast, was a close friend of Berenson and his wife Mary for nearly thirty years, visiting the Tuscan villa annually and hosting the Berensons in Hyères. Mary was the sister of Logan Pearsall Smith, one of Wharton's inner circle, adding to the intimacy of the group. Wharton invented the term "friendissimo" for Berenson (Balestra 209). The author's level of skill in Italian and her intimacy with the Berensons are markers of her age, her class, and her cosmopolitanism. Hemingway's rough-and-ready language, in contrast, places him in a modern Italy as a traveler who would not seek a permanent life in Europe. These differences are reflected in how Italy is represented in their fiction.

Wharton's novel *The Glimpses of the Moon* (1922) has central scenes set on Lake Como and in Venice; Hemingway's *A Farewell to Arms* likewise has scenes among the Italian Lakes, and his much later novel *Across the River and Into the Trees* (1950) is set in Venice. All three are novels of tourism and anti-tourism, and evoke Henry James's curmudgeonly remark, "Though there are some disagreeable things in Venice, there is nothing so disagreeable as the visitors" (*Italian Hours* 9). Both writers, moreover, offer subtexts on the rise of fascism.

The Glimpses of the Moon follows the marriage of Nick and Suzy Lansing as they conduct "the experiment" (1) of living in Europe for a year on the wedding gifts of wealthy friends, who offer their Italian and French houses to the newlyweds along with generous checks. Counting a flat in Chicago, they have five offers, and decide on the Italian Lakes: "Versailles in May would have been impossible: all our Paris crowd would have run us down within twenty-four hours. And Monte Carlo is ruled out because it's exactly the kind of place everybody expected us to go. . . . [I]t wasn't much of a mental strain to decide on Como." Suzy corrects Nick's reductive summary of her skill at planning: "It took a good deal of argument to convince you that we could face the ridicule of Como!" (2).

Writing in 1928 during travels in Italy that included a visit to the Lakes, Larz Anderson, a wealthy, well-traveled American diplomat, confirms the contemporary response to the region. He kept travel records later published by his wife that document the impressions of characters like those in Wharton's fiction:

> From Milan to Como there was a direct autostrada, a road built only for automobiles. As we whizzed along we saw the lights of little towns high above us on the hills.
>
> In the morning we looked from our window onto one of those incomparable views in which God and Man have collaborated to paint a perfect picture. Mountains of perfect proportions; lakes of indescribable beauty; villas fitting in as though they had grown there, rather than been built by man,—touches of mellow color against the terraced green slopes like cut velvet, and through it all, the black and orange and red rocky crests. Grey stone towers and ruins added a touch of age to even the age-old mountains.
>
> It was almost too beautiful! (534)

The first house the Lansings borrow is an Edenic site on Lake Como, the romantic setting that is a honeymoon cliché, and the cause of Suzy's fear of ridicule. Their enchantment mirrors the enthusiasm and awe that Anderson records, offering evidence that Wharton's style is grounded in contemporary American attitudes toward Italy. They are expelled from this earthly paradise when Suzy takes from the house expensive cigars for Nick, an act he finds reprehensible. The couple move on to Venice where, instead of a tourist's paradise, Suzy discovers she is "oppressed by the evidences of wealth," evidence of the fallen world they now inhabit. The Vanderlyns' Venetian palace is "out of scale" with its "great shadowy staircase" and high frescoed ceilings (*Glimpses of the Moon* 32–33). In the grand house, from which Suzy can see the Campanile of San Giorgio, she discovers the payment she must make in exchange for such luxurious surroundings: she must send out letters that will provide cover for Ellie's adulterous affair, and mind Clarissa, the Vanderlyns' neglected daughter. Thus Venice is tainted for Suzy by Ellie's adultery as well as the suggestions of illicit intentions for Clarissa hinted at by Strefford, one of the visitors who interrupt the Lansings' privacy in order to observe the "experiment" of the marriage.

The Lansings' clever plan to live at the expense of others begins to crumble. Suzy has planned on "indolent summer days on the lagoon, of flaming hours on the beach of the Lido, and evenings of music and dreams" (37). Isabel Anderson, Larz's wife, offers further documentation that the romantic description Suzy conjures reflects the rhetoric of wealthy travelers of the era. Writing of her visit to the city in 1929, she contrasts the "old Venice" of "mysterious canals winding like silver serpents in the moonlight; gondolas gliding by with whispering lovers" with the "new Venice": "the Lido with its myriad hotels and restaurants; the gaily painted bathing houses that now line the long beach; the pretty women with blond-tinted hair and sun-browned skins, grouped on the sands in their colorful chintz pajamas" (5). The languid city of tourist dreams has been invaded by the whizzing speed of the jazz age. Instead of time alone with Nick, Suzy finds herself among their curious acquaintances who, like Strefford, are arriving to watch the spectacle of their experiment. The marriage experiment puts the Lansings on stage; their wealthy friends have paid the price of admission to watch the unfolding of the plot. Their situation recalls the frescoed ceilings in Venetian palazzos which frequently display trompe l'oeil scenes of figures looking down on the inhabitants of the house as if from the balcony of a theater. "Strefford aimed his cigarette-end at a tourist in a puggaree who was gazing up from his guide-book at the palace. 'Ah,' he murmured with satisfaction, seeing the shot take effect" (51–52). The Lansings have become the object of the tourist gaze rather than being the gazers. Strefford's vulgar gesture makes him an animated fresco, but confirms the Lansings' loss of innocence as they flee Edenic Lake Como.

Just as she refuted the tourist sites of Milan, so Wharton avoids the lushly romantic portrayal of Venice common among visitors like the Andersons. While her characters do sip ices at Florian's (57), they admire the Campanile of San Giorgio, not the iconic Piazza San Marco. And, in a major plot point, Nick goes for a walk, absorbing the city's aging beauty of "bruised peach-tints," "worn canals," "half-decayed fruits and flowers," a "tumble-down palace," "a scrap of neglected garden" (91). He eventually reaches the Church of Mary of Nazareth, known as the Scalzi, near the railroad station, "not a church in which one was likely to run across sight-seers" (91). It is a church to which guidebooks can still be unfriendly. The current *DK Eyewitness Travel Guide* dismisses it as an "over-elaboration of polychrome" (Boulton and Catling 144). There he meets Coral Hicks, "applying her field-glass to the celestial vortex," guidebook in hand as she examines the Tiepolo ceiling. A Baedeker guide from 1906 contains the following entry: "Chiesa degli Scalzi . . . is perhaps the most imposing specimen of the Venetian baroque style. . . . The ceiling is decorated with a large fresco by Tiepolo, representing the miraculous removal of the house of the Virgin to Loreto. The high-altar . . . with its eight twisted columns, is a characteristic example of the architectonic perversities of the age of its construction" (320). The church is also the burial place of Venice's last Doge, an allusion to the collapse of the Republic in 1797, something that reinforces the theme of paradise lost.

Wharton was among the first of her contemporaries to admire this baroque style, and here, as with the Ospedale in Milan, she asserts her taste against Baedeker's conventional aesthetic. As Adeline R. Tintner noted, the ceiling was destroyed by Austrian bombs in 1915, though photographs of the original still exist. Having "restored" the Tiepolo fresco in her 1922 novel, Wharton clearly wants readers to pay attention to its subject: the transportation of the Virgin's house away from the Holy Land to the "safer" territory of the Adriatic coast of Italy near Ancona. Having driven through Ancona, Wharton would have seen the grandiose shrine at Loreto, an accretion of chapels and monuments to cover the tiny stone house at its center. Believing it to be the virgin's house, Crusaders dismantled it stone by stone and removed it from Nazareth to save the sacred relic from the Saracens in 1291. They carried the stones to Italy, where the house was reassembled. Greed of the local landowners led to problems, and the relic was again moved to its final site at Loreto. Over the centuries the house was embellished with chapels and shrines as the Catholic Church converted the Crusaders' piety into a miraculous event in which not men but angels delivered the house to its Italian site (Phillips 33–44). Tiepolo's ceiling fresco portrayed the Virgin riding on the little house as the heavenly movers carried it to safety. In fact, studies for the ceiling are on view in the Gallerie dell'Accademia in Venice, so the image would have been familiar both to Wharton and to tourists who came after the Great War despite the bombing. The Tiepolo appeals to Coral's interest in the archeology of the East, and gently mocks the Lansings' frequent moves from house to house.

Another reading is suggested by looking ahead to a scene in *Across the River and Into the Trees.* Colonel Cantwell, like Nick Lansing, wanders aimlessly in Venice, and stops to look at the church of Santa Maria del Giglio, the unusual design of which is completely secular: instead of saints' figures, it features the four wealthy Barbaro brothers who paid for its construction. Additional statues are "allegorical figures of Glory, Fame, and Wisdom extolling civil and military virtues," even though Barbaro was eventually "dismissed for ineptitude." Maps of fortifications along the Dalmatian coast and battles extolling Venetian sea power ornament the facade (*Venice Italy* 265; *Michelin Venice* 108). Cantwell compares the church to a P47, a World War II bomber, imagining it airborne. John Paul Russo suggests: "perhaps the heavy drinking may explain how this heavy baroque church could fly" (Lewis, *Hemingway* 163). Or, perhaps here too angels or Wharton intervened.

References to Browning in Wharton's novel further suggest that Venice wears battle scars. When Suzy and Strefford discuss Ellie's adultery, strains of a musical setting of "A Toccata of Galuppi's" float onto the balcony. The poem is an elegy for the city Browning loved: "'Dust and ashes, dead and done with, Venice spent what Venice earned.' . . . 'What of soul was left, I wonder, when the kissing had to stop?'" Wharton quotes the lines again when Nick discovers Suzy has gone out with friends after their argument, an action he reads as evidence of her indifference to him. Venice proves to be the site not of tourist romance, but of a war-torn world where churches are militarized and miracles are needed to save even holy shrines from advancing armies, whether Saracen or Fascist.

If Wharton writes a honeymoon guidebook to Lake Como, Hemingway revises the guidebook. If Wharton romanticized the Italian Lakes as Edenic, Hemingway in *A Farewell to Arms* demonizes them. The early days of Catherine and Frederic's romance are set in the tourist center of Milan, where we glimpse briefly the guidebook pleasures of the town. The chapters after the retreat from Caporetto portray the couple's escape to Switzerland from Stresa, as Henry rows them up Lake Maggiore across the border into Switzerland in a storm. As Emilio, the sympathetic barman in the Stresa hotel, warns Henry that he is about to be arrested as a deserter, and urges immediate departure, the dialogue maps the route up Lake Maggiore: "Past Luino, Cannero, Cannobio, Tranzano. You aren't in Switzerland until you come to Brissago. You have to pass Monte Tamara" (232). Emilio advises him to row past Isola Bella, Isola Madre, and Pallanza. The legendary beauty of the lakes is turned into a hellish nightmare of rain, wind, and cold. The thirty-five-kilometer trip is a cruel parody of a honeymoon, or even the Nativity, for the unmarried and pregnant pair. When they finally cross the border and meet the customs officer who asks why they have come to Switzerland, Henry replies, "For the winter sport. We are tourists and we want to do the winter sport." Noting that they have a good deal of cash, the suspicious official relents and advises them to visit Wengen, where his father runs "a very fine hotel" (241). They first find shelter in the mountains in the house of Mr. and Mrs. Guttingen. Later, they visit Montreux but do not live there, moving on to find a room in a hotel in Lausanne. Catherine enters the hospital in Lausanne, expecting to give birth, but dies along with the child. The honeymoon paradise has become a cold, wet town marked by corruption and finally death.

Across the River and Into the Trees, like *Glimpses of the Moon,* sets Venice as a place Cantwell longs to enjoy as a tourist, but one he finds he has reached too late. It is, like the disenchanted lakes, another place to die. In 1922, Hemingway had brought his first wife, Hadley, to the Veneto to visit the places he knew from the war. The writer and his fourth wife, Mary, stopped in Venice several times between 1948 and 1950, when they had brought their big blue Buick Roadmaster to Italy by ship from Cuba in order to have a comfortable touring car (McGrath C1). They returned again, by ship, in 1954 after two plane crashes in Africa when the author was so seriously injured that newspaper reports announced his death. They stayed often at the Gritti Palace, among the finest hotels in the city, which still preserves a Hemingway suite. The Venice of *Across the River and Into the Trees* is a site of memory and erotic encounter, of sex and death. The novel opens with Cantwell's arrival in the Veneto, as he stops the jeep to view the island of Torcello from the distance, the small island on which the city was founded. He offers the disinterested driver, Jackson, a lecture on the history and art of the region, explaining that, while he fought to defend Venice, "we never saw it. Then one time, I was back as far as Noghera[2] and it was clear and cold like today, and I saw it across the water. But I never got into it. It is my city, though, because I fought for it when I was a boy, and now that I am half a hundred years old, they know I fought for it and am part owner and they treat me well" (26). The narrative voice says: "This country meant very much to him, more than he could, or would ever tell anyone and now he sat in the car happy that in another half hour they would be in Venice" (33). We then hear a riff on *The Great Gatsby:* "They were coming up on Mestre fast, and already it was like going to New York the first time you were ever there in the old days when it was shining, white and beautiful. I stole that, he thought. But that was before the smoke. We were coming into my town, he thought. Christ, what a lovely town" (34).

Cantwell, a career soldier, walks the city like a tourist despite the cold weather: "Damn, I wish I might walk around this town all my life" (77). The novel offers a well-mapped walking guide as Cantwell wanders from the Gritti to Harry's bar and crosses the Grand Canal by traghetto and later by gondola with Renata. Later, he tells himself, "Only tourists and lovers take gondolas. . . . Except to cross the canal in the places where there are no bridges. I ought to go to Harry's, probably, or some damn place. But I think I'll go home" (163). But "home" is a temporary place, a hotel, much like an officers' mess but with better interior design.

One evening at Harry's Bar he watches a man at another table. The waiter tells Cantwell: "He condescends to me. He speaks bad Italian assiduously. He goes everywhere in Baedeker, and he has no taste in either food or wine" (124). He further notes that the man has "book-visited several palaces" (124). Mary Hemingway's autobiography *How It Was* suggests the man is Sinclair Lewis. She ruthlessly describes his face as "a piece of old liver, shot squarely with #7 shot at twenty yards" but concludes: "his mind was still sharp and glib and slick and I could accept him because he loved Italy" (269). What better way to satirize a competing author than by putting a Baedeker in his hand?

For both Wharton and Hemingway, then, Italy is a contested landscape.

The remarkable beauty entranced them, and each seemed to feel an entitlement to own it, separate from other visitors, and even from the Italians themselves. Both decried any change, whether through war or poverty or modernization. Wharton in 1903 writes to Margaret Chanler: "I think sometimes that it is almost a pity to enjoy Italy as much as I do, because the acuteness of my sensations makes them rather exhausting; but when I see the stupid Italians I have met here, completely insensitive to their surroundings, & ignorant of the treasures of art & history among which they have grown up, I begin to think it is better to be an American, & bring to it all a mind & eye unblunted by custom" (*Letters* 77–78). Her callous remark startles us today but captures the presence of the tourist gaze.

Hemingway, like Wharton, claims Venice as his own, assuring himself that the city, and even the country, would not have survived the war without his efforts. If it is "his" town, he still lives like a tourist, anchoring himself in the Gritti Palace Hotel and Harry's Bar as if he wrote for Baedeker. J. Gerald Kennedy argues, "Insofar as he mapped many enticing places for American readers between the World Wars, converting his encounters with new country into 'adventure' narratives, Hemingway participated in the promotion of tourism and the commodification of places like Pamplona and Key West" (327). He adds that Hemingway's travels "tended to be motivated not by touristic flaunting of privileged status but rather by his intuitive need for creative replenishment. Hemingway drew so many of his narrative ideas from terrain that he needed to relocate periodically both to take in new landscape and to clear his vision of previous scenery" (328). His letter to F. Scott Fitzgerald from the Riviera in 1926 supports this premise, but also his need to belong: "It's rained here every day for 3 weeks. I feel low as hell. Havent [*sic*] seen Bromfields, Edith Wharton, Conrad Bercovinci or any other of the little literary colony for some time. May be there will be a literary colony in Madrid" (*Letters* 203). Here he seems to crave "privileged status," but with his best work not yet published, he moves on to Spain and only later finds his Italian subject.

As much as both writers, then, swear emotional or aesthetic allegiance to Italy, neither commits to permanent residence. Their euphoric descriptions of an Edenic Italy are often contradicted by the representations of the country in their fiction. Wharton's Lake Como in *Glimpses* is overshadowed by the treacherous territory of Venice. The same Italian Lakes are turned dark and cold in *A Farewell to Arms,* whereas Cantwell's return to Venice opens as he views Torcello from a distance, the crumbling ruins on the island where Venice was founded, in which he sees "the fate of all things" (161) before entering the city in winter, encountering "wild, cold, wind from the mountain" (184).

What explains this contradiction? One likelihood is the very threatening political climate of Italy in the 1920s. The anti-tourist Italian scenes that dominate *Farewell* and *Glimpses* emerge in part from Hemingway's and Wharton's keen reading of the news from Italy. Still raw and tired from World War I, both writers watched the rise of the Fascist Party, which was officially launched in 1922, though manifestos like those of the Futurists foreshadowed the political changes. Among the most ardent anti-fascists was Bernard Berenson, who kept Wharton alert to the dangers he foresaw; he was to call Italy "Mussolinia" (Lee 740). By the 1930s, R. W. B. Lewis writes, Wharton "wondered if she could ever return to Italy" (505). Dale M. Bauer, writing about "Roman Fever," claims, "The marks of a changing and horrifying political climate are etched in Wharton's fiction" (682). Bauer quotes a letter Wharton wrote in 1935 to Royal Cortissoz: "I have not met anyone in France who is alarmed for the future, as far as one's own personal welfare is concerned; but politically, it does not look brilliant at present; nor does ours at home, either. So perhaps we had better turn to the Titians and the Giorgione, and try to forget it all" (683). Bauer reads the tone as ironic, and Wharton's active involvement in World War I supports that reading. Even the beauty of two of Venice's greatest painters cannot come to her aid as the signs of disaster were increasingly evident.

Like Wharton, Hemingway saw the rise of fascism as it threatened the country he so loved. Several news articles he wrote for the *Toronto Star* as early as 1922 condemn the Fascists "or extreme Nationalists" as "black-shirted, knife-carrying, club-swinging, quick-stepping, nineteen-year-old potshot patriots" ("Italy's Blackshirts"). In 1923, he writes an article on "Mussolini, Europe's Prize Bluffer." By 1937, in a speech he gave to the American Writers' Congress, Hemingway asserts that "fascism is a lie. . . . And when it is past it will have no history except the bloody history of murder that is well known" ("Fascism Is a Lie").

Rena Sanderson observes that between his marriages to Hadley and Pauline Pfeiffer, in 1927, Hemingway embarked on a trip to Italy with Guy Hickok, even though he had sworn to stay away from Italy as long as Mussolini was in power (Baker 182; Sanderson 16). She concludes: "For Hemingway, Italy has been ruined by Fascism and had become a painful reminder of the mutability of love. He would not return to it for another twenty years" (17).

Marinetti's Futurist rhetoric calling for the destruction of "past-loving Venice" in 1910 finds an eerie echo after World War II. Wharton had been dead for a decade by the time Hemingway survived his two African plane crashes. From Mombasa, he and Mary traveled by ship to Venice, heading for the Gritti to recuperate. Architect Ernest Hodgson discovered a curious Venetian link between Hemingway and Frank Lloyd Wright, both having lived in Oak Park, Illinois. Wright had been asked by the parents of an Italian student who died suddenly to design a three-story building to be constructed along the Grand Canal in the young man's memory. At the time that the Hemingways were arriving in Venice,

> Wright was in the middle of fighting City Hall. Heated discussions raged between those who hated the thought of a new building on the Grand Canal and those who were in favor of the project. On hearing the opposing views, Hemingway offered his solution to appease both sides: "Let them build it, and as soon as it is finished, burn it to the ground." When Wright's project was finally rejected by Venetian officials he "declared that tourism had won another victory." (Hodgson 46)

The rebuilding of the Campanile and the rejection of Wright's Masieri project should dispel Wharton's charge that the "stupid Italians" did not value their heritage. Here, in "Wopland," in the cherished architecture of the Italian past, she and Hemingway find common, if conservative, ground. In prose and mortar, each aimed to preserve the glorious beauty and the visible past of the place they loved more than anywhere else from the threats of fascism and rampant tourism. Emancipated from their Baedekers, these patient observers find their own "true Italy."

NOTES

1. Increasing interest in Wharton's importance as a gardener, garden historian, and designer of interiors and houses is evident in glossy texts such as Vivian Russell's *Edith Wharton's Italian Gardens* and academic studies including Annette Benert's *The Architectural Imagination of Edith Wharton* (2007), as well as related studies of Beatrix Farrand. A symposium at the Mount in 2006 resulted in a useful collection of papers, *Edith Wharton and the American Garden* (2009), edited by Robin S. Karson.

2. Presumably he means Maghera, now the industrial area of Venice. It is on a point visible from parts of the historic center.

WORKS CITED

Anderson, Larz. *Letters and Journals of a Diplomat.* Ed. Isabel Anderson. New York: Fleming H. Revell, 1940. Print.

Baedeker, Karl. *Italy from the Alps to Naples*. Leipzig: Karl Baedeker, 1906. Print.

Baker, Carlos. *Ernest Hemingway: A Life Story.* New York: Scribner's, 1969. Print.

Balestra, Gianfranca. "Edith Wharton's Italian Tale: Language, Exercise and Social Discourse." Colquitt, Goodman, and Waid, eds., *A Forward Glance* 206–20.

Bauer, Dale M. "Edith Wharton's 'Roman Fever': A Rune of History." *College English* 506 (1988): 681–93. Web. 21 June 2016. www.jstor.org/stable/377740.

Benert, Annette. *The Architectural Imagination of Edith Wharton: Gender, Class, and Power in the Progressive Era.* Madison, NJ: Fairleigh Dickinson UP, 2007. Print.

Benstock, Shari. *No Gifts from Chance: A Biography of Edith Wharton.* New York: Scribner's, 1994. Print.

Bittner, John Robert. Completed by Joseph M. Flora. "Anti-Fascist Symbols and Subtexts in *A Farewell to Arms*: Hemingway, Mussolini, and Journalism in the 1920s." Sanderson, ed., *Hemingway's Italy* 100–107. Print.

Boulton, Susie, and Christopher Catling. *Venice and the Veneto: Eyewitness Travel Guides*. New York: DK, 1996. Print.

Bruccoli, Matthew J., ed. *Conversations with Ernest Hemingway*. Jackson: UP of Mississippi, 1986. Print.

Cirino, Mark, and Mark P. Ott, eds. *Hemingway and Italy: Twenty-first Century Perspectives*. Gainesville: UP of Florida, 2017. Print.

Colquitt, Clare, Susan Goodman, and Candace Waid, eds. *A Forward Glance: New Essays on Edith Wharton*. Newark: U of Delaware P, 1999. Print.

Dwight, Eleanor. *Edith Wharton: An Extraordinary Life*. New York: Abrams, 1994. Print.

Flint, R. W., ed. *Marinetti: Selected Writings*. New York: Farrar, Straus and Giroux, 1971. Print.

Forster, E. M. *A Room with a View*. 1908. New York: Gramercy, 1993. Print.

Hemingway, Ernest. *Across the River and Into the Trees*. 1950. New York: Collier Macmillan, 1978. Print.

———. *A Farewell to Arms*. 1929. New York: Scribner's, 2012. Print.

———. "Fascism Is a Lie: Ernest Hemingway/1937." Bruccoli, ed., *Conversations with Ernest Hemingway* 193–95. Print.

———. "Fascisti Party Half-Million." *Toronto Daily Star*. 24 June 1922. White, ed., *Dateline Toronto* 172–73. Print.

———. "Italy's Blackshirts." *Toronto Star Weekly*. 24 June 1922. White, ed., *Dateline Toronto* 174–75. Print.

———. "Mussolini, Europe's Prize Bluffer." *Toronto Daily Star*. 27 January 1923. White, ed., *Dateline Toronto* 253–56. Print.

———. *Selected Letters, 1917–1961*. Ed. Carlos Baker. New York: Scribner's, 1981. Print.

Hemingway, Mary Welsh. *How It Was*. New York: Knopf, 1951. Print.

Hodgson, Ernest. "A Frank and Ernest Affair." *Canadian Architect*. 1 Oct. 2002: 43. Web. www.canadianarchitect.com/features/a-frank-and-ernest-affair/. Accessed 4 June 2018.

James, Henry. *Italian Hours*. New York: Horizon Press, 1968. Print.

Junkins, Donald. "The Poetry of the Twentieth Chapter of Death in the Afternoon: Relationships between the Deleted and Published Halves." Lewis, ed., *Hemingway in Italy and Other Essays* 111–21. Print.

Karson, Robin S., ed. *Edith Wharton and the American Garden*. Lenox, MA: Mount P, 2009. Print.

Kennedy, J. Gerald. "Doing Country: Hemingway's Geographical Imagination." *Southern Review* 35.2 (1999): 325–29. *Academic Search Complete*. Web. Accessed 20 Nov. 2016.

Le Blond, Aubrey. *The Old Gardens of Italy: How to Visit Them*. London: John Lane, Bodley Head, 1912. Print.

Lee, Hermione. *Edith Wharton*. New York: Knopf, 2007. Print.

Lewis, Robert W., ed. *Hemingway in Italy and Other Essays*. New York: Praeger, 1990. Print.

Lewis, R. W. B. *Edith Wharton: A Biography*. New York: Harper & Row, 1975. Print.

McGrath, Charles. "A Mutable Feast: Batch of Hemingway Ephemera from Cuba Digitized." *New York Times*, 10 Feb. 2014, C1. Print.

Michelin Venice. Watford, UK: Michelin Tyre, 1996. Print.

Moddelmog, Debra A., and Suzanne del Gizzo, eds. *Ernest Hemingway in Context*. New York: Cambridge UP, 2013. Print.

Phillips, G. E. *Loreto and the Holy House*. Fitzwilliam, NH: Loreto Publications, 2005. Print.

Platt, Charles A., and Keith N. Morgan. *Italian Gardens*. 1894. Portland, OR: Sagapress/Timber Press, 1993. Print.

Ramsden, George. *Edith Wharton's Library*. Settrington, York: Stone Trough Books, 1999. Print.

Reynolds, Michael S. *Hemingway's First War: The Making of "A Farewell to Arms."* Princeton, NJ: Princeton UP, 1976. Print.

Russell, Vivian. *Edith Wharton's Italian Gardens*. Boston: Little, Brown, 1997. Print.

Russo, John Paul. "To Die Is Not Enough: Hemingway's Venetian Novel." Lewis, ed., *Hemingway in Italy and Other Essays* 153–80. Print.

Sanderson, Rena, ed. *Hemingway's Italy: New Perspectives*. Baton Rouge: Louisiana State UP, 2006. Print.

———. "Hemingway's Italy: Paradise Lost." Sanderson, ed., *Hemingway's Italy* 1–37. Print.

Sinclair, Gail. "Reading." Moddelmog and del Gizzo, eds., *Ernest Hemingway in Context* 43–52. Print.

Sitwell, George. *On the Making of Gardens*. New York: Scribner's, 1909. Print.

Tintner, Adeline R. *Edith Wharton in Context: Essays on Intertextuality*. Tuscaloosa: U of Alabama P, 1999. Print.

Venice, Italy: Knopf Guides. New York: Knopf, 1996. Print.

"Venice's Famous Campanile Falls." *New York Times*. 15 July 1903. Online.

Wharton, Edith. *A Backward Glance*. New York: Appleton Century, 1934. Print.

———. *The Glimpses of the Moon*. New York: D. Appleton, 1922. Print.

———. *Italian Backgrounds*. New York: Scribner's, 1907. Print.

———. *Italian Villas and Their Gardens*. 1904. New York: Da Capo P, 1988. Print.

———. *The Letters of Edith Wharton*. Ed. R. W. B. Lewis and Nancy Lewis. New York: Scribner's, 1988. Print.

White, William, ed. *Ernest Hemingway: Dateline Toronto*. New York: Scribner's, 1985. Print.

Wright, Sarah Bird. *Edith Wharton A to Z*. New York: Facts on File, 1998. Print.

Zorzi, Rosella Mamoli, and Gianni Moriani. *In Venice and in the Veneto with Ernest Hemingway*. Venice: Supernova Edizioni, 2011. Print.

Dawn and Decline

Contrasting Spaces in Wharton's "False Dawn" and Hemingway's "A Very Short Story"

SIRPA SALENIUS

Every fictional story is in one way or another related to the space in which the action and events of the narrative take place. The spatial dimension of fictional stories may be conveyed to a reader in various ways: it can be described by one or several characters, or it may be a task given to a narrative voice. At times, literary scholars have considered fictional space as a mere setting for stories—often, however, with symbolic and metaphorical interpretative possibilities. More recent multidisciplinary scholarship that has engaged in literary studies operates, as Robert T. Tally Jr. explains, under different headings ranging from literary geography to spatial humanities and has brought attention to "the dynamic relations among space, place, and literature" (ix).[1] Such scholarship has pushed the concept of literary space from its simplistic conceptualizations as a mere geographical mapping and narrative setting toward more complex articulations of literary space as intimately connected with psychological states of fictional characters. The spatial presentations in Edith Wharton's novella "False Dawn" and Ernest Hemingway's "A Very Short Story" are connected to specific spaces of Italy and the United States, two different geographical locations that in these two short stories mirror and contrast each other in morals, emotions, ideals, and worldviews. Both stories have male protagonists, whose Italian experiences are characterized by open, outdoor spaces permeated with empowering emotions of freedom and control, passion and romance, which are in dramatic contrast with the suffocating, claustrophobic enclosures surrounding them in the United States.

The similarities that connect the two stories include, for instance, the initial scenes with highly positive cultural and emotional spaces, and the final spaces, which in both stories are closed and constraining, denoting shame and squalor. Descriptions of these spatial environments reflect the inner landscapes of the stories' characters while they also address dominant ideologies and prevailing trends of the characters' contemporary societies. Both stories are constructed around a journey from one space to another, and in both stories Italy figures prominently as a crucial location charged with thematic significance, empowerment, and the protagonists' symbolic rebirth. In "False Dawn" and "A Very Short Story," then, space is closely associated with mobility and the crossing of invisible borders separating contrasting realities.

Conceptualizing Space

Both Hemingway and Wharton render space significant in their discussion of opposing realities in these stories, as in others, in which space is "full of power and symbolism, a complex web of relations of domination and subordination" (Massey 265). In the two narratives discussed here, relationships are tied to specific spaces where such power relations are played out. The dominating figures are defined by their gender (male), while the subordinate are placed in that position either because of their gender (women) or their age (younger men).

Both authors, who knew of one another and read each other's works, had lived in Italy at various times, associating the place with intense intellectual and emotional experiences (Tintner 135–36). Both authors were young when they first visited Italy, both developed an attraction to the country and its atmosphere, and both kept returning there repeatedly. As scholars have noted, Italy featured prominently in their lives and their fiction. (For more about Italy in the life of Hemingway, see Sanderson, "Hemingway's Italy"; for Wharton and Italy, see Ricard.) In addition, in their texts both authors positioned Italy in dialogue with the United States.

Wharton compared such cities as Rome with New York, to the disadvantage of the latter. Such comparisons characterized her own life as well as her fictional works (see, for example, "Roman Fever"). She had been brought up in Europe, where she absorbed influences of foreign cultures and manners, and mastered foreign languages. When she returned to the

United States, she no longer felt a sense of belonging in her native society. In Wharton's life, Shari Benstock argues, "America represents deprivation, narrowness, and constraint; Europe offers plentitude and freedom" (20). Such contrasting impressions were shared by many Americans, especially artists and writers who had stayed in Italy for longer periods of time. Moreover, many, including Wharton, perceived American society, where she felt emotionally stifled, as permeated by pomposity and artificiality. It has been further suggested that Wharton praised the "dense old European order, all compounded of differences and *nuances*," which were interwoven with passions; these formed a contrast to the "safe, shallow, and shadowless" United States (Joslin and Price 5). In her life and narratives, Wharton criticized American socialites, and according to Katherine Joslin and Alan Price, "her harshest attack on the way American society treats women" appeared in *French Ways and Their Meaning*, published in 1919 (10). Italy, instead, represented youth, memories, vitality, romance, exoticness, and a place of alteration. In Benstock's view, Wharton was drawn to Italy's "art and gardens, but also to its religion and, most especially, to its music" (24), i.e. like so many other Americans and foreigners, she was attracted to its culture. For Hemingway, instead, Italy meant war, adventure, first love, and subsequent marriages.

Rena Sanderson argues that Hemingway "equated Italy with paradise; soon, he would revisit it and equate it with the loss of paradise" ("Hemingway's Italy" 2). Scholars have recognized that Hemingway's Italian stories abound in disillusionment, disappointment, and disconnections, or, to put it differently, in "emotional atmospheres" (14). The idea of place, then, for both authors intertwined with the intellectual, emotional, and sociocultural; it appeared as constantly changing, never static. Moreover, the two different locations served for construction and reconstruction of identities.

Indeed, scholars have defined place as an environment for a continuous production of identities and connections, "produced on many different levels by different modes of relation (cultural, social, emotional, psychological, global, and translocal)," which are tied to movement (Pultz Moslund 205, 210). Recent scholarship in literary geography has taken up similar ideas, examining fictional space not merely as a reference to existing locations but as a mobile and unstable process (Hones 686).[2] Hence, geographical boundaries and borders may define space which can be connected to a specific lifestyle and class, or, in the case of Wharton's and Hemingway's stories, also carry significance in relation to specific moments and episodes of life. In the two texts discussed here, the image of Italy is filtered through dominant national discourse, imagined as a space of art and culture, filled with historical and romantic associations. Italy in both stories features as a rejuvenating, empowering space that charges the protagonists with confidence, determination, optimism, and grand visions and plans for the future. The United States forms its dramatic opposite with contrasting social values and ideas, which are foregrounded through specific small and stifling spaces that are linked to commercial value, superficiality, emotional and financial decline, shame, and squalor. In addition, what Kathleen N. Drowne has noted as a tendency of James Baldwin's narratives "to infuse geographical spaces with psychological and moral significance" is also applicable to Wharton's "False Dawn" and Hemingway's "A Very Short Story" (73). Similarly to Baldwin's characters, the protagonists in these stories search for a place, a safe haven or an emotional home, which overlaps with their search for identity and agency. Such articulations of space reflect the psychological struggles of the protagonists. (For similar struggles of Baldwin's characters, see Drowne.)

Space as a Literary Device in "False Dawn"

Edith Wharton's novella "False Dawn" was published in 1924 by D. Appleton and Company of New York. It was in part influenced by the experience of the American art collector James Jackson Jarves, whose collection of Italian Primitives contemporary critics ridiculed; in part it was based on an earlier collector, Thomas Jefferson Bryan, and his "abortive attempt to educate the uncultivated New Yorker" (Tintner 156–57). In the story, Wharton intertwines geographical with cultural distance as she contrasts the New World with the Old, positioning the two spaces—and connected worldviews—as opposites that are evaluated against the backdrop of New York. In this way, Wharton returns to the examination of the "international theme," first articulated and developed by Nathaniel Hawthorne and Henry James, and its exploration of antonyms, contrasting ideals and ideologies. New York epitomizes the New World in art appreciation, trends, society, and fashion, which are measured against those of its Old World counterpart, Italy. New York in this story and in Wharton's *The Age of Innocence* has a similar function: "Cautious, conservative, resistant to indiscreet expenditure, New York reigns in passions and capital" (Knights 34). Through its society, it stands for materialistic and mercenary ideals, profit and social prominence, whereas Italy is depicted as richer in art, culture, history, and innovation in artistic trends. The story is characterized by an interplay of the two opposing spaces and realities that fail to be reconciled until years later when the Christian art collection the protagonist, Lewis Raycie, has put together during his journey in Italy is found in the closed space of forgotten, useless objects, the attic. In this way, the two worlds represented by New York and Italy are reconciled through appreciation of art and the discovery of an invaluable collection of Italian artworks buried in the confining New York attic.

New York, which is the setting dominating both the beginning and ending of the novella with the protagonist's Grand Tour in its center, represents upper-class appearances and superficiality that initially form the world of the protagonist. The opening scene of the narrative takes place on the verandah of Lewis Raycie's father, Mr. Halston Raycie, an upper-class art collector, whose country house at High Point "stood on a height above the Sound," at a driving distance from his house in Canal Street (Wharton 9). The narrative voice's mention of Mr. Raycie's various possessions—art and abode—announce him as a wealthy and prominent figure. The verandah where the opening scene finds him is an open space, linked with the domesticity of the rural house located on a geographically elevated position, further underscored in the name of the country town. All the various elements defining the space Mr. Raycie possesses contribute to the impression of financial and patriarchal dominance. In the scene, luxury and leisure are enveloped in the heat of the "languid July day," which renders Mr. Raycie's brow "steaming" (9). Everything appears quite still due to the stifling heat, turning the verandah into a static, somewhat oppressive, open space.

Unlike the porch in Zora Neale Hurston's *Their Eyes Were Watching God*, which appears as a liminal space (see Pattison 19), the verandah is a limiting barrier that forms a border between the socially, psychologically, and physically elevated and dominating position of Mr. Raycie and his guests and others who reside outside the verandah. It is evident right from the first paragraph that Mr. Raycie is opinionated and stubborn, and he holds a position of authority. Such impressions come across through references to his elderly guests on the hot verandah "furtively" slapping their mosquito-bitten cheeks because, as the narrator explains, Mr. Raycie refused to "admit that there were mosquitos at High Point" (Wharton 9). The obliging guests, sitting on the verandah, being bitten by the mosquitoes, languidly sip their drinks and savor fresh strawberries. The verandah, closely associated with the authority of its owner, is an exterior that foregrounds the importance Mr. Raycie places on exteriors and appearances, and it functions as his private social space employed for entertaining prominent guests. Like Hurston's porch, the verandah is a masculine space, "both an intimate space connected to the house and an exterior space accessible to the public" (Pattison 13); it is a space that belongs to its owner, Mr. Raycie.

The scholar Judith Fryer notes, "There are spaces for greeting guests, for dining, for taking a quiet cup of tea before the fire, for intimate conversation, for concentration," and for other social activities. According to Fryer, Wharton believed that, "'whatever the uses of a room, they are seriously interfered with if it be not preserved as a small world itself'" (71). The house Mr. Raycie lives in appears as an example of such a miniature world: his residence is an imitation Tuscan villa, which attests to his admiration of everything Italian, but it also demonstrates the importance he places on appearances. He is satisfied with an imitation of a Tuscan abode, of one implying elegance and wealth, rather than desiring an authentic architectural design, which perhaps could have been American and thus would have linked him more closely with his native country. He prefers a replica of an Italian villa, which clearly indicates his desire to emphasize his fashion-consciousness, sense of style, appreciation of foreign elegance, willingness to foreground his financial well-being, and overall intention to give the outside world an impression of his sophistication.

The owner of the "majestic" villa himself is described as "a monumental man," a definition that further links him to Italy: it evokes an image of a monument, immovable and massive, while it also connects Mr. Raycie with the art world to which he is so keen on belonging. He is further associated with a specific space, that of "a great agricultural estate of which not an acre is untilled" (Wharton 11). The land, then, is fully taken advantage of, with not an acre left free and out of his control, and it is filled with agricultural produce, such as the strawberries Mr. Raycie's guests are enjoying on the porch, or rather, on the Italian villa's verandah. The great estate further foregrounds Mr. Raycie's patriarchal position of power that extends through every acre, which is cultivated and controlled, thus covertly including control and dominance over his wife and son.

If Mr. Raycie appears as a monumental figure and an estate, his wife, instead, is linked with stylish feminine clothing as she appears on the scene in her "lace ruffles and clustered purple grapes of her newest Paris cap" (12). In addition to her fashionable cap from France, she also uses the best French soap. Similarly to Tuscany, the French capital denotes sophistication, high fashion, and implies that perhaps the Raycies themselves have visited Paris and Tuscany. And yet, despite the material possessions associated with France and Italy, the Raycies are convinced of American superiority over Europe. Wharton, then, underscores the contradictory attitudes of such New Yorkers as the Raycies toward Europe and emphasizes the characters' dedication to the cultivation of American values.

The older generation of Raycies, Lewis's mother and father, belong to a world of class-conscious snobbery. They are incapable of recognizing true artistic talent as they merely follow ideals introduced in mainstream artistic discourse. The brief mention of Edgar Allan Poe in the text as marginalized because of his poverty exemplifies the failure of New York high society to recognize artistic talent because the vision of such upper-class snobs as the Raycies is blurred by class prejudice. Moreover, Poe is described as an atheist, or in Mr. Raycie's words "a blasphemer," who fails to sustain conventional values. (For the passage on Poe, see 22–23.) New York as urban space reflective of its upper-class society becomes a character in its own right to personify such a society's arrogance and callousness, which are linked to wealth. Wharton examines the power play inherent in social hierarchies whose stability precludes any recognition of lower-class artistry or acknowledgment of any fresh ideas in cultural and artistic expression. Nonetheless, as a stage for social power relations and an active player in transmitting cultural knowledge, the city becomes a changing space whose initial immobility is contrasted with the mobility of the protagonist, Lewis Raycie, on his Grand Tour of Europe.

The couple's son, Lewis, dramatically differs from his father: he is described as having been "a shrimp of a baby, a shaver of a boy, and now a youth as scant as an ordinary man's midday shadow" (12). In other words, the narrator who admiringly portrays the father as a strong, monumental, and authoritarian man, introduces the son as small, weak, and insignificant. Therefore, the overpowering Mr. Raycie wishes to send his "scant" son on a journey through Continental Europe, to encourage the son to embark on his Grand Tour whose goal, in accordance with the eighteenth-century tradition, was to train boys into men and further into gentlemen. Lewis, who is eager to explore the wonders of the Old World, has already formed his expectations of Europe, Italy in particular. His impressions and ideas are partially based on stories he has heard from his father's cousin, Mr. Donaldson Kent, Esquire, whose niece (his brother's daughter), Beatrice, also has told stories of Italy where she was born and had resided in until Mr. Donaldson's brother, Julius, and his wife had both died there. Italy, then, epitomizes art and culture but also death and decline. The opposing ideas are intimately tied to specific characters—Lewis and Mr. Raycie versus Julius and Mr. Donaldson Kent Esquire—who are rooted in specific locations (the United States and Italy).

Lewis, then, leaves the United States to explore the Old World and to collect artworks for his father's new gallery. Lewis's geographical and physical distance from New York—and from his father—triggers a growing awareness of the real character of the place he has left behind and the people who surround Lewis in his native country. The mental smallness of America is contrasted with Lewis's growing self-reliance implied in the act of "confidently" surveying "the sublime spectacle of Mont Blanç" (39). As he gazes on the spectacular monumental mountain in front of him, Lewis is at his own High Point, both mentally and physically. His experience in Europe provides him with an agency, which is empowering and which he lacked when living in his father's house. Europe becomes an emotional refuge from the imprisonment of the New York milieu of wealth and intellectually limited society. It is during his Grand Tour, "attenuated by time and distance," when Lewis, initially depicted as "fluid," "insubstantial," and fearful (39), starts to rebel against the social codes of his previous life, realizing how his dominating father had always imposed his views and values on his son. Proceeding on his journey of initiation, his pilgrim's progress,

Lewis wonders "what could be left in his mind of Canal Street and the lawn above the Sound?" (41). Everything is different, even the mosquitoes that buzzed "in scenes so different" from that of New York "encased in security and monotony" (41).

As he gains knowledge in the vaster cultural richness of Europe, Lewis recognizes his father's arrogance and incompetence in artistic judgment. Indeed, Mr. Raycie's attitude toward art is superficial, and his interest lies in collecting the works of such famous artists as Raphael or Salvator Rosa, mainly because of the fame these artists enjoyed among American art admirers. The purpose of his collection of masterpieces by well-known artists is to underscore his own superiority and importance. Lewis, instead, reflects on the differences between New York and Europe where he has an opportunity to witness the evolution of trends in art appreciation that had occurred through the influence of John Ruskin and the Pre-Raphaelite movement. These trends are transmitted to him and influence the change of direction in his selection of artworks to take back to the United States.

It is "in a tiny Venetian church, no more than a chapel, that Lewis Raycie's eyes had been unsealed" (46). The moment of revelation occurs in a religious, holy space, in an authentic church unspoiled by tourist hordes, thus underscoring Lewis's understanding of authenticity. "His eyes had been opened to a new world of art. And this world it was his mission to reveal to others—he, the insignificant and ignorant Lewis Raycie. . . . His excitement had something of the apostle's ecstasy," and he was ready to "preach the new gospel to them that sat in the darkness of Salvator Rosa and Lo Spagnoletto" (48). The church, thus, renders such fervent artistic ecstasy possible and emphasizes the almost religious nature of Lewis's recognition of his mission and role in promoting new ideals in art to an American audience. His courage in choosing to become a pioneer in promoting Christian art contrasts with his earlier fearfulness. Hence, his initial insignificance is replaced by bravery, enthusiasm, vitality, and vision, which give form to his confident self exploring Italy.

After being exposed to the influence of European culture, which has a significant impact on his personal development, the protagonist returns to New York a different man. The first thing he notices is "the smallness of the house on the Sound, and the largeness of Mr. Raycie" (48). His father's overwhelming presence in the seemingly small-scale imitation villa transforms Lewis's impression of Mr. Raycie. He now seems "narrow, juvenile, almost childish," and what Lewis realizes was, "above all, the arrogance and incompetence of his artistic judgements" (48–49). When the father is ready to question his son about his European tour, however, the study in which they find themselves "seemed to grow even smaller," a change that mirrors Lewis's emotional state as he starts to lose confidence and once more begins to feel insecure when facing his controlling father (50). The study, hence, becomes a projection of Lewis's shrinking self-esteem. Wharton's choice to place the scene in the father's study, a locus of education, of teaching and learning, underscores the father's refusal to be guided by his more cultured and informed son. It is in the study that relates "spatiality to the social and to power," where the father-son relationship returns to the previously established system of control and authority (Massey 4). Hence, space is tied to ideological systems, to influences of patriarchal power, and to losing and gaining authority. In the scene, the study echoes the philosopher George Santayana's pictorial space, which moves in accordance with its center, here Lewis, who continuously has to adjust to his changing environment and position in the fluctuating circumstances. In Santayana's perception of space, the spiritual and moral, or psychological and emotional, intertwine with the physical. In such a double dimension of spatiality, pictorial space becomes "an accurate and detailed map, drawn according to a private projection, and covering the field of action" (Santayana 51).[3]

The physical space of the studio triggers a psychological and emotional change in Lewis. Since "social relations are bearers of power," as Massey suggests, the space in which such relations are enacted becomes "an important element in the constitution of power itself" (22). The decline in Lewis's confidence, caused by his father's emotional and financial power over the son, continues "in the Canal Street house where the unpacked pictures had been sent": "Lewis felt himself shrinking and his father expanding" (Wharton 53). If Mr. Raycie had hoped to hang a Raphael on the walls of his city house, being satisfied even with "an inferior specimen," he had not expected to get originals—of a different time period and by artists whose names he is unable to pronounce. The dream of the Raycie Gallery dies, and a year later Mr. Raycie himself dies. "New York agreed it was the affair of the pictures that had killed him" (60). New York becomes a character to personify its wealthy and snobbish, yet ignorant, society when

"New York agreed" it was not ready for new artistic trends. Arrogance and meanness are linked to the upper class, whereas other social classes and the idea of a heterogeneous city are excluded from the judgmental city. The generational gap is played out in the Canal Street residence, the canal referring to a divide that separates the old from the new. For both, Lewis and his father, the house as space had carried its traditional significance: it had been "a nest for dreaming, a shelter for imagining" (Stilgoe viii), except their dreams had been different. The townhouse becomes a separating line that anchors the old New York with its traditional values and snobbery, completely detached from the future, whose dawn is played out in other sections of the city.

Reminiscent of Wharton's "The Valley of Childish Things," in which, as Fryer suggests, the author addresses the "consequences of deviating from cultural patterns" (8), Lewis realizes upon his return to New York that his understanding of art had progressed beyond the American art colony's comprehension, which had remained anchored in conventional ideas. His aims of mapping art development and generating new models of artistic appreciation by placing Italian art in its historical context of production turn into utter failures. His modern views clash with the stubborn, stagnant conventionality of his father and the New Yorkers of the father's generation.

Lewis, who is disinherited, moves to an unfashionable part of the city, into a house "on the corner of Third Avenue and Tenth Street," which is ironic because he is the most fashionable man in New York, years ahead of his time (Wharton 62). As he no longer fits into the society he had left behind, a dramatic transformation takes place not only in him but also in his environment. The house, inherited from cousin Ebenezer, is "an admired specimen of domestic architecture," not an imitation of a foreign villa like that of Lewis's father (75). Lewis, hence, values originality, which is associated with him through his new inherited residence and the artworks he has collected. He turns his home, a domestic environment, into a public museum which is open to other serious art appreciators; unfortunately, there are none in New York. In addition, the unenlightened high society mocks him for displaying his Christian art collection in his own house. Hence, New York as space becomes fluid, reflective of values and trends which are tied to different sections of the city and linked to mobility as the art collection is variously praised (in Europe) and rejected (in America), finally ending up in the crammed attic from where it is recovered when New York has become ready to accept the novelty of Christian art. By then, the Raycies are forgotten, "like so many of the descendants of the proud little Colonial society" (74). By then also Louisa Raycie, the daughter of Lewis, had died "of a decline" (75).

It is only years later that the Raycie collection is recognized as "one of the most beautiful collections of Italian Primitives in the world," with some of the most magnificent paintings by Mantegna, Giotto, Piero della Francesca, and Carpaccio (76). After the deaths of Louisa Raycie and her parents, a cousin—an old Miss Raycie—had inherited the house with the pictures she never bothered to take a look at, stored in the attic. She had lived in the house on Tenth Street "for nearly half a century, with five millions' worth of pictures shut up in the attic over her head" (77). The pictures that had caused the financial ruin of Lewis Raycie, rendered him a target of ridicule, and made his sisters ashamed of him, were now stored among forgotten, insignificant items in the small, stifling attic of the American house. Similarly to the High Point, imitation Italian villa of the opening scene, the attic where the paintings are buried is located at the highest point of the house, which is an example of original American architecture.

In "False Dawn" Wharton projects her analysis of society's moral and social codes against the backdrop of New York as she explores conventionality reflected against new trends in art appreciation. The story is as much about New York and the New World as it is about its contrast, the Old World, both geographical territories overlapping with a discussion about generational gap—the pompous upper-class conservative parents' disapproval of their child who supports the poor genius, the poet Poe, and rejects the parents' provincial mind frame. "False Dawn" is characterized by an interplay of these two opposing spaces and realities that clash and contrast each other until the very end of the story when the Christian art collection the protagonist has put together is found in the attic of his home. In this way, the two worlds are reconciled through art appreciation, eventually closing the gap between different spaces and generations. However, by the time the pictures are found in the attic of Lewis's former home, "the proud little Colonial society" has vanished, and the collector of the masterpieces has died in poverty and shame.

Gendered Spaces in "A Very Short Story"

In Ernest Hemingway's "A Very Short Story," which was composed in June–July 1923, the narrative spaces carry similar meanings and echo some of the same themes as in Wharton's "False Dawn." In addition, for many readers, as Thomas Strychacz observers, Hemingway was an author who glorified machismo (*Hemingway's Theaters* 3). Hence, in interpreting his fictional men, Hemingway's readers need to "activate cultural codes about manly behavior" as the author depends on "preexisting codes about how men should perform for other men" (6). And yet, Strychacz correctly notes that "Masculinity in Hemingway can be seen more profitably as a trope that must be negotiated into meaning by means of a changing structural relationship between character, masculine code, and legitimating audience" (8). The wounded soldier who is afraid to reveal his vulnerability corresponds to the image of Philip Young's "code hero" with "existential courage" (63–64). He also reflects Judith Butler's theory of gender-as-performance in revealing the ways in which "men enact, and try to stabilize, a pose of masculine authority" (Strychacz, *Dangerous Masculinities* 3); his performance of masculinity offers a critique of dominant gender codes and men's fashioning of ontological conceptions of manhood. As Strychacz puts it: "Under the trope of masculine self-fashioning, masculinity is held to be theatrical, rhetorical, and relational; it is a pose, a demonstration, an act of persuasion" (22).

The very short short story has been recognized as an early example of Hemingway's "deliberate strategy of leaving out vital information" (Pfeiffer 101). Hemingway himself maintained that, "If you leave out important things or events that you know about, the story is strengthened" ("The Art of the Short Story" 3). According to Scott Donaldson, "A Very Short Story" "went through at least three versions"; the revisions rendered it "more impersonal and more bitter" (100). The romantic tone was replaced by "a sardonic resentment," and the first-person narration was substituted with a more distant third-person "he" who had been mistreated. The story in which "the deck," as Donaldson observes, had been "stacked against Luz," depicts gender as a power structure (102). In the end, Luz is turned into the destroyer of the young man's life, or as Robert Scholes puts it, "the agent of the [his] unhappiness" (40). The overall effect of the revisions was aimed at arousing sympathy for the wounded soldier, and the details, such as the selection of space, offer indirect interpretative clues that render gendered power-play accentuated.

The story, which reflects Hemingway's relationship with the nurse Agnes von Kurowsky, as scholars argue, resonates with "the author's resentful imagination" (Pfeiffer 100). It stems from a real-life episode: in July 1918, Hemingway was wounded and taken first to a hospital near Treviso, then to Ospedale Croce Rossa Americana in Milan, where, according to Hemingway's biographer Carlos Baker, Hemingway fell "'wildly' in love with Agnes von Kurowsky" (50). The story's autobiographical basis has been discussed by several Hemingway scholars and biographers, in a way similar to the autobiographical relevance of the character Nick Adams as Hemingway's alter ego, a "second self," noted by many (see, for example, Daiker 35–36). Consequently, the scholar Donald A. Daiker for one argues that "A Very Short Story" should be read in relation to the preceding vignette, which renders it obvious, according to him, that the protagonist of this story is no other than Nick Adams. To sustain his argument, he points out verbal echoes between the vignette and the story, refers to the same setting (World War I, Italian-Austrian front, summer), mentions that Italian is spoken and Italian cities are named, and notes that the events seem to continue from the vignette into "A Very Short Story" (29–30). Daiker questions why Hemingway scholars have resisted identifying the young soldier in "A Very Short Story" as Nick Adams. Hemingway, as is well known, paid great attention to his choice of words, omissions, and sentence structures. Therefore, it seems rather obvious how in this particular story the author's decision not to name the protagonist renders the wounded soldier a universal character, making him a representative of any man. The nameless hero, afraid to express his emotions and show his sensitivity, a brave soldier wounded physically and emotionally, becomes a prototype of man, a realistic man, vulnerable and afraid, who is expected to use his physical and emotional strength to protect others, his compatriots, by killing other men, equally sensitive and frightened. Hence, Hemingway's nameless male protagonist becomes a statement against war.

The plot of "A Very Short Story" follows the male protagonist's emotional decline from a moment of euphoria stemming from his idealized relationship with Luz, the nurse he had fallen in love with during his convalescence in Italy. It proceeds with a discussion of the couple's plans for a brilliant future together; such optimistic projections are rendered possible by the atmosphere of Italy. The story descends from the emotionally euphoric high point set on a rooftop to its ending, a scene of utter squalor conveyed through the male protagonist's ride in a taxicab through Lincoln Park of Chicago with a salesgirl from whom he contracted gonorrhea. Hemingway's brief story, which is rich in interpretative possibilities, places Padua, Italy, in conversation with the United States, contrasting the two different realities and the protagonist's experiences there.

As Scholes points out, the narrative "increases its speed throughout and achieves its effect of culmination by the use of the infinite terms in the last paragraph" (37). It opens similarly to Wharton's "False Dawn" with a heat-emanating scene taking place, not on a verandah like Wharton's story, but on a roof, "one hot evening in Padua." The space of the initial scene is outside, and like Wharton's verandah, the roof is an open space, up above and away from the realities of the town, and seemingly close to the sky, which implies psychological and physical domination. Since the protagonist is physically so high, by implication, as the philosopher Gaston Bachelard has argued about philosophers of domination, "he is great, the height of his station is proof of his own greatness" (173). The male dominance in the initial scene is similar to Wharton's conceptualization of Mr. Raycie. Such masculine power is contrasted with the soldier's helplessness: he is carried up, implying his incapacity to move, by an insignificant, faceless, and nameless "they." After the others, or the anonymous "they," have gone down, only "he" and Luz remain looking out "over the top of the town" in this euphoric moment taking place "in the hot night."

The sexual connotations are present in the heat of the night but also in introducing Luz sitting on a bed, "cool and fresh in the hot night." The heat, then, is both sexual and climatic. The tempting coolness of Luz in the heat that surrounds her sets her apart. Hence, the love and sexual heat seem to permeate the protagonist's entire universe. The paragraph denotes perfection as it starts with "one hot evening" and comes full circle, closing with "hot night" (Hemingway 65). The sentence about Luz on her bed, cool despite the heat, remains in the center of the paragraph, making her the alluring center of the male protagonist's universe.

Luz, the cool nurse in the hot Italian night, frames also the subsequent paragraph, which starts with the words "Luz stayed on night duty" and ends with "Luz in his bed." Hence, the protagonist is unable to think of anything other than the erotic woman and his passion for her while he is nearly immobile in his hospital bed, which Luz shares with him when she is on night duty. The secrecy of the sexual encounters is imposed by the space, the hospital, which denotes curing and healing but also clinical sterilization. The hot and cold pairing in the description of the space and atmosphere reappears in a different variation of human warmth and sterile coldness echoed in the author's choice of a place for the love affair, the hospital. Moreover, the wounded soldier, a prototype of masculinity, is portrayed as a silent macho hero, afraid of revealing his true feelings when he is being prepared for his operation. When he "went under the anesthetic," afraid to "blab" about his love, he is depicted on the operating table, which implies that he will be cured and rendered strong again, perhaps both physically and mentally. Hemingway responds to hegemonic constructions of masculinity by depicting a soldier as afraid of blabbing about his true feelings, an act which would reveal his sensitivity; at the same time, such emotional honesty would create a stronger intimate tie with and bring him closer to the object of his love, Luz.

Luz and "he" in the next paragraph lose their individuality when they are united, here indicated in the use of the third-person plural, "they." They pray in the dim and quiet Duomo, the silent cathedral where they are surrounded by others praying. It is a sacred episode during which they, together, discuss their plans to marry. The church where the events take place renders the passage spiritual, eternal, and holy, and it transforms their relationship from what initially could have been a casual love affair into an officially endorsed engagement. Regrettably, they lack the required documents needed for a marriage, and the soldier is forced to return to the front without the church's sanction of his intentions to spend the rest of his life with Luz. The serene silence of the cathedral plays a significant role in the interpretation of the couple's relationship at this precise moment, which becomes a turning point in their relations. The revelation of the couple's desire to render their love permanent and public resembles Lewis Raycie's revelation of his mission to render Primitive art known in the United States.

In Hemingway's story, "they" are thus separated, Luz back at the hospital curing other soldiers and "he" back at the front killing them. Their realities are contrasting: Luz remaining within the protective walls of the hospital and the soldier trying to be brave and strong in the open battlefield. In this passage, Luz's letters are briefly summarized, creating a profound sense of distance, not only in respect to time but also in relation to physical and growing psychological distance. The paragraph with its contrasting spaces separates and alienates the protagonists. The final detachment is conveyed in the negative image of the night: the sexual heat is gone, but it is "terrible" for Luz to miss him at night. The ending of this paragraph foreshadows the soldier's replacement in Luz's life, and bed, by another man.

The letters subsequently exchanged between Luz and her lover portray none of the initial passion. The main topic of their discussion now is the plan to move to the United States. The planned life in America forms a direct contrast to the romance lived in Italy: the projections are all about ordinary life, about jobs, marriage, promises, and goodbyes. The extensive use of the conditional renders the couple's plans theoretical, and in the middle of the subsequent paragraph stands a short sentence revealing that their relationship had turned into a duty, an incomplete reality, which is expressed in an incomplete static sentence: "Only to get a job and be married" (66). The weight of the obligation is palpable. In addition to the change in location and their relationship from passionate to ordinary, Luz and he quarrel; then they kiss in their last attempt to connect and reconcile, but they continue quarreling as they say goodbye. Their final argument, which takes place in Milan, which is neither Padua nor the United States, is about an abstract "home." In this instance, Milan becomes a no-man's-land located between two realities, one euphoric and the other one of obligations.

The point of view throughout the story is the nameless narrator's who assumes control and possession of the spaces he inhabits, oppressing Luz in the process. "How he seems to her," Scholes observes, "or how she feels about him are not considered relevant" (38). Teasing out Luz's interpretation of the love story reveals the ways in which gender-power mechanisms are at play. The soldier's initial possession of the space he inhabits overlaps his masculinist domination over Luz, whose resignation is detectable in such instances as when she "stayed on night duty for three months," working the least desirable shift, which her colleagues are glad to have her take on. There is no indication of her willingness or desire to work through the night while simultaneously keeping the narrator, who is lying in his bed, satisfied.

As Rena Sanderson notes of Hemingway's short stories: "Contrary to the charge that Hemingway prefers to depict men without women, these stories stress the interdependence, however unhappy, between the sexes" ("Gender History" 176). Hemingway's questioning of traditional gender attributes comes across in gender dislocation, especially in the depiction of Luz as independent, sexually active, career-oriented, in charge of her life; she thus epitomizes the modern New Woman who challenges the normative female submissiveness. And yet, the crippled soldier, temporarily caged in inactivity, tries to assert masculine domination over her. The quarrel they have in Milan further implies her reluctance in giving up her successful career in Italy (soon after their separation, she becomes responsible for opening a hospital in Pordenone), only to move to the United States where he had no employment, but only hoped to find a job, any job.

In the United States, the soldier's decline hits a psychological and social lowest point when "he contracted gonorrhea from a sales girl in a loop department store while riding in a taxicab through Lincoln Park" (Hemingway 66). Such a squalid affair with a nameless girl reveals the depth of his emotional wound inflicted by the unsuccessful idealized love affair with Luz; its impact on the sensitive young soldier is devastating. Thus, the nurse working in the hospital to cure and heal suffering soldiers has dramatically wounded one of them. The emotional and sexual heat, the centrality of Luz in the protagonist's life, their plans to get married, the entire episode set in Italy, all of it seems far away from the final fleeting scene in a car. The taxicab, indeed, forms a direct contrast to the opening scene: it is a closed space, moving fast through a Chicago park. Its movement transforms the ride into a passing moment with no prospects of rendering the relationship a lasting one. In this context, "riding" obviously can be interpreted in two ways: riding in the taxi and having sexual intercourse with the nameless salesgirl. To define her as a "sales girl" implies that perhaps she sold sexual favors in addition to working in a Loop department store. Hence, there is nothing emotional or even remotely reminiscent of any sort of emotions in the sentence that summarizes the extent of their relationship. Hemingway's wounded man finds himself in an emotional vacuum inside a moving car.

Nearly a year has gone by from the hot evening in Padua (summer) to the squalid taxi ride in the spring. The taxicab, a small, closed, suffocating space, contrasts with the initial open space above the town when "he" seemed able to conquer the world. The male protagonist is once again sick, this time with a sexual disease, gonorrhea. The story has come full circle, but there is nothing left of the romantic passion and sexual heat associated with Italy. It has been replaced by hurried, commercialized sex taking place in the United States. The open and public yet intimate space of the rooftop forms a direct contrast to the small and private, yet public, interior of the moving taxi.

In their short stories, Hemingway and Wharton explore social relations and interaction in spaces that are constituted by difference and conflict. (For more about such spaces, see Massey 139.) If Hemingway is known for "the recurrence of failed communication" between genders (Sanderson, "Gender History" 190), Wharton explores a similar failure in relation to generational distrust. Both authors link their contrasting spaces with behavior and power, or its opposite, powerlessness. The scenes in which space figures prominently create specific worlds where the characters act, and react. In both stories, what also is at stake is "mobility, and control over mobility," which, as Massey notes, "both reflects and reinforces power. . . . [T]he mobility and control of some groups can actively weaken other people" (150). In these two stories, the gendered control suppresses the artistic son and independent woman.

Both Wharton and Hemingway present male protagonists who are offered a glimpse of the dawn of their futures: they experience passion and inspiration, feelings of competence and limitless potential. Such positive emotions are associated with their physical presence in Italy. The foreign destination becomes an evasion: "place and locality are foci for a form of romanticized escapism" (Massey 151). The return from the idealized Italy to the native United States results in defeat; both authors end their stories with decline, physical and emotional, reflected in the repressive spaces of an attic and a taxicab, and in the narratives, both enclosures are located in the United States. The protagonists are removed from the central position of their narratives to the margins of their societies. The small spaces of shame and squalor represent the narrow-mindedness and commercial pursuits of rushed, modern Americans, whose vision is blurred by social conventions and prejudice. The authors skillfully convey their social criticism of modern America through an interplay of opposite fictional realities. In this way, Wharton and Hemingway charge their stories with sociocultural significance through the depiction of fictional narrative space.

NOTES

1. Scholars have associated space with belonging, hybridity, exile, mobility, cosmopolitanism, regionalism; space appears as critical, cultural, political, gendered, domestic, public, or racialized space; as a ghetto, enclave, or community in urban or rural settings; and often with enclosing walls, borders, or frontiers that are limiting or liminal, confining, or contrasting, and which may be crossed from one reality into an altered, and altering, experience.

2. Sheila Hones, for instance, quite correctly argues that "setting cannot be separated out from narrative voice and treated as a geographical frame of reference, something which simply situates plot action or reflects its themes" (697). Following a similar line of theorizing, William A. Gleason has taken this idea further, suggesting that "Stories rooted in specific places and housed in particular structures can tell us a great deal not only about past practices but also about meanings and ideologies, both shared and contested" (2).

3. For more about pictorial space, see Santayana, chap. 4: "Pictorial Space and Sentimental Time"; Santayana's pictorial space is also discussed in Sprigge 138–43.

WORKS CITED

Bachelard, Gaston. *The Poetics of Space: The Classic Look at How We Experience Intimate Places.* Boston: Beacon Press, 1994. Print.

Baker, Carlos. *Ernest Hemingway: A Life Story.* New York: Charles Scribner's Sons, 1969. Print.

Benstock, Shari. "Landscapes of Desire: Edith Wharton and Europe." *Wretched Exotic: Essays on Edith Wharton in Europe.* Ed. Katherine Joslin and Alan Price. New York: Peter Lang, 1993. 19–42. Print.

Daiker, Donald A. "In Search of the Real Nick Adams: The Case for 'A Very Short Story.'" *Hemingway Review* 32.2 (2013): 28–41. Print.

Donaldson, Scott. "'A Very Short Story' as Therapy." *Hemingway's Neglected Short Fiction: New Perspectives.* Ed. Susan F. Beegel. Tuscaloosa: U of Alabama P, 1992. 99–105. Print.

Drowne, Kathleen N. "An Irrevocable Condition: Constructions of Home and the

Writing of Place in *Giovanni's Room*." *Re-Viewing James Baldwin: Things Not Seen*. Ed. D. Quentin Miller. Philadelphia: Temple UP, 2000. 72–87. Print.

Fryer, Judith. *Felicitous Space: The Imaginative Structures of Edith Wharton and Willa Cather*. Chapel Hill: U of North Carolina P, 1986. Print.

Gleason, William A. *Sites Unseen: Architecture, Race, and American Literature*. New York: New York UP, 2011. Print.

Hemingway, Ernest. "The Art of the Short Story." *New Critical Approaches to the Short Stories of Ernest Hemingway*. Ed. Jackson J. Benson. Durham, NC: Duke UP, 1990. 1–16. Print.

———. "A Very Short Story." *In Our Time* (1925). New York: Simon and Schuster, 1996. 65–66. Print.

Hones, Sheila. "Literary Geography: Setting and Narrative Space." *Social and Cultural Geography* 12.7 (2011): 685–99. Print.

Joslin, Katherine, and Alan Price. "Introduction." *Wretched Exotic: Essays on Edith Wharton in Europe*. Ed. Katherine Joslin and Alan Price. New York: Peter Lang, 1993. 1–16. Print.

Knights, Pamela. "Forms of Disembodiment: The Social Subject in *The Age of Innocence*." *The Cambridge Companion to Edith Wharton*. Ed. Millicent Bell. Cambridge: Cambridge UP, 1995. 20–46. Print.

Kort, Wesley A. *Place and Space in Modern Fiction*. Gainesville: UP of Florida, 2004. Print.

Massey, Doreen. *Space, Place and Gender*. Cambridge: Polity Press, 2007. Print.

Pattison, Dale. "Sites of Resistance: The Subversive Spaces of *Their Eyes Were Watching God*." *MELUS* 38.4 (2013): 9–31. Print.

Pfeiffer, Gerhard. "'She Expected, Absolutely Unexpectedly': A Freudian Wordplay in 'A Very Short Story.'" *Hemingway Review* 21.1 (2001): 100–101. Print.

Pultz Moslund, Sten. *Literature's Sensuous Geographies: Postcolonial Matters of Place*. New York: Palgrave Macmillan, 2015. Print.

Ricard, Virginia. "Legendary Spell: Edith Wharton's Italy." *American Authors Reinventing Italy: The Writings of Exceptional Nineteenth-Century Women*. Ed. Sirpa Salenius. Padua: Il Prato, 2009. Print.

Sanderson, Rena. "Hemingway and Gender History." *The Cambridge Companion to Hemingway*. Ed. Scott Donaldson. Cambridge: Cambridge UP, 1996. 170–96. Print.

———. "Hemingway's Italy: Paradise Lost." *Hemingway's Italy: New Perspectives*. Ed. Rena Sanderson. Baton Rouge: Louisiana State UP, 2006. 1–37. Print.

Santayana, George. *The Realm of Matter: Book Second of Realms of Being*. New York: Charles Scribner's Sons, 1930. Print.

Scholes, Robert. "Decoding Papa: 'A Very Short Story' as Work and Text." *New Crit-*

ical Approaches to the Short Stories of Ernest Hemingway. Ed. Jackson J. Benson. Durham, NC: Duke UP, 1990. 33–47. Print.

Sprigge, Timothy L. S. *Santayana: The Arguments of the Philosopher*. London: Routledge, 2005. Print.

Stilgoe, John R. "Foreword to the 1994 Edition." Bachelard, *The Poetics of Space*. vii–x. Print.

Strychacz, Thomas. *Dangerous Masculinities: Conrad, Hemingway, and Lawrence*. Gainesville: UP of Florida, 2008. Print.

———. *Hemingway's Theaters of Masculinity*. Baton Rouge: Louisiana State UP, 2003. Print.

Tally, Robert T. Jr., ed. *Literary Cartographies: Spatiality, Representation, and Narrative*. New York: Palgrave Macmillan, 2014. Print.

Tintner, Adeline R. *Edith Wharton in Context: Essays on Intertextuality*. Tuscaloosa: U of Alabama P, 1999. Print.

Wharton, Edith. "False Dawn." *Old New York: Four Novellas by Edith Wharton*. 1924. New York: Scribner Paperback Fiction, 1995. Print.

Young, Philip. *Ernest Hemingway: A Reconsideration*. Rev. ed. New York: Harbinger, 1966. Print.

IV

GENDER AND MODERNITY

Too Bad Hemingway Never Reached *The Reef*

Wharton's Anna Leath and Hemingway's Brett Ashley

LINDA WAGNER-MARTIN

The second half of this essay compares Edith Wharton's character Anna Leath from her 1912 novel *The Reef* and Ernest Hemingway's character Brett Ashley from his 1926 novel *The Sun Also Rises.* But to fill in those intervening years, the literary critic must become something of a literary historian. Eager as the young midwestern Hemingway was to leave his poems and prose poems behind as he moved into longer stories and even a novel, he realized the immense gaps in his education. Through Ezra Pound's patient teaching, he had become a passable Imagist poet. Through Gertrude Stein's equally patient admonitions, he had learned to draw from his inner consciousness. Through his voracious reading from all kinds of fiction borrowed from Sylvia Beach's Shakespeare and Company bookshop, Hemingway—along with Hadley, herself an avid reader—had learned the fundamentals of the novel in English, French, and Russian (in translation). But his education was enhanced immeasurably in 1924 when *Scribner's Magazine* began the serialization of Edith Wharton's prolegomenon about the craft that so attracted him. *The Writing of Fiction,* which would appear in book form in 1925, was tailored to aid the inexperienced writer.

Wharton was not only a best-selling novelist; she had already received the Pulitzer Prize in Fiction for her 1920 novel, *The Age of Innocence,* and her works had been made into movies. Even though F. Scott Fitzgerald preferred Willa Cather (praising Cather's 1923 novel *A Lost Lady* to everyone who would listen), he also revered Wharton: neither Fitzgerald nor Hemingway made their admiration visible, however, since the innovation of *the new* associated with the modern demanded a masculine facade.

Through Hadley's enthusiasm for Henry James, as well as for Wharton and Dorothy Richardson, Hemingway became an accomplished reader in these premodern texts; much of Hemingway's and Hadley's correspondence during the year of their courtship—she in St. Louis, he in Chicago—discusses their reading.[1]

What Wharton says in *The Writing of Fiction* draws repeatedly on her understanding of Henry James's novels. For instance, she describes what she terms "the illuminating incident," a means of impacting the fusion of character and plot so that "the more threads of significance are gathered up into each one, the more pages of explanatory narrative are spared" (113). Going beyond Pound's insistence on the use of image, and the paring away of unnecessary words, this "incident," a wide-reaching scene, creates for the reader a kind of epiphany. In illustration Wharton refers to the scene in James's *The Golden Bowl* in which

> the deeply, the doubly betrayed Maggie, walking up and down in the summer evening on the terrace at Fawns, looks in at the window of the smoking room, where her father, her husband and her step-mother (who is her husband's mistress) are playing bridge together, unconscious of her scrutiny. As she looks she knows that she has them at her mercy, and that they all (even her father) know it; and in the same instant the sight of them tells her that to feel about them in any of the immediate, inevitable, assuaging ways, the ways usually open to innocence outraged and generosity betrayed, would have been to give them up, and that giving them up was, marvelously, not to be thought of. (*Writing of Fiction* 112)

From Pound, Hemingway learned about the power of the image, but Wharton's compounding that imagistic power here, fusing it through an almost surging language rhythm, brings in what she had referred to as a "fourth dimension" of knowing. (Hemingway pursued the "fourth dimension" through P. D. Ouspensky as well as Stein, and of course, Wharton.) Wharton knew that a novel whole, a complete aesthetic work, had to show more than the mechanics of technical prowess. She wrote, "nothing shows the quality of the novelist's imagination more clearly than the incidents he singles out to illuminate the course of events and the inner workings of his people's souls" (*Writing of Fiction* 161). It comes later in Hemingway's career, any mention of a character's *soul*, but such a presence is implicit in his emphasis on both *motivation* and his own sense of completion as writer.[2]

Wharton points out decisively that "modern fiction really began when the 'action' of the novel was transferred from the street to the soul." (So much for the trappings of realism, should any vestige of that style remain here in 1925.) She explains that no character could be "stock"; rather, invented characters must be "breathing and recognizable human beings." Using the works of Balzac and Stendhal as examples, she then explains that characters in themselves provide "the springs of social action" (*Writing of Fiction* 3–5). Returning to the dilemma of realism, Wharton emphasizes that "The stream of consciousness method differed from the slice of life in noting mental as well as visual reactions, but resembles it in setting them down just as they come, with a deliberate disregard of their relevance in the particular case, or rather with the assumption that their very unsorted abundance constitutes itself the author's subject" (12).

Moving beyond considerations of sheer craft, Wharton then describes the significance of the well-chosen incident—nothing betters her term, "the illuminating incident"—within a wider context.

> All things held together in the practice of any art, and character and manners, and the climaxes spring out of them, cannot, in the art of fiction, be dealt with separately *without diminution to the subject.* It is a matter for the novelist's genius to combine all these ingredients in their due proportion; and then we shall have "Emma" or "The Egoist" if character is to be given the first place, "La Pere Goriot" or "Madame Bovary" if drama is to be blent with it, and "War and Peace," "Vanity Fair," "L'Education Sentimentale" if all the points of view and all the methods are to be harmonized in the achievement of a great picture wherein the individual, the group and their social background have each a perfectly apportioned share in the composition. (146–47)

It goes without saying that Hemingway read all the books Wharton mentioned, drawing from the stock at Shakespeare and Company as well as working from his mentors' suggestions. As he aged, Hemingway himself provided countless reading lists for would-be writers, but the texts never varied much from Edith Wharton's examples here.

Perhaps unanticipated is Wharton's insistence on a novel's providing a moral perspective. In tandem with her comment that "True originality consists not in a new *manner* but in a new *vision,*" she continues that discussion to state, somewhat bluntly, "A good subject, then, must contain in itself something that sheds a light on our moral experience" (*Writing of Fiction* 18, 28). Although she discusses only Proust from the writers contemporary with her, and she has some reservations about his work, she relies on traditional views (and moral ones) of such writers as Jane Austen (whose characters she praises as "speaking portraits") and James and Tolstoy (choosing his "The Kreutzer Sonata" as his deft masterpiece, telling her readers that "No one remembers who the people in 'The Kreutzer Sonata' were, or what they looked like, or what sort of house they lived in—but the very roots of human jealousy are laid bare in the picture of the vague undifferentiated husband") (127–28).

In the case of Proust, whose originality Wharton admires with few reservations, she notes that, when his subject allows him (describing his central subject as "the mysteries of love and death"), she thinks that he rivals Tolstoy. But her underlying reservation is that he seems unsure of his own moral position toward his art. She considers him "erratic in applying moral principles." Pointing specifically to his sense of courage, Wharton discusses at some length what she sees as his failing: "That quality, moral or physical, seems never to have been recognized by him as one of the mainsprings of human action. He could conceive of human beings as good, as pitiful, as self-sacrificing, as guided by the most delicate moral scruples; but never, apparently, as brave, either by instinct or through conscious effort" (171, 177). Stepping far outside the boundaries that marked her earlier discussions of writers and their works, Wharton in this case says emphatically, of Proust: "Fear ruled his moral world; fear of death, fear of love, fear of responsibility, fear of sickness, fear of draughts, fear of fear. It formed the inexorable horizon of his universe and the hard delimitation of his artist's temperament" (177).

Wharton was proud of her essay on Proust; she had written to Galliard Lapsley (to whom *The Writing of Fiction* was dedicated), and she had written letters of praise to both Fitzgerald (after he had sent her a copy of *The*

Great Gatsby) and to Sinclair Lewis (thanking him for dedicating *Babbitt* to her), but she admitted to finding the truly contemporary difficult reading—she thought that it lacked the moral underpinning she expected. As she said then, she was not sure American readers could follow irony (Benstock 389; Wharton, *Letters* 481, 448). One opinion Wharton never changed was her displeasure at what James Joyce had achieved in *Ulysses*.

Most of Wharton's pronouncements would have continued to lead Hemingway in the directions he had already established. As he moved from the poems and prose poems and short fiction that appeared in *Three Stories & Ten Poems*, *in our time* (a limited-edition volume of eighteen vignettes), and *In Our Time*, published between 1923 and 1925, he was practicing the fragmentary edicts that would be stated in *The Writing of Fiction*. Although many of his readers thought they had found evidence of Hemingway's early career as a journalist in his early fiction writing, they were responding more directly to the unstated authorial control—a new kind of objectivity—of not only word selection taken from strong nouns and verbs (and fewer adjectives) but of the moral underpinning that his choice of scenes and incidents gave the reader. Maggie Verver's observing her husband and father and the father's unfaithful wife found its counterpart in Nick Adams's observing his and Rinaldi's wounded bodies, in the war-ravaged streets littered with shells, the debris of damaged walls, and the bodies of the dead. Terse as Hemingway's descriptions were in the *In Our Time* vignettes, they contributed to *scenes* rather than to fragments of dialogue. Hemingway talked about the beauty of "cablese" to Lincoln Steffens,[3] but he was early on building scenes readers would not soon forget. Considering that so few words appear on the pages of both *in our time* and *In Our Time*, Hemingway's creation of the *scenes* that readers absorb from these vignettes is surprising. In fact, when he writes to Edmund Wilson in 1925, giving the important critic instructions for reading *In Our Time* before it is published, he emphasizes those scenes: "Like looking with your eyes at something, say, a passing coast line, then looking at it with 15X binoculars. Or rather, maybe, looking at it and then going in and living in it—and then coming out and looking at it again" (*Selected Letters* 128).

In 1912, when Wharton's *The Reef* was published by Appleton (who had outbid Scribner's for serialization rights and therefore became Wharton's publisher), it is safe to conjecture that Ernest Miller Hemingway knew very little about Henry James, or Joseph Conrad, or Balzac—and he had most likely never heard of either Edith Wharton or Dorothy Richardson. As a high-school student, he was writing bad Ring Lardner pieces for English classes, as well as for the school newspaper, and he was trying to pattern his relatively unathletic young body on the hunter-explorer model of Theodore Roosevelt. Not a sports star, Hem was a swimmer and a would-be boxer; he liked to hike and camp and fish. And when he was a few years older than he was in 1912, he pledged to himself that he would excel in scientific discoveries, and would hopefully work in a largely unexplored continent such as Africa.

Even with Hadley's urging him to read Henry James and Wharton and George Eliot, there is no evidence that Hemingway had ever crossed paths with Wharton's carefully drawn, and eminently less than moral, Anna Leath. Yet Hemingway was such a voracious reader, no observer can be sure of even that statement. It goes without saying, however, that when the Hemingways moved to Paris, and quickly began the extensive borrowing from Shakespeare and Company that became a lifeline to the literary aspirations the young Hemingway had, he could have found Wharton's *The Reef.* He was being swept away then on the cultural interest in the New Woman: he understood reader interest in a free-living, self-determining heroine who, in some cases, might replace a hero. Knowing about the twentieth-century New Woman was as much a part of modernism as was the avoidance of unnecessary adjectives.

What Hemingway tried to achieve with the strong woman character he placed at the center of his first serious novel—Lady Brett Ashley of *The Sun Also Rises*—was a woman who usurped the sexual privileges that had previously belonged only to men. Barely twenty-six when he wrote this novel, comfortably married to Hadley Richardson (and supported in large part by her family inheritance), Hemingway used the observational skills he had sharpened during his four years in journalism; there were, however, few models for a genteel, privileged, yet promiscuous modern beauty. Hemingway's narrative method was in some ways self-protective. He never tried to do interior consciousness for Brett Ashley; in fact he seldom did interiority for Jacob Barnes, the war-wounded journalist who was the center of life in both Paris and Pamplona. Distancing of perspective, cryptic dialogue scattered through the white spaces of page after page, covered a multitude of errors that grew from the author's sheer ignorance.

When Edith Wharton wrote *The Reef*, in contrast, she was for the first time in her writing life drawing from her own battered psyche. As she wrote to her dear friend Bernard Berenson when she sent him a copy of the novel, "Anyhow, remember it's not *me*, though I thought it was when I was writing it" (*Letters* 284).[4]

Remarkably, even though Fullerton had put Wharton through a number of somewhat classic moves in his effort to end their relationship—delaying for months writing the letters she expected, for instance; keeping the facade of his love in place long after it had diminished—Wharton had asked him to read *The Reef* as she was writing it. At one point she said, with keen desperation, that she could "see the end" but, without his help, she did not think she could "go on alone" (Benstock 266). The novel was two-thirds done at that point. (In her 19 June 1912 letter to Fullerton, she told him she would not be sending him the chapters after all.)

What Wharton created in *The Reef*, a novel in which the title noun never occurs, is the story of the strangely ennobled Anna Leath, now widowed after the death of her French spouse, caring for their daughter Effie and her stepson Owen on the French estate of Givré (glossed as "frosted" in her notes). When Charles Darrow, the man who was her first suitor back in the States, finds her again, he has become a career diplomat of a low level. He is thirty-seven; he has never married. He claims to once again love her. Anna is close to being thrilled: Fraser Leath had appeared to care more for his collection of snuff boxes than he had romance. She felt that any sort of passion had long been missing from her life.

As Darrow travels from the United States to London, expecting to be with Anna within hours, he receives a brief wire telling him not to come and reassuring him that a letter will follow. This is the starting point for Wharton's novel. Anna Leath does not appear in *The Reef* until page 79, chapter 9. Darrow, disappointed by the delay, plays hero for a pretty young American in a pink opera cloak. Sophy Viner seems vaguely familiar to him because she had worked for the Mrs. Murratt who ran a dubious place of business in Washington, DC. Sophy, charmingly young, has come to England to study for the stage. And from the first page of *The Reef* until book II, she is alone in London, as is Darrow; they are staying at the same hotel. It is a master stroke of fiction that the character of Anna Leath does not appear except as she figures in the early telegram and then, ten days later, as the author of the fulsome letter that Darrow throws into the fire, unopened.

The content of book I, those first seventy-eight pages, is Darrow's deciding to win Sophy Viner, an almost reasonless act but, once sexually fulfilled, he cannot spare any time to read Anna's long-anticipated letter. Book I is the story of the month of May. Book II is the story of the month of October. When Anna does not hear from Darrow at all, once he should have received her letter, she spends the summer bewildered. The man who had asked her to marry him (the reason he was coming to Givré to receive her answer) had seemingly fallen from the face of her earth. Practical beyond reader expectations, Anna writes to Darrow again, telling him what she had already said in the May letter: yes. In October, Darrow replies, and book II brings him to Givré, finally able to meet Owen and Effie, finally able to hold Anna's hand in commitment, and finally able to assume what he had thought would be his rightful place in May.

What Wharton does to create a believable Anna Leath is exactly right. The Lady Anna, the expectant Anna, the unsuspicious Anna never thinks to question Darrow. We first see Anna Leath in the silence of her thoroughly content persona at Givré. It is one of Wharton's "illuminating incidents" as Anna moves from thinking of the stately Givré to being herself presented as embodying the most important of those subtle qualities:

> The court was very still, yet full of a latent life: the wheeling and rustling of pigeons about the rectangular yews and across the sunny gravel; the sweep of rooks above the lustrous greyish-purple slates of the roof, and the stir of the tree-tops as they met the breeze which every day, at that hour, came punctually up from the river. Just such a latent animation glowed in Anna Leath. In every nerve and vein she was conscious of that equipoise of bliss which the fearful human heart scarce dares acknowledge. She was not used to strong or full emotions; but she had always known that she should not be afraid of them. She was not afraid now; but she felt a deep inward stillness. (*Reef* 81)

Wharton signals the centrality of Anna Leath by creating this still space in the novel. The reader has no choice but to identify thoroughly with Anna, whose consciousness speaks to all our consciousnesses: hope, vested in the arrival of Darrow, the true beloved, colors our understanding of this discreetly silent woman.

Then Darrow makes his second appearance. We already know him from his days in London. But we do not know the Darrow that Anna Leath thinks she knows. The truly impossible situation seems to have been put to rest: he had not come in May, he had not written in May, he had not broken four months of his silence during the summer until Anna had again written to him, restating what she had said in the May letter, and Anna pretends to believe his explanation: that *she* had taken so long to write that he had found himself to be bitter and brokenhearted.

Then, as Wharton describes Anna the following morning, arranging salmon pink geraniums and feeling "thrice-alive," Wharton lays beside the image of Anna, completely satisfied at Givré, and now "thrice-alive" there, the second of her "illuminating incidents," this one of Darrow—now her beloved—coming toward her:

> Darrow stood framed in the door-way of the farthest drawing-room, a light-grey figure against the black and white flagging of the hall; then he began to move toward her down the empty pale-panelled vista, crossing one after another the long reflections which a projecting cabinet or screen cast here and there upon the shining floors. As he drew nearer, his figure was suddenly displaced by that of her husband, whom, from the same point, she had so often seen advancing down the same perspective. Straight, spare, erect, looking to right and left with quick precise turns of the head, and stopping now and then to straighten a chair or alter the position of a vase, Fraser Leath used to march toward her through the double file of furniture like a general reviewing a regiment drawn up for his inspection. (103–4)

The tone of Anna's memory of her husband, now dead but still figured as being in control of his house, is chilling: the military description of the man clashes with whatever romance Anna believed to be inherent in Darrow's love for her. Because the dramatic irony Wharton had created by giving her readers early insight into Darrow's faithlessness is already tainting his and Anna's relationship, the shift from Darrow in her vision to Fraser Leath in a memory vision is not startling: it becomes a confirmation of book I of the novel.

Although Anna does not yet realize it, she holds the outcome of the novel in her impassioned hands. Her hopefulness is the fulcrum for not only Darrow and herself but for Sophy Viner and for Owen Leath. Wharton lets the reader believe that resolving Darrow's faithlessness will be easy; at the close of Darrow's first few days at Givré, the "illuminating scene" is convincing though brief: "For a long moment they looked at each other without speaking. She saw the dancing spirit in his eyes turn grave and darken to a passionate sternness. He stooped and kissed her, and she sat as if folded in wings" (112).

The layers of complicating situations begin with Sophy's horror when she sees Darrow at Givré; another set of layers takes shape as Owen begins observing how strangely Sophy behaves around Darrow. It does not take long for Owen to connect the pink-cloaked woman he had seen with Darrow in London with his betrothed. In this novel about the utter lack of honest disclosure, Wharton characteristically discloses a great deal. There are scenes of Anna and Darrow, scenes of Sophy trying to escape Darrow, scenes of Owen standing wistfully between his grandmother and his step-mother: no observer could fail to ferret out the pattern of misbehavior that implicates Darrow. It is not only the militaristic ghost of Fraser Leath, whose only fault might have been those snuff boxes, that dooms these heterosexual relationships. Masculine pride, masculine acquisitiveness, masculine angers, and the masculine need to express power are all embodied in Darrow's questionable romantic aura.

Against that wash of masculine ego, Anna's subtle powers are inconsequential. She believes in her own powers, and she believes that she can draw Darrow into the stillness of her accepting soul. It is Anna who can create that beneficent calm. But even if Darrow can enter her aura, he cannot create a like mood. She "had an extraordinary sensitiveness to the implacable elements of happiness."[5] Darrow does not have that. What Darrow has is unreasonable haste: he has only six weeks before his work takes him to a post in South America. Anna *must* accompany him; they *must* marry before that move. The reader becomes an integral part of Darrow's urgent plot, asking the key question: so why has this man just wasted four months of his courtship time avoiding Anna?

Sophy Viner, the naturally cultured naïf, becomes a noble figure—and a precursor to Charity Royall in *Summer.* In creating her, Wharton shows her lack of familiarity with lower-class life, yet she draws Sophy behaving with true honor: loving Darrow as she does, and having genuine affection for both Anna and Owen, she chooses not to marry the latter. Instead she takes another job—this time abroad—with the Mrs. Murratt about whom Darrow has been so disdainful. But first Wharton makes the reader acknowledge Sophy's "absolute candor, her hard ardent honesty" (*Reef* 146).

The scenes that build to Sophy's relinquishment of her engagement and her work with the Leath family, Owen's anticipated heartbreak over the broken engagement, and Anna's conviction that she must give up Darrow (for Sophy's sake? as condemnation of his unfaithfulness?) are less fully explored. They serve as narrative stepping stones. What moves the novel to its end, skirting those "reefs" the title suggests, is Anna's singularly personal realization that she wanted to have Darrow as her sexual partner. Despite the moral costs, she wanted Darrow. Biographer Shari Benstock compares Anna's words with lines from Wharton's diaries about Fullerton: the possessive "mine, mine" becomes Anna's cry. "Every drop of blood in my body whispers: 'Mine—mine—mine!'" becomes Wharton's. No more self-abnegation, no more idealization: Darrow is what Darrow is, and Anna, the modern woman, will take him as that (Benstock 267).

But first, Anna tries her own act of relinquishment. She goes to Sophy's sister's house, looking for the girl. There she sees a kind of gaudy culture parading as high-classed life. The timing of her visit, however, is significant—it is very late, and Sophy has already left England. Before Anna makes this physical effort, however, she has her night with Darrow—off-stage, of course. She has yearned to know the passion of true consummation, and she has now indulged herself in sexual completion. But that act—along with her love for Darrow, despite his weaknesses—becomes the snare that traps Anna no less than it has changed the direction of Sophy Viner's life. Wharton refers to the memory of their night of love-making as "humiliation."

It is little wonder that reviewers responded to *The Reef* with questions, even with unease. Where is the morality in this account? Whose is the courage that Wharton would find so necessary by the time of her 1925 book about writing fiction? With the narrative of *The Reef* echoing the patterns of romance throughout history, were readers meant to find Anna's staying with Darrow a positive ending? Was it possible that Wharton found the outcome of Sophy Viner's unrequited love for Darrow of little consequence? Given the autobiographical circumstances of Wharton's life between 1908 and 1912, the reader must see Anna as a courageous woman, intent on taking the man she loves for her own. Whatever society's opinion is, Anna Leath makes a choice almost beyond reason: she has her beloved, whatever his worth.

There are similarities between Wharton's treatment of Anna and Hemingway's creation of Lady Brett Ashley, and there would have been more had Hemingway not jettisoned his first long opening to *The Sun Also Rises.* In his 1925 draft, Hemingway began the novel with Brett, rather than with Robert Cohn: "This is a novel about a lady. Her name is Lady Ashley and when the story begins she is living in Paris and it is Spring. That should be a good setting for a romantic but highly moral story. As every one knows, Paris is a very romantic place. Spring in Paris is a very happy and romantic time. Autumn in Paris, although very beautiful, might give a note of sadness or melancholy that we shall try to keep out of this story."[6] With only one well-borne lady, and the author's somewhat tongue-in-cheek emphasis on this book's being "highly moral" (as well as French, although Brett is British but, like the American characters, expatriate), *The Sun Also Rises* maintains a sense of the exotic.

In the later version of the novel, Brett does not appear until she enters a café with a group of homosexuals. Anna Leath convinced readers of her position and her ladyhood through that emanation of stillness: Brett Ashley is lively and hedonistic, living now to erase the devastation of the First World War. Drawing on what he knew so thoroughly, Hemingway was positioned to write a war novel. Of the characters he created for *The Sun Also Rises,* he pretends that Brett Ashley is among the most seriously damaged. He asks his readers to accept her debility as somehow equal to Jake Barnes's physical wounding. He also asks them to accept the quantity of drinking and dancing, of lives given to partying at the bullfights once the group moves to Spain. Although Hemingway spoke of this novel as being "moral" and attempted to show Brett's sexuality as a positive realization for women, the novel made little use of Wharton's "illuminating incidents."

Brett's first appearance, flirting with the gay men, deflects the reader from any serious study of her character. Hemingway's description of the men signals that their arrival is itself a travesty: "I could see their hands and newly washed, wavy hair in the light from the door. The policeman standing by the door looked at me and smiled. They came in. As they went in, under the light I saw white hands, wavy hair, white faces, grimacing, gesturing, talking. With them was Brett. She looked very lovely and she was very much with them" (*Sun Also Rises* 20).

The next two scenes create some sense of Brett's frustration—crowded against Jake in the taxi, she professes her love for him and her frustration at his war injury; later that night she invades his bedroom, bringing Count Mippipopolous and his champagne with her. Then the pace becomes hectic: Brett with Robert Cohn, Brett with Mike, Brett telling Jake she cannot see him, Jake enjoying his friend Bill, Jake and Bill fishing with Wilson-Harris, and finally all parties arriving in Spain for the bullfighting extravaganza. Nearly half the novel has passed in rapid-fire action: readers could not have kept track of Brett, even if that had been their intention.

It is more than a hundred pages later that Brett is given her illuminating scene. The Pamplona San Fermin fiesta "exploded. There is no other way to describe it" (152). Rockets colored the sky. The male dancers were everywhere. And with them was Brett. Hemingway did not use that phrase again, but he did create the startling effect of Lady Brett's having become the center of the dance:

> [T]here was a smell of incense and people filing back into the church, but Brett was stopped just inside the door because she had no hat. . . . Some dancers formed a circle around Brett and started to dance. They wore big wreaths of white garlics around their necks. They took Bill and me by the arms and put us in the circle. Bill started to dance, too. They were all chanting. Brett wanted to dance but they did not want her to. They wanted her as an image to dance around. When the song ended with the sharp *riau-riau!* they rushed us into a wine-shop. . . . They had Brett seated on a

> wine cask. It was dark in the wine-shop and full of men singing, hard-voiced singing. (155)

Like the rhythm of Hemingway's intentionally paced scene, as Jake Barnes's voice describes segment after segment, this portrait of Lady Brett has little to convey to the reader. As a sentient person, Brett has small importance to the narrative: men surround her, but—except for Jake—they are not affected by her. By the end of the novel, Lady Ashley is more significant as *scene* than as *character,* and that, according to Edith Wharton, is not the impact a writer wants to achieve. As Wharton had determined in *The Writing of Fiction,* "the chief difference between the merely sympathetic and the creative imagination is that the latter is two-sided, and combines with the power of penetrating into other minds that of standing far enough aloof from them to see *beyond,* and to relate them to the whole stuff of life out of which they but partially emerge" (15). To Hemingway, his creation of Brett Ashley seemed to be a stroke of genius, capitalizing on readers' interest in the New Woman, the sexually liberated woman, the war-damaged woman. But Brett Ashley was not so fully formed as she might have been. Whatever moral lessons Hemingway thought this flamboyant woman character might convey in 1926 reached few readers with the power he tried to instill: it may have been "pretty to think so," but reviews of *The Sun Also Rises* saw the book as a man's soliloquy, a testament to the bullfight, a canvas of Spanish life, an exciting study of alcoholism, sexual experience, and postwar apathy. Lady Brett was mentioned only peripherally.

One might also have noticed that Wharton's advice, after the writer had found the true "illuminating scene," that the structure of the work allow repetition and added emphasis through incremental returns, does not occur in *The Sun Also Rises.* It is likely that Hemingway had decided that Brett's relinquishing Pedro Romero was an illustration of her moment of both morality and courage, but he fails to give her enough space to explain that choice. In the rush of the novel's ending, the reader finds the irony, but—quoting Bill—not the pity—and very little of Lady Brett's substance. Wharton too had cautioned about achieving a strong ending for a novel. As she wrote in 1925, there must be "the touch of inevitableness to the conclusion of any work of art. . . . [The book] should be seen as a slowly built-up monument in which every stone has its particular weight and thrust to carry and of which the foundations must be laid with a view to the proportions of the highest tower" (*Writing of Fiction* 50).

All writers sometimes fail. It could be that Wharton felt she had failed in *The Reef.* But she would have been less than honest had she let people praise Hemingway's Lady Brett in *The Sun Also Rises* for an achievement that never came close to her own success in drawing Anna Leath in *The Reef.*

NOTES

1. See my *Ernest Hemingway: A Literary Life*, 19–29, drawing from the Hadley Richardson correspondence, in the Hemingway Archive, John F. Kennedy Library.

2. A passage in the restored edition of Hemingway's *A Moveable Feast* offers this candid explanation of the source of his stories: "In the early days writing in Paris I would invent not only from my own experience but from the experiences and knowledge of my friends and all the people I had known. . . . I was very lucky always that my best friends were not writers and to have known many intelligent people who were articulate. . . . My own small experience gave me a touchstone by which I could tell whether stories were true or false and being wounded was a password" (180–88).

3. According to Carlos Baker, Hemingway told Lincoln Steffens (as they were reporting in Europe), "just read the cablese, only the cablese. Isn't it a great language?" (Baker 102).

4. Wharton's impassioned sexual affair with Morton Fullerton, a younger bisexual journalist she had met through Henry James, had lasted several months in 1908. The positive outcome of this debilitating affair was that, in both *The Reef* and *Summer*, her characterization of women governed by their passions rang vividly true. The negative was years of Wharton's self-scrutiny about her behavior, her honesty, her courage, and her role in twentieth-century culture. See Benstock (177–287) and the selection of her letters to Fullerton in Wagner-Martin, ed., *The Portable Wharton* (581–88). (Other stories that stem from this same situation are "The Choice" and "The Letters," both in *Portable Wharton*, 69–83 and 213–49.)

5. "For the first time, everything in her, from hand to foot, seemed to be feeding the same full current of sensation. . . . Nothing really mattered but this light in her veins" (*Reef* 119–20).

6. Manuscript #200, Hemingway Collection, John F. Kennedy Library; see also Svoboda.

WORKS CITED

Baker, Carlos. *Ernest Hemingway: A Life Story.* New York: Scribner's, 1969. Print.

Benstock, Shari. *No Gifts from Chance: A Biography of Edith Wharton.* New York: Scribner's, 1994. Print.

Hemingway, Ernest. *Ernest Hemingway: Selected Letters, 1917–1961*. Ed. Carlos Baker. New York: Scribner's, 1981. Print.

———. *A Moveable Feast: The Restored Edition*. Ed. Sean Hemingway. New York: Scribner's, 2009. Print.

———. *The Sun Also Rises*. New York: Scribner's, 1926. Print.

Svoboda, Frederic J. *Hemingway and The Sun Also Rises: The Crafting of a Style*. Lawrence: UP of Kansas, 1983. Print.

Wagner-Martin, Linda. *Ernest Hemingway: A Literary Life*. New York: Palgrave Macmillan, 2007. Print.

———, ed. *The Portable Edith Wharton*. New York: Penguin, 2003. Print.

Wharton, Edith. *The Letters of Edith Wharton*. Ed. R. W. B. Lewis and Nancy Lewis. New York: Scribner's, 1988. Print.

———. *The Reef*. New York: Appleton, 1912. Print.

———. *The Writing of Fiction*. New York: Scribner's, 1925. Print.

Wharton, Hemingway, and the Architecture of Modernism

Gendered Tropes of Architecture and Interior Decoration

LISA TYLER

Frederic Henry, the protagonist of Ernest Hemingway's 1929 novel *A Farewell to Arms,* tells a Swiss customs official that before the war he studied architecture in Italy, but "With the war going on you cannot study architecture" (280). While not everything Frederic tells the Swiss customs official is true, his description of his reason for being in Italy seems to be, for elsewhere in the novel Frederic privately tells his friend Simmons, whom he has turned to for help after deserting the Italian army, "I wanted to be an architect" (242).

In a 2008 essay, "My Problems in Teaching *A Farewell to Arms,*" a skeptical Peter Hays writes, "I cannot believe Frederic Henry ever studied architecture: he never says anything about any building's shape, size, or structure, except for the barn he hides in later in the novel; he never mentions building materials, stresses, or engineering principles" (165–66).[1]

Hemingway did observe in a 1922 *Toronto Star* article that Swiss hotels were "built on the cuckoo clock style of architecture" (*By-Line* 16), and he does have Colonel Richard Cantwell of *Across the River and into the Trees* call the Basilica of San Marco "that damned cinema palace" (161). Apart from these occasional passing comments, however, Hemingway himself was apparently not much interested in the built environment, either. A discussion of architecture in Hemingway's writings occupies just under nine pages of the monograph *Ernest Hemingway and the Arts* (199–207), and even its author, Emily Stipes Watts, admits that it's really only the architecture of cathedrals that interests Hemingway at all.

There is no chapter on architecture in the admirably comprehensive

Cambridge University Press volume titled *Ernest Hemingway in Context*, as there is in the comparable volume on Edith Wharton (Macheski).[2] The nearest equivalent is Frederic Svoboda's essay on Hemingway's "Houses and Museums," but Hemingway's wives had more to do with finding, selecting, and decorating his various homes than Ernest did. So, given Frederic Henry's and Ernest Hemingway's apparent lack of interest in the field, why does Hemingway choose to make him an architecture student at all?

Hemingway grew up in Oak Park, Illinois, outside of Chicago at a time when Chicago was, in the words of one architectural historian, "the capital of American architecture" (Zukowsky 15). Hemingway was born in 1899, just six years after the 1893 World's Columbian Exposition. Daniel Burnham, the internationally influential architect now perhaps best known as one of the protagonists of Erik Larson's nonfiction best seller *The Devil in the White City*, was responsible for creating the White City in his role as chief of construction for the World's Fair (Zukowsky 22). Frederick Law Olmsted, now probably best known as the landscape architect of Central Park in New York City, planned the fair's site in collaboration with Burnham (Draper 110). The fair's neoclassical white structures were so startlingly lovely that spectators frequently fainted or burst into tears at the sight of them, and they inspired the line "Thine alabaster cities gleam: Undimmed by human tears" in one of the verses of "America the Beautiful" (Sherr 78).[3]

Louis H. Sullivan, now considered the father of both skyscrapers and architectural modernism, came to Chicago after the Great Fire of 1871 and "made major contributions to the American cityscape, and Chicago in particular" (Zukowsky 22). His most prominent student was Frank Lloyd Wright, arguably the most famous American architect of the twentieth century, and Wright's home was in Oak Park, the birthplace of Ernest Hemingway. In his essay on Wright's artistic and cultural influence on Ernest, Hays has noted, "Hemingway, growing up on Kenilworth Avenue, almost around the corner from the architect's studio on Chicago and Forest, could not help but notice the houses that Wright was building in Oak Park, some thirty-six in all, one just across the street from the Hemingway house" ("Wright" 54). So young Ernest was exposed to excellent, ground-breaking examples of American modernist architecture every time he looked out the window or walked down the street. As one architectural historian suggests, "[Chicago's] role in the development of the tall office building of the Chicago School and the single-family house of the Prairie style have both been considered, internationally, the epitome of America's contributions to the history of world architecture" (Zukowsky 15). In early twentieth-century Chicago, then, architects were the most prominent modernist artists successfully making a break with the past.[4]

So it is hardly surprising that, as a writer, Hemingway identified with architects as fellow creators of carefully constructed works of art. He once wrote, in a fragment published in Frank Scafella's edited collection, "I have always thought of writers as combining many of the attributes of whores, *architects* and veterinary surgeons" (Hemingway, "Item 841"; emphasis added). He might well have been gratified, then, by Cecelia Tichi's comment about his prose in her book *Shifting Gears: Technology, Literature, Culture in Modernist America:* "That swift movement of the eye along the flush planes and vertical thrusts of the skyscraper has implications for literary style. It calls to mind the Hemingway sentence, a direct statement proceeding without digression or qualification. It is the architectural equivalent of the straight line without curves, the column without entablature" (291). Hays further develops this analogy between modernist architecture and Hemingway's prose, noting the author's avoidance of complex sentences, his preference for basic vocabulary, and his rejection of rhetorical flourishes in his writing ("Wright" 55).

As Hemingway himself famously wrote in *Death in the Afternoon*, "Prose is architecture, not interior decoration, and the Baroque is over" (91). He employs architecture as a trope for the art of writing modernist literature. In so doing, he carefully distinguishes the (masculine and therefore superior) art of architecture from the (feminine and therefore inferior) art of interior decoration. In making this distinction, he is reacting not just to the architecture of Frank Lloyd Wright but also to the writings of Edith Wharton, a worthy literary opponent.

Wharton was, after all, pronounced a "poet of interior decoration" by Edmund Wilson when he damned her with faint praise in his article "Justice to Edith Wharton," published shortly after her death (201). Architecture and interior decoration figured importantly in many of Wharton's works, including *Sanctuary, The House of Mirth, The Custom of the Country, Summer,* and *The Age of Innocence*, and her first published short story, "Mrs. Manstey's View," concerned an elderly woman who would lose her view to a planned building extension. Wharton was flattered when her editor praised the structure of *The House of Mirth* in 1905, writing to tell him, "So your seeing a certain amount of architecture in it rejoices me above everything" (*Letters* 94).

Wharton's first book was an interior-decoration manual titled *The Decoration of Houses*, published in 1897 and coauthored by professional architect Ogden Codman. In that book Wharton and Codman write, "All good architecture and good decoration (which it must never be forgotten *is only interior architecture*) must be based on rhythm and logic" (13; Wharton's emphasis). Wharton was aware of the gender implications, noting in her memoir *A Backward Glance* that "the architects of that day looked down on house-decoration as a branch of dressmaking, and left the field to the upholsterers" (106). Even in the twenty-first century, the gendered implications persist: "Interior design is perceived as feminine, superficial, and mimetic as opposed to a male, rational, and original architecture. Although the subtext is not said out loud, it is still clear: interior design is inferior to architecture" (Havenhand 33). As one interior designer notes, "the duality that places architecture as the dominant term in a binary opposition with interior design remains largely undeconstructed" (Havenhand 33). In calling decoration "*only interior architecture*," then, Wharton collapses the (historically gendered) distinction between interior decoration and architecture. In his apparently throwaway comment in *Death in the Afternoon*, Hemingway is resurrecting that distinction and that (gendered) binary opposition.

But Hemingway's harshest attack on Wharton is more oblique. When Hemingway says in *Death in the Afternoon* that "the Baroque is over," the remark is generally taken as a modernist rejection of ornament, comparable to Hemingway's famous rejection of adjectives as a result of the rules for style he learned as a reporter for the *Kansas City Star* early in his writing career: "Avoid the use of adjectives, especially such extravagant ones as splendid, gorgeous, grand, magnificent, etc." (Fisher). As early as 1929, Morley Callaghan recalls a conversation in which Hemingway articulated this modernist aesthetic: "The decorative style, the baroque based on a literary adornment of perceptions, was an affectation in our time, he said. Only the clear direct stripped statement belonged to our time" (233). In *A*

Moveable Feast, Hemingway refers to his own adherence to this principle: "If I started to write elaborately . . . I found that I could cut that scrollwork or ornament out and throw it away and start with the first true simple declarative sentence" (12).[5] The Hemingway sentence, Tichi suggests, "is the architectural equivalent of the straight line without curves, the column without entablature" (291).

Certainly rejection of ornament was an important element of modernist architecture. The "Manifesto of Futurist Architecture 1914" trumpets, "THE DECORATIVE MUST BE ABOLISHED" (Sant'Elia 367). In "Ornament and Crime," Adolf Loos argued, "*The evolution of culture is synonymous with the removal of ornament from objects of daily use*" (349; emphasis in original). Note that Wharton's original working title for *The House of Mirth* was *A Moment's Ornament* (Wolff 109), an allusion to a poem by William Wordsworth. As Tichi points out, "Hemingway's persistent distaste for such nonfunctional ornament, whether in architecture or literature, marks him as a modernist" (227).

But there is a second, less obvious meaning to Hemingway's contention that "the Baroque is over": The single best known example of baroque architecture in the world is the Palace at Versailles. Wharton and Ogden Codman Jr. included several photographs from Versailles as models of exemplary decorating taste in their book *The Decoration of Houses.* Even more important, Wharton was part of a rival literary salon that met at the Versailles home of Prince and Princesse Bassiano, and it was there that she met both Paul Valéry and André Gide. Her circle and Hemingway's were more or less mutually exclusive: "While Gertrude Stein was offering counsel to James Joyce, Ernest Hemingway, Sherwood Anderson, and many others, Edith Wharton was playing hostess to Paul Valéry, André Gide, Sinclair Lewis, Aldous Huxley, and Kenneth Clark" (Lewis 440). It's true that the two worlds nearly collided when F. Scott Fitzgerald sent her a dedicated copy of *The Great Gatsby* and in return was invited to bring his wife to tea at Edith Wharton's home, but he was drunk and flustered, and the meeting was not a success (Lewis 465–66). As R. W. B. Lewis notes of Wharton and Stein, "The two rich human and artistic Paris worlds of these two expatriate American writers astonishingly failed to overlap to any real extent" (440).[6]

The thirty-three-year-old author of *Death in the Afternoon* must have resented his exclusion from the salon of the seventy-year-old Wharton. In May 1926, he wrote sarcastically in a letter to F. Scott Fitzgerald, "Havent seen the Bromfields, Edith Wharton, Comrade Bercovinci [a slightly misspelled reference to the successful and prolific Romanian-American writer Konrad Bercovici] or any other of the little literary colony for some time" (*Selected Letters* 203, my addition; *Letters* 2: 70–71).

The people who *did* join Wharton's "literary colony" received especially harsh treatment at Hemingway's hands. Louis Bromfield was invited to join Wharton's literary circle, although Daniel Bratton, who has edited their correspondence, argues that they probably did not become acquainted with each other until 1931 (xiii n1). Bromfield, who had volunteered for the Army Ambulance Service during World War I and "served in seven major battles on the Western front" (xxvi), also trumped Hemingway by writing regularly for a slew of mainstream publications (including the *New York Times, New York Herald Tribune, New York City News, The Bookman, Musical America,* and *Time*) at a time when Hemingway was still struggling to get published. It didn't help that Bromfield also published a bestselling novel, *The Green Bay Tree,* in 1924 (Bratton xxvii). Bromfield eventually wrote thirty-three books, twenty-six of them novels, and won the Pulitzer Prize in 1927 for his novel *Early Autumn* (Loesch 9–10). Wharton must have valued the younger writer's friendship and counsel, for she consulted him about a publishing problem with a Hearst publication (Loesch 47).

Hemingway's letters suggest that he met Bromfield in 1925 (*Letters* 2: 428, 434), and Bromfield went out of his way to help Hemingway, asking his own publisher, Harcourt, if he would be interested in taking Hemingway on—a kindness that Hemingway himself described as "damned decent" (460). He signed his next letter to Bromfield and his wife "Affectionately" and told the writer, "You and [Ford Madox] Ford seem the most generally admired novelists in N.Y." (*Selected Letters* 196; *Letters* 3: 38, 37). Unable to accept any assistance gracefully, Ernest then retaliated by calling him "Bloomfield" in private (*Selected Letters* 249; *Letters* 3: 221) and mocking Bromfield savagely in his letters, writing to F. Scott Fitzgerald in 1927:

> Old Brommy [Hemingway's nickname for Bromfield] has certainly swept the women's clubs. It was a sure thing that he would

> encounter my mother "Mother of Four Takes Up Painting at 52" and he did. He told her he was certain he had recognized her although he couldn't place her because Ernest was his best friend and how wouldn't he know Ernest's mother. Now my mother has a new cause to weep because I don't write [like] Brommy. (*Selected Letters* 267, Baker's additions; see also *Letters* 3: 342)[7]

Hemingway slammed Bromfield one last time in a 1933 letter to Maxwell Perkins: "Poor old Gertrude Stein. Did you read the August *Atlantic?* She's finally found a writer she can love and not be jealous of—the real american writer [*sic*]—Bromfield. It's damned wonderful how the story ends. She lost all sense of taste when she had the menopause" (*Selected Letters* 395).

Aldous Huxley and his wife Maria, Wharton's neighbors on the French Riviera (Lee 699), also successfully became part of Wharton's "literary colony," and Huxley received similarly harsh treatment from Hemingway. As one of her biographers reports, "Edith would exchange half a dozen visits with the Huxleys each winter for . . . years, and her delight in them only grew with every season" (Lee 497). Wharton called Huxley's 1932 novel *Brave New World* "a masterpiece of tragic indictment of our ghastly age of Fordian culture" and urged a friend, "Get it at once"; she was also flattered by his praise of her own 1927 novel: "He wrote to me that I had 'put the case already in *Twilight Sleep*, & I own I was much set up by his recognition of the fact!'" (*Letters* 547). Given that Huxley and Wharton were on such friendly terms, it's probably not coincidental that Hemingway attacks Aldous Huxley so prominently in *Death in the Afternoon* a page before his reference to the baroque (190). As a result of Huxley's critical comments about Hemingway's reference to Mantegna in *A Farewell to Arms*, Hemingway despised Huxley's whole literary circle.[8]

Hemingway's brusque implication that Wharton and her literary circle are obsolete ("the Baroque is over") echoes a very similar overt statement that he had made in 1927 (five years earlier) about Virginia Woolf:

> The Virginia Woolf review was damned irritating—She belongs to a group of Bloomsbury people who are all over 40 and [. . .] they dislike what they consider the intrusion of anybody much under 40 into the business, though God knows one doesn't wish to intrude.

> They live for their Literary Reputations and believe the best way to keep them is to try and slur off or impute [impugn] the honesty of anyone coming up. (*Selected Letters* 264, Baker's addition; see also *Letters* 3: 315)

He famously spoke of metaphorical boxing victories over the great male writers of an earlier time period: "I started out very quiet and I beat Mr. Turgenev. Then I trained hard and I beat Mr. de Maupassant. I've fought two draws with Mr. Stendhal, and I think I had an edge in the last one. But nobody's going to get me in any ring with Mr. Tolstoy unless I'm crazy or I keep getting better" (Ross 35). But he could hardly write about battling Woolf or Wharton in the ring. He was forced to resort to other ways to express his supposed metaphorical victories over their work, and castigating women writers he admired as now hopelessly dated was one way to accomplish that goal.

But Hemingway might have had special reason for disparaging Wharton personally. A page after his comment about prose being architecture rather than interior decoration, Hemingway introduces his famous "iceberg theory" of literature: "If a writer of prose knows enough about what he is writing he may omit things that he knows and the reader, if the writer is writing truly enough, will have a feeling of those things as strongly as though the writer had stated them. The dignity of movement of an iceberg is due to only one-eighth of it being above water" (*Death in the Afternoon* 192). This passage sounds suspiciously similar to one in Wharton and Codman's *Decoration of Houses:* "There is a sense in which works of art may be said to endure by virtue of that which is left out of them, and it is this 'tact of omission' that characterizes the master hand" (Wharton and Codman 192).

Similarly, Alan Price suggests that Paul Dastrey's words in Wharton's 1923 novel *A Son at the Front* anticipate Frederic Henry's famous meditation on the meaninglessness of highblown language in Hemingway's 1929 novel *A Farewell to Arms* (Price 176): "'I was considering how the meaning had evaporated out of lots of our old words, as if the general smash-up had broken their stoppers. So many of them, you see,' said Dastrey smiling, 'we'd taken good care not to uncork for centuries. Since I've been on the edge of what's going on fifty miles from here a good many of my own words have lost their meaning, and I'm not prepared to say where honour lies in a case like yours'" (Wharton, *A Son at the Front*, 187–88).

Surprisingly, even Hemingway's celebrated literary style may owe something to Wharton. Tichi argues that the style of Wharton's 1911 book *Ethan Frome* "announced the engineering aesthetic Hemingway would display in his own fiction of the 1920s" (217). Hemingway "enacted the values of engineering in his tight, functional prose style," and his "terse, economical lines brought engineering values into the very sentence itself" (216). But he might well have learned them from Wharton's novel, in which her narrator, an engineer, favors declarative sentences, an emotionally restrained style, and "an economy of phrasing that never compromises—in fact, intensifies—the emotional impact of the discourse" (218). In her brief introduction to the book, Wharton herself explains that she was trying to present her subject "without an added ornament" (*Ethan Frome* vii). While Tichi says that there is no evidence Hemingway read *Ethan Frome*, he did own the book by 1955, and he was reading his parents' copy of *Scribner's Magazine* during the years when *Ethan Frome* would have been serialized in it.

Wharton and Hemingway were not the only modernist writers to draw on the tropes of architecture and interior decoration. American novelist John Dos Passos wrote in his introduction to the 1932 Modern Library edition of his novel *Three Soldiers*, "A writer who writes straight is the architect of history" (viii). A generation earlier, in his preface—composed between 1906 and 1908 (James vii)—to *The Portrait of a Lady*, Henry James defends his writing against a common charge against it, which he describes, in French, as "*que cela manqué souvent d'architecture*"—in other words, "it often lacks architecture" (43). While here James may use the term *architecture* to mean "plot" or "structure," his later reference in the same prefatory essay to "the house of fiction" that "has in short not one window, but a million," suggests that he also refers here to the literary canon.

If only "a writer who writes straight" becomes an "architect of history," to use Dos Passos's felicitious phrase, then Hemingway, like Dos Passos, is prescribing what kind of writers and what kind of prose will enter the modernist canon when he asserts, "Prose is architecture, not interior decoration, and the Baroque is over." As architecture historian Beatriz Colomina reminds us, "The heroic male figure—energetic, cool and detached—was the figure of architectural modernity" (45). If only architects can build modernist structures, and the unspoken corollary is that only men can become architects, women (like little girls banned from their brothers' tree house) can never build a modernist novel worthy of entrance into the house of fiction that is the modernist literary canon. Hemingway engages with Wharton, then, only to pointedly exclude her from the canon, the house of fiction, literary modernism. No girls allowed.

NOTES

1. For the genesis of this project, I am indebted to Peter Hays's observations about Frederic Henry and his curious lack of interest in architecture despite being a former architecture student. I am also grateful to Shari Rethman, dean of the College of Arts and Sciences at Sinclair Community College and former chair of the Design Department, for reading an earlier version of this essay and suggesting relevant sources.

Steven Florczyk offers an alternate explanation for Henry's lack of passion for architecture, the subject "that seemed to bring him to Italy in the first place," arguing that "his interest in the vocation he pursued prior to his enlistment has become another 'casualty' of the war" (109).

2. On the relationship between architecture and Edith Wharton's writings, see Benert, Chase, Fryer, Kovács, Macheski, Stephenson, and Williams.

3. Katharine Lee Bates, who wrote the poem that became the lyrics for the song "America the Beautiful," visited the White City at the World's Columbian Exposition with Katharine Coman and her family (Burgess 101). Bates, a professor of English at Wellesley College, and Coman, a professor of economics and history at Wellesley, lived together in a "Boston marriage"—a long-term lesbian relationship—for more than twenty-five years (Proctor and Burns). Like Frank Lloyd Wright and Ernest Hemingway, Coman came from Oak Park, Illinois (Sherr 78). For a spirited discussion of Bates's lesbianism (and her socialist politics), see Dreier.

4. Ironically, Hemingway was highly critical of one of Wright's proposed projects later in life. When Hemingway arrived in Venice on 23 March 1954, after his two African plane crashes, Italian reporters asked him to comment on Wright's plan to construct the Masieri Memorial, a residence hall and library for architecture students, along the Grand Canal in Venice. The project would also be a memorial to Italian architect Angelo Masieri, who was killed in a car crash. Wright's design was exhibited in New York in 1953 before he received permission to build, and the plans provoked controversy. While press reports varied, Hemingway evidently responded that the building should be constructed and then burned to the

ground, an attitude which garnered him the affection of many Venetians. Even under these circumstances, however, he conceded Wright's genius: "He is a great architect for America, but not for Venice" (qtd. in Ainsworth 33). See Troy Ainsworth for a detailed discussion of the controversy and ensuing press reports.

5. Hemingway's disdain for the word "ornamental" is evident in both his private and public writings. In July 1926, he wrote Maxwell Perkins, his editor at Scribner's, defending his language in the manuscript of *The Sun Also Rises*: "But in the matter of the use of the *Bitch* by Brett—I had never used this word ornamentally nor except when it was absolutely necessary and I believe the few places where it is used must stand" (Hemingway, *The Only Thing* 43).

In *Green Hills of Africa*, he writes of his hunting guide, "He hated to have anything killed except what we were after, no killing on the side, no ornamental killing, no killing to kill" (16). When Hemingway later offers his wife the book he is reading, she tells him "Don't be ornamental" (110)—presumably meaning that he should not make the offer insincerely. Nevertheless, it is clear that for Hemingway the word is coded as feminine. Pauline objects when Philip Percival repeatedly compares her to "a little terrier" (64, 116, 155). As Hemingway notes, "If she must be like any dog, and she did not wish to be, she would prefer a wolfhound, something lean, racy, long-legged, and ornamental" (64).

6. Robert A. Martin and Linda Wagner-Martin have argued that literary history and comparative textual analysis prove that the real nature of the relationship between Wharton and Fitzgerald was much more complicated and much richer than the lone anecdote about their meeting might suggest.

7. In their annotations to the third volume of *The Letters of Ernest Hemingway*, editors Sanderson, Spanier, and Trogdon confirm that "EH's mother attended Bromfield's lecture at the Nineteenth Century Club meeting in Oak Park on 10 October 1927 and told EH in a letter of 14 October 1927 that she had introduced herself to Bromfield after his talk and he said that EH was one of his best friends (JFK)" (344n2). They also point out that Grace—a mother of six—was featured in the *Lynchburg* [Virginia] *Advance* under the headline "Mother of Four Becomes Artist! Wins Notice for Portraits at 52" (344n2).

8. See Comley and Scholes (111–17) for a detailed discussion of Hemingway's resentment of Aldous Huxley.

WORKS CITED

Ainsworth, Troy. "Modernism Contested: Frank Lloyd Wright in Venice and the Masieri Memorial Debate." PhD diss. Texas Tech University, 2005. Texas Tech University DSpace Repository. Web. Accessed 12 Jan. 2016.

Benert, Annette. *The Architectural Imagination of Edith Wharton: Gender, Class, and Power in the Progressive Era*. Madison, NJ: Fairleigh Dickinson UP, 2007. Print.

Bratton, Daniel, ed. *Yrs. Ever Affly: The Correspondence of Edith Wharton and Louis Bromfield.* East Lansing: Michigan State UP, 2000. Print.

Burgess, Dorothy. *Dream and Deed: The Story of Katharine Lee Bates.* Norman: U of Oklahoma P, 1952. Print.

Callaghan, Morley. *That Summer in Paris: Memories of Tangled Friendships with Hemingway, Fitzgerald, and Some Others.* New York: Dell, 1963. Print.

Chase, Vanessa. "Edith Wharton, *The Decoration of Houses,* and Gender in Turn-of-the Century America." *Architecture and Feminism.* Ed. Debra Coleman, Elizabeth Danze, and Carol Henderson. New York: Princeton Architectural P, 1996. 130–60. Print.

Clark, Suzanne. "Roosevelt and Hemingway: Natural History, Manliness, and the Rhetoric of the Strenuous Life." *Hemingway and the Natural World.* Ed. Robert P. Fleming. Moscow: U of Idaho P, 1999. 55–67. Print.

Colomina, Beatriz. "Sex, Lies and Decoration: Adolf Loos and Gustav Klimt." *Gustav Klimt: Paintings, Design and Modern Life.* Ed. Tobias G. Natter and Christoph Grunenburg. London: Tate Publishing, 2008. 43–51. Print.

Comley, Nancy R., and Robert Scholes. *Hemingway's Genders: Rereading the Hemingway Text.* New Haven, CT: Yale UP, 1994. Print.

Dos Passos, John. Introduction. *Three Soldiers.* New York: Modern Library, 1932. v–ix. Print.

Draper, Joan E. "Paris by the Lake: Sources of Burnham's Plan of Chicago." *Chicago Architecture, 1872–1922: Birth of a Metropolis.* Ed. John Zukowsky. Munich: Prestel-Verlag, 1987. 106–19. Print.

Dreier, Peter. "Rush Limbaugh's Favorite Lesbian Socialist—Author of 'America the Beautiful'—Inspired the Super Bowl Coke Ad." *Huffington Post.* 5 Feb. 2014. Web. Accessed 11 Apr. 2016. www.huffingtonpost.com/peter-dreier/america-the-beautiful_b_4728976.html.

Fisher, Jim. "Of '*Star*' Style and a Reporter Named Hemingway." *Kansas City Star.* July 29, 2007. Web. Accessed 2 January 2019. https://www.kansascity.com/entertainment/arts-culture/article294964/Of-i%60Stari-Style-and-a-reporter-named-Hemingway.html.

Florczyk, Steven. *Hemingway, the Red Cross, and the Great War.* Kent, OH: Kent State UP, 2014. Print.

Fryer, Judith. *Felicitous Space: The Imaginative Structures of Edith Wharton and Willa Cather.* Chapel Hill: U of North Carolina P, 1986. Print.

Gerard, Albert. "Romanticism and Stoicism in the American Novel: From Melville to Hemingway, and After." Trans. Elaine P. Halperin. *Diogenes* 23 (1958): 95–110.

Havenhand, Lucinda Kaukas. "A View from the Margin: Interior Design." *Design Issues* 20.4 (Autumn 2004): 32–42. Print.

Hays, Peter L. "Conrad and Hemingway." *American Notes and Queries* 14 (1976): 87–88. Print.

———. "Hemingway's Bartlebys." *North Dakota Quarterly* 68.2–3 (Spring–Summer 2001): 85–90. Print. Rpt. in *Fifty Years of Hemingway Criticism*. Blue Ridge Summit, PA: Scarecrow P, 2013. 161–65. ProQuest. Web. 13 Jan. 2016.

———. "My Problems in Teaching *A Farewell to Arms*." *Teaching Hemingway's "A Farewell to Arms."* Ed. Lisa Tyler. Kent, OH: Kent State UP, 2008. 164–73. Print.

———. "Wright, Cezanne, and Hemingway." *Fifty Years of Hemingway Criticism*. Blue Ridge Summit, PA: Scarecrow P, 2013. 53–58. ProQuest. Web. Accessed 27 Feb. 2015.

Hemingway, Ernest. *Across the River and into the Trees*. New York: Scribner's, 1950. Print.

———. *By-Line: Ernest Hemingway*. Ed. William White. New York: Bantam, 1967. Print.

———. *Death in the Afternoon*. New York: Scribner's, 1932. Print.

———. *Ernest Hemingway: Selected Letters, 1917–1961*. Ed. Carlos Baker. New York: Scribner's, 1981. Print.

———. *A Farewell to Arms*. New York: Scribner's, 1929. Print.

———. *Green Hills of Africa*. New York: Collier, 1935. Print.

———. "Item 841." In *Hemingway: Essays of Reassessment*. Ed. Frank Scafella. New York: Oxford UP, 1991. 32. Print.

———. *The Only Thing That Counts: The Ernest Hemingway–Maxwell Perkins Correspondence*. Ed. Matthew J. Bruccoli with Robert Trogdon. Columbia: U of South Carolina P, 1996. Print.

———. *The Letters of Ernest Hemingway*, Vol. 2: *1923–1925*. Ed. Sandra Spanier, Albert J. DeFazio III, and Robert W. Trogdon. Cambridge: Cambridge UP, 2013. Print.

———. *The Letters of Ernest Hemingway*, Vol. 3: *1926–1929*. Ed. Rena Sanderson, Sandra Spanier, and Robert W. Trogdon. Cambridge: Cambridge UP, 2015. Print.

———. *A Moveable Feast*. New York: Scribner's, 1964. Print.

James, Henry. *The Art of the Novel: Critical Prefaces*. Boston: Northeastern UP, 1984. Print.

Kovács, Agnes Zsófia. "The Uses of Architecture as a Metaphor for the Critique of American Culture: Henry James' *The American Scene* and Edith Wharton's *Italian Villas and Their Gardens*." *Americana: E-Journal of American Studies in Hungary* 8.1 (1 Mar. 2012). Web. *Ebscohost*. Accessed 2 Dec. 2014.

Lauer, Kristin Olson. "Can France Survive This Defender? Contemporary American Reaction to Wharton's Expatriation." *Wretched Exotic: Essays on Edith Wharton in Europe.* Ed. Katherine Joslin and Alan Price. New York: Peter Lang, 1993. 77–95. Print.

Lee, Hermione. *Edith Wharton.* New York: Knopf, 2007. Print.

Lewis, R. W. B. *Edith Wharton: A Biography.* New York: Harper & Row, 1975. Print.

Loesch, Harold G. "A Study of the Life of Louis Bromfield from 1925–1939 with Emphasis on His Association with Edith Wharton." MA thesis, Kent State U, 1964.

Loos, Adolf. "Ornament and Crime." *The Architecture of Adolf Loos.* Ed. Joanna Drew. London: Arts Council of Great Britain, 1985. 100–103. Rpt. in *Architecture and Design in Europe and America, 1750–2000.* Ed. Abigail Harrison-Moore and Dorothy C. Rowe. Madden, MA: Blackwell, 2006. 348–54.

Macheski, Cecilia. "Architecture." *Edith Wharton in Context.* Ed. Laura Rattray. Cambridge: Cambridge UP, 2012. 189–98. Print.

Martin, Robert A., and Linda Wagner-Martin. "The Salons of Wharton's Fiction." *Wretched Exotic: Essays on Edith Wharton in Europe.* Ed. Katherine Joslin and Alan Price. New York: Peter Lang, 1993. 97–110. Print.

McNeil, Peter. "Designing Women: Gender, Sexuality and the Interior Decorator, c. 1890–1940." *Art History* 17 (1994): 631–57. Print.

Mellow, James R. *Hemingway: A Life without Consequences.* Reading, MA: Addison-Wesley, 1992. Print.

Meyers, Jeffrey. "Conrad's Influence on Modern Writers." *Twentieth-Century Literature* 36.2 (Summer 1990): 186–206. *Academic Search Complete.* Web. 13 Jan. 2016.

Philbrick, Nathaniel. "A Window on the Prey: The Hunter Sees a Human Face in Hemingway's 'After the Storm' and Melville's 'The Grand Armada.'" *Hemingway Review* 14.1 (Fall 1994): 25–35. Print.

Proctor, Judd, and Brian Burns. "Katharine Lee Bates: Author of 'America the Beautiful.'" *The Gay History Project: Documenting LGBT History. Philadelphia Gay News,* n.d. Web. 11 Apr. 2016. gayhistoryproject.epgn.com/historical-profiles/katharine-lee-bates-author-of-america-the-beautiful/.

Price, Alan. *The End of the Age of Innocence: Edith Wharton and the First World War.* New York: St. Martin's Press, 1996. Print.

Reynolds, Michael. *Hemingway: The 1930s.* New York: Norton, 1997. Print.

———. *Hemingway's Reading, 1910–1940: An Inventory.* Princeton, NJ: Princeton UP, 1981. John F. Kennedy Presidential Library. Web. 27 May 2015.

Ross, Lillian. *Portrait of Hemingway.* New York: Simon and Schuster, 1961. Print.

Sanford, Marcelline Hemingway. *At the Hemingways, with Fifty Years of Correspon-*

dence between Ernest and Marcelline Hemingway. Centennial ed. Moscow: U of Idaho P, 1999. Print.

Sant'Elia, Antonio. "Manifesto of Futurist Architecture 1914." *Futurist Manifestos.* Ed. Umbro Apollonio. Trans. R. W. Flint. London: Thames & Hudson, 1973. 160–72. Rpt. in *Architecture and Design in Europe and America, 1750–2000.* Ed. Abigail Harrison-Moore and Dorothy C. Rowe. Madden, MA: Blackwell, 2006. 364–67.

Sherr, Lynn. *America the Beautiful: The Stirring True Story behind Our Nation's Favorite Song.* New York: PublicAffairs, 2001. Print.

Small, Judy Jo, and Michael Reynolds. "Hemingway v. Andersen: The Final Rounds." *Hemingway Review* 14.2 (Spring 1995): 1–17. Print.

Stephenson, Liisa. "Decorating Fiction: Edith Wharton's Literary Architecture." *University of Toronto Quarterly* 79.4 (2010): 1096–1104. Print.

Svoboda, Frederic. "Houses and Museums." *Ernest Hemingway in Context.* Ed. Debra A. Moddelmog and Suzanne del Gizzo. New York: Cambridge UP, 2013. 130–40. Print.

Tichi, Cecelia. *Shifting Gears: Technology, Literature, Culture in Modernist America.* Chapel Hill: U of North Carolina P, 1987. Print.

Tintner, Adeline R. "Edith Wharton, Ernest Hemingway and Vivienne de Watteville, *Speak to the Earth.*" *Edith Wharton in Context: Essays on Intertextuality.* Tuscaloosa: U of Alabama P, 1999. 134–38. Print.

Watts, Emily Stipes. *Ernest Hemingway and the Arts.* Urbana: U of Illinois P, 1971. Print.

Wharton, Edith. *A Backward Glance: An Autobiography.* 1933. New York: Touchstone, 1998. Print.

———. *Ethan Frome.* New York: Scribner's, 1911. Print.

———. *Hudson River Bracketed.* New York: Scribner's, 1929. Print.

———. Letter to Bernard Berenson. 18 June 1930. MS. Biblioteca Berenson. I Tatti—The Harvard University Center for Italian Renaissance Studies, Florence, Italy.

———. *The Letters of Edith Wharton.* Ed. R. W. B. Lewis and Nancy Lewis. New York: Scribner's, 1988. Print.

———. *A Son at the Front.* New York: Scribner's, 1923.

Wharton, Edith, and Ogden Codman Jr. *The Decoration of Houses: The Revised and Expanded Classical America Edition.* New York: Norton, 1997. Print.

Whitley, Edward. "Race and Modernity in Theodore Roosevelt's and Ernest Hemingway's African Travel Writing." *Issues in Travel Writing: Empire, Spectacle, and Displacement.* Ed. Kristi Siegel. New York: Peter Lang, 2002. 13–17. Print.

Williams, James. "Gopher Prairie or Prairie Style? Wright and Wharton Help

Dodsworth Find His Way Home." *Sinclair Lewis: New Essays in Criticism*. Ed. James M. Hutchisson. Troy, NY: Whitston, 1997. 125–46. Print.

Wilson, Edmund. *The Wound and the Bow: Seven Studies in Literature*. New York: Oxford UP, 1947. Print.

Wolff, Cynthia Griffin. *A Feast of Words: The Triumph of Edith Wharton*. New York: Oxford UP, 1977. Print.

Zukowsky, John. "Introduction to Internationalism in Chicago Architecture." *Chicago Architecture, 1872–1922: Birth of a Metropolis*. Ed. John Zukowsky. Munich: Prestel-Verlag, 1987. 15–25. Print.

Motor Flight

Gender, Power, and the Automobile

ANNA GREEN

MODERNISM, TRANSPORTATION, AND THE POLITICS OF TRAVEL

Throughout the twentieth century, the most important and energizing locale for American authors was France, which hosted numerous expatriates eager to escape the constraints of their home country and keen to encounter the aesthetic ideals of their European counterparts. Edith Wharton and Ernest Hemingway were two of these authors whose fiction and nonfiction works betray the significant influence of their own travel to and movement within France. Wharton's preoccupation with French culture and art influenced the interior designs of her book *The Decoration of Houses*; motivated the writing of her ethnographic guide, *French Ways and Their Meaning*; and appeared as the setting of her novels *The Custom of the Country* and *The Reef*. Similarly, Hemingway's careful observations of Paris informed the geographic backdrop of his first novel, *The Sun Also Rises*, and the French Riviera figures prominently in his last, posthumously published novel, *The Garden of Eden*. It is, however, through their respective travel memoirs that Wharton and Hemingway's parsing of France and French culture can be best understood. These texts—Wharton's *Motor-Flight through France* and Hemingway's *A Moveable Feast*—provide two distinct impressions of French travel as both a physical and a conceptual intersection for the social and technological transformations of the twentieth century.[1]

A Moveable Feast and *A Motor-Flight through France* lend themselves to comparison for several reasons. First, as two purportedly factual, nonfiction accounts produced by two famous expatriates, these texts illustrate the important influence of travel and travel writing on American modernist literature. In his book *Modernist Travel Writing*, David Farley underscores modernism's internationalism as one of its "most distinguishing features," pointing out that writers often invoked the "vocabulary of travel" both through the "citation of foreign literary works and tradition" and through the creation of "works that drew directly on the experience of foreign travel" (2). Craig Monk echoes this sentiment, emphasizing that the intersection of travel, modernism, and the autobiography reveals some of the ways that "American artists forged an art that both expanded their own national tradition and participated in a wider, international enterprise" (3–4). Especially because these writers belong to two different generations of modernism—Wharton associated with other *fin de siècle* figures like Henry James, Hemingway with interwar writers and fellow authors of the "lost generation"—depictions of travel in *A Moveable Feast* and *Motor-Flight* suggest the enduring importance of travel as a practice of personal and aesthetic discovery. The comparison also showcases the changing significance of travel across the twentieth century as the decline of empire increasingly fostered an understanding of global space as finite and fully mapped and the large-scale violence of the Great War irrevocably transformed existing paradigms for meaning-making.

Second, both writers are perhaps best known for their outspoken negotiation of existing gender roles with Wharton famously critiquing an idealized Victorian femininity and Hemingway anxiously asserting a traditional masculinity based, as Thomas Strychacz has described, on "autonomy, self-control, courage, grace under pressure" (49).[2] Thus exploring *A Moveable Feast* and *Motor-Flight* through the gendered languages of travel and transportation technologies offers an opportunity to expand and further specify but also complicate the gender politics attributed to both authors. Examining the travel discourses woven throughout both of these texts demonstrates the vital interaction between technological development and gender, working to undo established associations between femininity and stability, masculinity and movement. Giuliana Bruno's *Atlas of Emotion* stresses that overcoming this reductive view of women's mobility is especially important for scholars of modernism: "A regretfully persistent resistance to acknowledging the mobilities of woman's place especially in modernity and its discourse, informs the binary assumption that equates the figure of the male with voyage and the woman with home—a static, enclosed space" (81). As such, Wharton's text provides a sense of how women attempted to negotiate this binary and how travel, in particular, became especially "transgressive for Western women who sought both escape and pleasure abroad" (Kelley 357).

At the same time that travel became more *possible* for women, it *continued* to play an integral role in the formation of masculinity, a process Sidonie Smith describes: "Ever in the process of becoming 'men,' travelers affirm their masculinity through purposes, activities, behaviors, dispositions, perspectives and bodily movements displayed on the road and through the narratives of travel that they return home to the sending culture. Thus, travel functions as a defining area of agency" (xi). In other words, women's efforts to loosen their associations with home and stability did not necessarily undermine traditional linkages between men and travel. From the colonial journey into "unknown territory" to the Grand Tour, physical movement facilitated the psychological and emotional movement from boyhood to manhood. This idea marks both Hemingway's and Wharton's texts. Wharton offers an idea of the journey that borrows heavily from romanticized ideals of colonialism as she attempts to secure a place for women within this predominantly masculine mode of travel writing. *A Moveable Feast* also works within this framework but resists linking masculinity to large-scale movement or monumental discovery; instead, masculinity becomes bound up with Hemingway's identity as an artist and writer whose psychological transformation is facilitated only by fully and completely apprehending and aesthetically capturing the significance of the repetitions and details of a single city.

These historical and gendered discourses of travel further influence both *A Moveable Feast* and *A Motor-Flight through France* through their respective representations of transportation technologies. The car, in particular, takes on a specific meaning in each text, symbolizing women's freedom and individual agency in Wharton, indicted by Hemingway for its complicity in the erosion of masculine free will. In short, travel and movement technologies in both texts are inextricable from their broader engagements with travel narrative and, concomitantly, gender politics. Therefore, through their divergent views, *A Moveable Feast* and *Motor-Flight* demonstrate travel and transportation technologies as key conceptual sites for the revision and restaging of twentieth-century gender roles.

Finally, the gendered significance of travel and movement technologies in *A Moveable Feast* and *Motor-Flight* also reveals the extent to which Hemingway's and Wharton's respective aesthetic choices remain inextricably tied to their gender politics. As Joyce Kelley emphasizes, "travel of the body may encourage mental journeying," and the aesthetic productions of Hemingway's and Wharton's journeys are profoundly influenced by the specific ways they traverse French territory, registering, embracing, and rejecting specific transportation technologies based on the modes of perception enabled or disabled. Wharton embraces the car not just as an object that offers her freedom and independence but also as a means of seeing and apprehending the world through a technological lens aligned with her individualist, feminist politics. Hemingway rejects the mode of perception offered by the car in favor of walking precisely because this latter mode of seeing achieves the meticulous perceptual control always denied by the blur created by a speeding automobile. As Sara Danius has argued, "modernist aesthetics . . . is an index of a technologically mediated crisis of the senses," and investigating these two texts alongside one another reveals two ways of "indexing" this crisis while also suggesting that, at least in the context of travel writing, a technologized crisis of the senses remains entwined with the crisis of shifting gender roles (1).

Both Wharton and Hemingway represent travel and transportation technologies, specifically the automobile. Wharton celebrates the individualized freedom of the car as evidence of her desire to situate women within the mythos of the heroic (and colonial) journey of discovering by charting unknown paths in known territory, by tapping into a kind of ethnographic authenticity absent in tourist-dominated railway towns, by showcasing travel as an opportunity for women to intervene and participate in shaping perceptions of a given location. Hemingway offers a starkly different portrait of automobile travel, depicting the car as a technology complicit in the wartime disablement of the male body and the removal of his free will. Emphasizing walking as the means of transport that best maintains a hold on the free will and the agency to govern the movement of one's own body, Hemingway's memoir coheres with Mark Seltzer's notion of "relocation of the topography of masculinity to the surrogate frontier of the natural body" (104). These contrasting attitudes toward the gendering of travel and of transport technologies have aesthetic consequences. The technologized and non-technologized modes of perception that emerge from travel literature move beyond mere historical register and begin to provide a framework for reading transportation technologies through the lens of modernist aesthetics.

A MOTOR-FLIGHT THROUGH FRANCE: WOMEN AND THE RE-GIFTING OF ADVENTURE

A Motor-Flight through France opens by extolling the virtues of the automobile as a highly individualized mode of travel; situating the car as the comparative opposite of the train, imbuing it with the power to "re-enchant" travel, Wharton prioritizes the role of individual agency in shaping the course of the journey as well as the aesthetic insight that might result from such an endeavor, declaring: "The motor-car has restored the romance of travel. Freeing us from all the compulsions and contracts of the railway, the bondage to fixed hours and the beaten track, the approach to each town through the area of ugliness and desolation created by the railway itself, has given us back the wonder the adventure and the novelty which enlivened the way of our posting grand-parents" (1).

Wharton's description of the train emphasizes her objection to its physical and temporal restrictions of the individual traveler, condemning, in particular, its inherent capacity to destroy a passenger's opportunity to access and appreciate unexpected beauty. The functioning of the train, Wharton reminds us, is only possible through the production of smoke clouds that obscure views and through the construction of vast railway networks that flatten or forever transform landscapes both natural and manmade. As such, Wharton's text is framed by what Sidonie Smith has described as a condemnation of the train as an "engine of destruction, cultural intervention, and bankrupt modernity, alienated and routinized" (122).

The first lines of *Motor-Flight* thus illuminate the critique of modernity woven throughout the text and foreground the importance of individualism to Wharton's gender politics. Her specific objection to the train's "compulsions and contracts" underscores Wharton's understanding of this as a technology complicit in stripping away the individual agency of the traveler by bonding her to the patterns, needs, and limitations of the machine. Exploring the notions of compulsion in American naturalist fiction, a genre with which Wharton is commonly associated, Jennifer Fleissner defines compulsion as "the opposite of the will to act," noting that in many cases references to and depictions of compulsion "indicate more of a participation, even an investment in one's own reduction from agent to automaton" (39).[3] At the same time, Wharton's references to the problem of the "beaten path" intone a familiar modernist elitism, objecting to the democratization of travel and the concomitant transformation of the "masses" into movable herds of uneducated and undiscerning tourists.[4] We might expect a more moderate or measured criticism of the train from Wharton, given the train's important role in providing women with greater access to movement.[5] As part of Wharton's gender politics, however, this must be seen as an attempt to parse individual, cerebral women from the feminized masses; though women had indeed benefited from the democratization of travel and particularly through the invention of the steam engine, Wharton demonstrates a desire to carve out a new and differentiated space for herself on this new frontier of travel and travel writing, a desire to configure herself as the active agent and adventurer rather than a passive railway passenger. As Helen Carr points out, Wharton, along with many twentieth-century writers and intellectuals, worried that the proliferation of inexpensive train tickets and cheap Baedeker guides would overturn longstanding associations between freedom, discovery, and travel, instead offering only routinization, repetition, and uniformity of experience (72). Wharton illustrates this notion with her repeated references to the ruinous effects of the Baedeker; when, for example, she reflects on the beauty of Rouen, she states: "Only one trembles lest it should cease to shine in its own twilight heaven when it has become a star in Baedeker," suggesting that the town's appearance in a tourist guide will surely rob it of its special beauty (23).

Wharton's elitism and contempt for popular travel thus again highlights the desire for individual agency that motivates her enthusiasm for the automobile. According to Smith, "Restoring the individualizing logic of travel, automobility distinguishes the true traveler from the mere tourist who proceeds by railway" not only by offering Wharton and other woman motorists greater physical freedom but greater imaginative freedom as well, capable of "respond[ing] to the traveler's imagination, desire, and energy" (179). The importance of physical freedom and agency infuses Wharton's descriptions of motoring, which often obfuscate the identities of driver and passengers and elide the body with the automobile using such phrases as "We climbed" and "we pushed south," which serve to emphasize exertion and distance covered by the individual motorist. These highly physical descriptions aim to position Wharton as an agent rather than obverse of adventure; with the car acting as her aide, Wharton resists the configuration of woman as "earth, shelter, enclosure," as "home," as an "anchoring . . . compass point," and rejects the notion of woman as "that which must be left behind in the pursuit of agency" (Smith x). Indeed, these descriptions of movement seem to borrow from the vocabulary of masculine adventure, cultivated through the narration and interpretation of a man's *physical* movements and as such harken back to Wharton's opening nostalgia for the wonder of discovery experienced by previous generations who, though Wharton does not explicitly say so, experienced travel primarily as a mechanism and result of colonialism (Smith xi). Wharton's rhetorical move here can be seen as a part of her need to distinguish her cerebral, aesthetically minded work from travel writers catering to the average tourist, a strategy necessary for Wharton, who was eager to emphasize the individual woman's ability to stand apart from, rather than blending into, the faceless and feminized traveling masses.[6] Read within the historical discourses of travel, Wharton's stress on movement becomes suggestive of her romanticization of a form of adventure deeply imbricated with colonialism.

These colonial underpinnings become clearer later in Wharton's text when she states: "Above all these recovered pleasures must be ranked the delight of taking a town unawares, stealing on it by backways, and unchronicled paths, and surprising some intimate aspect of past time, some silhouette hidden for half a century by the ugly mask of railway embankments and the iron-bulk and a huge station" (1–2). Wharton's comments thus illustrate two related aspects of this colonially derived fantasy of travel: First, that motorists can literally discover new territories not yet "chronicled" by English-language writers. This sense of motoring suggests that in a very tangible way motorists can indeed recapture the magic of discovery. Within the scheme of Wharton's gender politics, this suggests a way that women might participate in the process of discovery and as such also participate in the individualizing journey of moving through, discovering, and possessing territories—a privilege traditionally made available only to men. Second, and perhaps more importantly, Wharton suggests that the automobile *also* creates unique *creative* opportunities for women, carving out spaces for woman drivers to capture and interpret images, for women to take part in the conceptual mapping of a given territory, providing alternative ways for women to "possess" the places they encounter while motoring.

Bruno reminds us that the process of image-making through travel represents another facet of coloniality as a process that "is directed toward taking possession—conquering sites and their inhabitants. Viewed from this perspective, the culture of travel exhibits its historical bond with colonialism" (71). Compiling both images and text, Wharton participates in the process Bruno describes, possessing through her particular mode of representation. The photographs serve to frame each town through its architectural and aesthetic import, often featuring cathedrals and other famous buildings in ways that are quite similar to the typical travel guide. Wharton's text, however, more fully interprets the meaning of the pictures she provides as well as the pictures she describes. For instance, when Wharton says, "Here in northern France, where agriculture has mated with poetry instead of banishing it, one understands the higher beauty of land developed into relation to life and history as compared with the raw material with which the greater part of our own hemisphere is still clothed," she casts an approving glance at the land carefully cultivated in conjunction with the manmade beauty, simultaneously offering a disapproving assessment of the wild and untamed interior of her home nation (5). Such a passage participates in a colonizing practice of image-making not only by interpreting for her readers the significance of France's territorial organization as the *right* form of organization but also by projecting her visions of how other landscapes might be shaped through a similar framework. The car thus furnishes Wharton with the material to practice this colonially derived form of image-making, and thereby also entering into a masculine narrative of travel through the practice of movement, discovery, and possession. At same time, this act of possession is also one of authorial assertion. By creating and interpreting these images for readers, Wharton's travel narrative claims a degree of ownership for these territories as one of few writers physically equipped to move beyond the well-worn paths of the railway and intellectually equipped to encounter them with a critical eye.

Wharton's understanding of the car therefore remains entwined not only with its capacity to differentiate passenger from traveler, adventurer from conformist, but also with her nostalgia for and desire to participate in the colonial journey of discovery experienced by previous generations of travelers. Using her text to "possess" by showcasing unknown pathways and "capture" French territory through her image-making process, Wharton uses her writing as a means of inserting women into existing narratives of adventure and implicating them in the processes of discovery from which they had been traditionally excluded. Wharton's text reveals the importance of the automobile not just as the mechanism of physical liberation for women but conceptual liberation as well, providing an image of a woman's agency that although problematic nevertheless manipulates existing paradigms to enable women's interventions in map- and meaning-making across the globe.

ERNEST HEMINGWAY AND THE AGENCY OF THE MALE BODY

Though primarily a memoir of a pedestrian's urban flânerie, *A Moveable Feast* offers sparing mention of the car, corresponding with some of memoir's key moments, particularly those where Hemingway encounters fellow American expatriate authors. In each anecdote, the car appears as a broken object in need of repair, a trend that broadly bespeaks Hemingway's ambivalence towards automotive technology. The car first appears in an episode that recounts Stein's famous labeling of Hemingway's as the "lost generation," a comment that, as Hemingway records it, actually arises as a result of Stein's disgruntled interactions with a Parisian auto-repair worker and his boss:

> [Miss Stein] had some ignition trouble with the old Model T Ford that she then drove and the young man who worked in the garage and had served in the last year of the war had not been adept, or perhaps had not broken the priority of other vehicles in repairing Miss Stein's Ford. Anyway he had not been *sérieux* and had been corrected severely by the *patron* of the garage after Miss Stein's protest. The *patron* had said to him "You are all a génération perdue." (Hemingway 29)

In part, Hemingway here illustrates the vindictiveness that scholars have routinely attributed to his memoir. According to Jacqueline

Tavernier-Courbin, *A Moveable Feast* remains preoccupied with a desire to "settle old scores," an idea echoed by Suzanne del Gizzo's argument that the memoir performs as a "killshot" that strikes down Hemingway's old rivals (Tavernier-Courbin 44; Del Gizzo 122).[7]

Undergirding Hemingway's denigration of Stein, however, is a particular objection to the complex gender interactions routed through her broken automobile. Hemingway identifies the mechanic as "a young man" and chafes at the paternalistic and condescending treatment delivered to the young mechanic first by Stein and then by the garage owner. Speculating on the rationale for Stein's ire, Hemingway suggests that it is not poor workmanship—something the text silently insinuates that Stein would not recognize—but rather the young man's apparently unaccommodating attitude, his failure to immediately acquiesce to Stein's demands, his lack of "seriousness." These problems however are, for Hemingway, explicitly related to the war as evidenced by his framing of the incident by foregrounding the young stranger's military record. The garage owner's subsequent remarks *also* emphasize the important role of the war when he refers to the mechanic's (and, by extension, Hemingway's) generation as "lost." As Tony Fong has noted, Hemingway objects to Stein and the garage owner's flattening and reductive narrative that "reduces the young man with an individual history into a type: an unserious and drunken lout who did not respect his elders" (273). Stein's extension of the pronouncement to include Hemingway intensifies the identification Hemingway already feels with the mechanic and subsequently his resentment of Stein's "dirty easy labels" (Hemingway 31).

That the car is the impetus for Hemingway's staging of these generational differences, however, is not incidental; when Hemingway again revisits the incident in the garage to provide what Fong has described as "an alternative narrative for the mechanic" that projects "memories onto the young man so as to flesh out Stein's caricature," the car again figures prominently (273):

> That night walking home I thought about the boy in the garage and if he had ever been hauled in one of those vehicles when they were converted to ambulances. I remembered how they used to

> burn their brakes going down the mountain roads with full load of wounded and braking in low and finally using reverse, and how the last ones were driven over the mountainside empty so they would be replaced by big Fiats and good H-shift and metal-to metal brakes. (Hemingway 30)

This passage is interesting for several reasons. First, although biographically it makes sense that Hemingway would immediately think of the ambulance, a vehicle also specifically associated with the disenfranchisement of male bodies. As a mode of transport for wounded soldiers, ambulances both concretize the war's creation of helpless male bodies and technology's complicity in both destroying and repairing those bodies. Hemingway's memories of "burned out brakes" and his allusion to the potential for plummeting over the mountainside similarly position the car as a fickle technology that threatens to overturn its driver's control at any moment.

At the same time, this passage uses the car to meditate on the idea of obsolescence. Hemingway's descriptions of the automobile as an object casually discarded to make room for newer, more cutting-edge models are suggestive of his indictment of a wartime culture of wastefulness. This is further underscored by Hemingway's troubling insinuation that young men's bodies and cars share a condition of easy expendability. According to Deborah Clarke, the twentieth century witnessed the transformation of masculinity into something "no longer solely grounded in the human body . . . inextricably linked to technology and the automobile," producing an anxiety over the possibility that men might become "interchangeable, valued less for their individuality than for their efficiency and conformity" (49). Such an anxiety certainly emerges from Hemingway's complex portrait of wartime vehicles which at once showcase the vulnerability of the male body, offer technology as a troubling prosthetic extension of the male body, and work to extend the military control by restraining and constraining masculine free will. Amelia Jones's *Irrational Modernism* describes the radical transformation of masculinity produced by World War I: pressure to join the army and the concomitant demand for militarized discipline and obedience both harnessed and disrupted traditional associations between masculinity and free will. According to Jones, the obligation placed on young men to run into battle simultaneously required soldiers to submit to military authority while also performing a kind of heroic masculinity (49, 51). Viewed through this lens, then, the car becomes a means of unraveling Hemingway's skepticism of the automobile as an object of individuation, freedom, or agency, providing a portrait of technology that significantly diverges from Wharton's.

Though Hemingway's other descriptions of the car move away from his memories of the war, they also reiterate associations between the automobile and the loss of agency. The second significant automobile incident in *A Moveable Feast* occurs within Hemingway's narrative of his early friendship with F. Scott Fitzgerald, in which the two embark on a motor journey that, like the garage episode, slowly unravels Hemingway's tenuous relationship with a fellow American expatriate writer. Using the car as a mechanism for critiquing Fitzgerald's devotion to his controlling wife and his willingness to "whore" by compromising his writerly craft in favor of commercial success, the automobile in this instance begins to more clearly position Hemingway's aversion to the car and its perceived ability to strip away agency as an aesthetic concern.

The story itself recounts a road trip that Hemingway undertakes with Fitzgerald. Having left his broken-down car in Lyon, Fitzgerald proposes that Hemingway accompany him to retrieve the newly repaired car. Hemingway initially agrees, sure that the road trip back to Paris will give him the opportunity to "learn much that would be useful to know," with the car functioning as a mobile literary salon (155). As Hemingway's persistent use of the conditional foreshadows, however, his enthusiasm for the journey wanes almost immediately. When they reach the garage where Fitzgerald's car has been repaired, an exasperated Hemingway discovers that the car lacks a top, apparently because Fitzgerald's wife dislikes them. In mentioning this detail, Hemingway silently critiques Fitzgerald for acquiescing to his wife's impractical demands that also feminize the car, subtly eliding the altered car with Zelda's absent body and also with her power. Like Zelda herself, the car possesses the capacity to manipulate Fitzgerald, drawing out another (perhaps more familiar) dimension of Hemingway's objection to the car and its erosion of agency.

As the story goes on, Hemingway is further annoyed when the garage owner approaches to appraise him of some of the car's other problems: "The garage man explained to me that the car needed new piston rings and had evidently been run without sufficient oil and water. He showed me how it had heated up and burned the paint off the motor. He said if I could persuade monsieur to have a ring job done in Paris, the car, which was a good little car, would be able to give the service it was built for. . . . 'One has an obligation to a vehicle . . . try and make Monsieur be serious,' he said pleadingly, 'At least about the vehicle'" (162). The mechanic's use of "serious" echoes the words of the Parisian garage owner. In both instances "seriousness" gestures to a man's apparent obligation to the machine, an obligation to permit the vehicle to operate at its fullest potential, to allow the car to "give the service it was intended to give." Thus beyond its status as a fairly scathing critique of a fellow author, Hemingway's description of the car here again raises the issue of a man's relationship to technology, suggesting that he is beholden to the machine. Combined with his initial references to Zelda, Hemingway perhaps rather cynically suggests that the obligations of marriage and soldiering represent an equal threat to masculine agency.

Hemingway's contempt for the car can elsewhere be located via his privileging of other forms of transportation and movement including train, horseback, and walking. While the train, like the car, remains bound up with forces beyond Hemingway's control, the latter forms of transport—those especially appreciated by Hemingway—epitomize an idealized kind of movement unaided and unfettered by technology. In Hemingway's descriptions of the train, however, we see crossover with the automobile's tendency to strip away the traveler's freedom. Throughout *A Moveable Feast* the train serves to conduct Hemingway and his wife, Hadley, away from Paris, to the Parisian suburbs and beyond. Though Hemingway conveys excitement at the idea of travel, the memoir makes clear that the pragmatic realities of travel, namely the financial components, raise for Hemingway the issue of his poverty, a partial marker of his inadequacies as a writer as well as his inability to support his wife and son. This is clear when he states: "I knew how severe I had been and how bad things had been. The one who is doing his work and getting satisfaction from it is not the one the poverty bothers, recognizing the hardship that his career places on his wife and child" (50). And though Hemingway's memoir aims to cast this poverty as evidence of his more profound commitment to art—certainly more genuine than that of the wealthy but pandering Fitzgerald—Hemingway's repeated mentions of his need for third-class passage mark the moments of financial and hence also writerly and masculine anxiety for him.[8]

The anxieties raised by transport technologies thus help to account for Hemingway's apparent gravitation towards forms of movement that emphasize the role of the idealized, natural body. When Hemingway describes his and Hadley's enthusiasm for visiting the racetrack, he refers to the activity as "going racing": "It was gambling on horses but we called it racing" (61). Elsewhere, Hemingway mentions, "That day after I finished work, we would go racing," thereby eliding himself with the horse-and-jockey team, inserting himself into a competition fundamentally associated with the power and strength of the horse's body. Hemingway's enthusiastic narrations of the horse race even go so far as mentioning his apparent feeling of physical exertion by proxy, at one point telling Hadley that he can "still feel it inside me" (52)—revealing a distinct departure from his descriptions of both car and train. Racing therefore shows Hemingway's imaginative attraction to physical exertion, his tendency to configure the relationship between horse and rider as a mutual athleticism rather than a mechanized prosthetic, and suggests that an idealization of an apparently natural bodily power animates Hemingway's chosen forms of movement.

Because technologized movement denies or threatens the agency that fundamentally undergirds Hemingway's conception of masculinity, the exercise of the idealized, natural body therefore seeks to subvert this threat to masculine autonomy. This idea is particularly evident in Hemingway's insistent mention of walking, revealing the extent to which this ideal guides his choices of movement: "I was always hungry with the walking and the cold and the working" and later, "it was wonderful to walk down long flights of stairs knowing that I'd had good luck working" (12). Only two of the many descriptions of walking throughout *A Moveable Feast*, these passages illustrate not only the sense of independence that stems from this kind of movement, but also the sense of empowerment that comes from the body's combined physical and mental exertion.

Considering the car and other automotive cognates in *A Moveable Feast* illustrates not the embrace of a prosthetic masculinity that we might expect of a man renowned for his green Rolls Royce and his yellow Chrysler convertible, but rather an anxiety that seeks to return masculinity to a legible and non-technologized form. Thus while the memoir in some ways reinscribes the mythologies of virile masculinity that have long been attributed to Hemingway, it also complicates easy affiliations between masculinity and technology, and masculinity and movement for Hemingway are not a man looking to colonize or possess new geographic territory. Instead he looks to repossess the territory of his own body.

TOWARD A GENDERED AESTHETIC

Comparing the car and movement technologies in the nonfiction texts of these quintessential American authors demonstrates the car as a potent site for the working out of gender politics and reveals the extent to which differing attitudes towards movement technology mark the aesthetic interventions offered by Wharton and Hemingway. It is, of course, no accident that the car appears in two incidents that critique Hemingway's literary peers, nor is it a coincidence that the car is heavily implicated in Wharton's ability to produce material that distinguishes her as a discerning and literary travel writer. More specifically, however, the car's impact on the way each memoir describes and chooses to represent perception reveals that Hemingway's and Wharton's aesthetic principles remain irrevocably linked to their respective understandings of gender and agency.

After motoring back to Paris with Fitzgerald, for instance, Hemingway admits, "I cannot remember all the details of that afternoon" (162, 164). As we might expect, Hemingway's failure to recall any distinguishing details of his motor trip through the French countryside contrasts sharply with the almost compulsive level of detail offered in his recollections of his Parisian walking routes. Early in *A Moveable Feast*, Hemingway recalls that "there were many ways of walking down to the river from the top of the rue Cardinal Lemoine" (41). He goes on to describe one such "way," apparently the shortest, where he reconstructs not just the official topography of the city but also the architecture, the sounds of clattering traffic, and the feel of the air along the river. Hence bound up with Hemingway's "ways" of walking are actually ways of seeing, feeling, and experiencing the city's aesthetic potentialities, of its various dimensions. For "ways" connotes "method" as it does direction. Walking allows Hemingway to be fully in control of his perception; his comparatively slower speed allows him to see completely, to appreciate intricacies, to apprehend more completely, and to exert maximum power over the way details are aesthetically received and replicated on the space of the page. Conversely, Wharton's concern for "discovering" new pathways and for discovering novel ways to frame those pathways prompts her to embrace the perceptual limits created by the car's speed, going so far as to laud the sense of continuity produced by motoring across an entire country: "Had we visited by rail the principal places named in this itinerary, necessity would have detained us longer in each, and we should have had a fuller store of specific impressions; but we should have missed what is, in one way, the truest initiation of travel, the sense of continuity of relation between different districts" (37). In keeping with Wharton's underlying romanticization of the car as a vehicular return to the adventure of a colonial past, she here reveals her interest in characterizing the wholeness of a place, even at the cost of sacrificing the individual details precisely because it is the broader portrait that cannot be accessed or apprehended by passive passengers of the train by those without her sense of independence and adventure, which differentiates her from other types of travelers and reasserts her agency as an active, mobile adventurer.

Hence, beyond revealing the ways in which gender politics infuse both Hemingway's and Wharton's representations of travel and transportation technologies, these memoirs gesture to the importance of travel memoirs as a site where the contestation of gender roles, the impact of new technology, and the evolution of aesthetic perception collide and mutually influence each other. Delving into the gendering of movement and of the car in particular in *A Moveable Feast* and *A Motor Flight through France* demonstrates the key ways that technology prompts and props up the mechanisms through which writers negotiate the changing landscape of the twentieth century and beckon us to more firmly advocate for the place of travel narratives within our broader understanding of interventions of modernist aesthetics.

NOTES

1. *Motor-Flight* was published in 1908 using a collection of travel essays that appeared in *Atlantic Monthly* in 1906 and 1907. See Schriber (259) for more information on the publishing history of Wharton's several travel books, including *Italian Backgrounds*. Hemingway's memoir was published posthumously but was assembled using fragments written during his stay in Paris from 1921 to 1926; see the introduction to *A Moveable Feast*.

2. Strychacz and others are rightly critical of this uncomplicated view of Hemingway's masculinity. He offers a corrective to existing narratives of Hemingway's approach to gender by sketching a more complex and varied understanding of the multiple masculinities explored in Hemingway's writing.

3. Barbara Hochman points out that "since the late 1980's [Wharton] has frequently been seen as a part of the realist, and even the naturalist, company" (129).

4. Helen Carr emphasizes the correlation between modernist elitism and travel writers' concern with the popularization of travel: "Such dismay at the democratisation of travel was widely shared among travel writers, many of whom showed the same suspicion of popular travel that modernists exhibited towards popular culture in general" (72).

5. According to Smith, "Newly gained freedom and prowess" were "made possible by the new technologies of motion that drove modernity. Large numbers of women began to leave home for the lure of the road as a result of the emergence of faster, safer, cleaner, and more comfortable machines of motion," and the railway serves as a particularly salient example of this process (xii).

6. Huyssen's chapter "Modernism's Other: Woman as Mass Culture" argues that high modernism tended to feminize popular or mass culture.

7. Suzanne Del Gizzo ponders the significance of Hemingway's claim that *A Moveable Feast* was a "biography by remate." Del Gizzo points out that "remate" can be translated not only as "reflection," as many scholars have argued, but also as "killshot," and therefore we might read the text as a deliberate, final blow to each of the various people it describes, including Stein (122).

8. Hemingway's anxiety about money is especially clear in his description of his train trip, the first leg of his journey to retrieve Fitzgerald's car from Lyon. When Fitzgerald fails to appear at the assigned time, Hemingway is forced to purchase his own train ticket, setting in motion the financial anxiety which dominates his recollections of the trip: "I got aboard and walked through the train hoping only that he would be aboard. It was a long train and he was not on it. I explained the situation to the conductor, paid for a ticket second class—there was no third" (Hemingway 157). The train ticket becomes metonymic of Hemingway's worry about the finance of the trip, which he reiterates at several points: "I had never before accepted any invitation to go on any trip that was paid for, instead of the cost split, and in this one I had insisted that we split the cost of the hotels and meals" (157). Similarly, Hemingway later mentions, "Since the start of the trip I had felt a little complicated about it emotionally and I found I felt much better the more things I could pay for" (161).

WORKS CITED

Bruno, Giuliana. *Atlas of Emotion: Journeys in Art, Architecture, and Film*. London: Verso, 2002. Print.

Carr, Helen. "Modernism and Travel (1880–1940)." *The Cambridge Companion to Travel Writing*. Ed. Peter Hulme and Tim Youngs. Cambridge: Cambridge UP, 2002. 70–86. Print.

Clarke, Deborah. *Driving Women: Fiction and Automobile Culture in Twentieth-Century America*. Baltimore: Johns Hopkins UP, 2007. Internet resource.

Danius, Sara. *The Senses of Modernism: Technology, Perception, and Aesthetics*. Ithaca, NY: Cornell UP, 2002. Print.

Del Gizzo, Suzanne. "Redefining Remate: Hemingway's Professed Approach to Writing *A Moveable Feast*." *Hemingway Review* 28.2 (2009): 121–26. Web. Accessed 15 Aug. 2016.

Farley, David G. *Modernist Travel Writing: Intellectuals Abroad*. Columbia: U of Missouri P, 2010. Print.

Fleissner, Jennifer. *Women, Compulsion, Modernity: The Moment of American Naturalism*. Chicago: U Chicago P, 2004. Print.

Fong, Tony. "The Fictional Selves of *A Moveable Feast*." *Auto/Biography Studies* 31.2 (2016): 261–83. Print.

Hemingway, Ernest. *A Moveable Feast: The Restored Edition*. New York: Scribner's, 2009. Print.

Hochman, Barbara. "The Good, the Bad, and the Literary: Edith Wharton's *Bunner Sisters* and the Social Contexts of Reading." *Studies in American Naturalism* 1.1–2 (2006): 128–43. Print.

Huyssen, Andreas. *After the Great Divide*. Bloomington: Indiana UP, 1986. Print.

Jones, Amelia. *Irrational Modernism: A Neurasthenic History of New York Dada*. Cambridge, MA: MIT UP, 2004. Print.

Kelley, Joyce. "Increasingly 'Imaginative Geographies': Excursions into Otherness, Fantasy, and Modernism in Early Twentieth-Century Women's Travel Writing." *Journal of Narrative Theory* 35.3 (2005): 357–72. Web. 15 Aug. 2016.

Monk, Craig. *Writing the Lost Generation: Expatriate Autobiography and American Modernism*. Iowa City: U of Iowa P, 2010. Print.

Schriber, Mary Suzanne. "Edith Wharton and Travel Writing as Self-Discovery." *American Literature* 59.2 (1987): 257–67. Web.

Seltzer, Mark. *Bodies and Machines*. New York: Routledge, 1992. Print.

Smith, Sidonie. *Moving Lives: Twentieth-Century Women's Travel Writing*. Minneapolis: U of Minnesota P, 2001. Print.

Stoneback, H. R. “Freedom and Motion, Place and Placelessness: On the Road in Hemingway’s America.” *Hemingway and the Natural World.* Ed. Robert Fleming. Caldwell: U of Idaho P, 1999. 203–19. Print.

Strychacz, Thomas F. *Dangerous Masculinities: Conrad, Hemingway, and Lawrence.* Gainesville: UP of Florida, 2008. Print.

Tavernier-Courbin, Jacqueline. “Fact and Fiction in *A Moveable Feast.*” *Hemingway Review* Fall 4.1 (1984): 44–51. Print.

Wharton, Edith. *A Motor-Flight through France.* New York: Scribner’s Sons, 1908. Print.

V

INTERTEXTUALITIES

Wharton, Hemingway, Ecclesiastes, and the Modernist Impulse

DUSTIN FAULSTICK

When Edith Wharton's adviser at Scribner's, William Crary Brownell, tried to include an epigraph from Ecclesiastes at the beginning of Wharton's 1905 novel *The House of Mirth,* the author responded by "drawing an inexorable blue line through the text" (*Letters* 94). Her fear, as she indicates in her letter to Brownell, was that she "might surely be suspected of plagiarizing from Mrs. Margaret Sangster's beautiful volume, 'Five Days with God'" (94), a pious text devoted to religious duty. "Seriously," she explained of her title borrowed from the biblical Ecclesiastes, "I think the title explains itself amply as the tale progresses" (94). Ernest Hemingway does include an epigraph from Ecclesiastes to accompany his Ecclesiastes-titled 1926 novel *The Sun Also Rises,* but few readers of this Lost Generation novel full of drinking, sexuality, and bullfighting would accuse the young Hemingway of plagiarizing a pious religious text. A casual reader might consider any biblical reference as an indication of moralizing, but for readers familiar with Ecclesiastes, the book is less likely to convey this association. In fact, the interpretation history of Ecclesiastes includes endorsements from such notable skeptics as Voltaire, Volney, and Arthur Schopenhauer. John Franklin Genung, in his 1904 commentary on Ecclesiastes, claims, "One never hears of the skeptics rejecting this book. It seems rather to warm and nourish them" (*Words of Koheleth* 3). Likewise, Samuel Cox's 1903 commentary acknowledges, "From Schopenhauer downward, this Book is constantly cited by them as if it confirmed the conclusion for which they contend, [Agnes] Taubert even going so far as to find 'a catechism of pessimism' in it" (4–5).[1]

Beyond being the beloved scripture of the skeptics, Ecclesiastes enjoyed widespread popularity in the early twentieth century. Cox sees the book as primary among Christian readers as well: "few books were, or are, more popular than the book Ecclesiastes. [. . .] Brief as the Book is, I am disposed to think it is better known among us than any other of the Old Testament Books except Genesis, the Psalter, and the prophecies of Isaiah" (289). Genung sees the views of its main author—the Preacher, or Qoheleth[2]—as "eminently timely" (*Words of Koheleth* 159), and, in 1906, William Forbush calls Ecclesiastes "the most modern book in the Bible" (3). In his 1919 commentary *A Gentle Cynic*, Morris Jastrow identifies the book's twofold appeal for early twentieth-century readers: "The book is not only intensely human, it is also remarkably modern in its spirit" (8).

Ecclesiastes' modernity rests largely on its compatibility with contemporary science and philosophy. Darwin, Freud, and Nietzsche had recently established a climate at odds with much of the Bible, but markedly consistent with Ecclesiastes. Although most of the Bible claims a superior role for humans, Qoheleth agrees with Darwin and Freud that humans "themselves are beasts" (3:18). And while Ecclesiastes doesn't share Nietzsche's proclamation of the death of God, it is largely compatible with that proclamation because it focuses less on God's imminence than does much of the Bible and concludes that life is foundationally meaningless. From the book's second verse—"vanity of vanities; all is vanity" (1:2)—Qoheleth rejects inherent meaning. "Vanity" or the Hebrew *hebel* appears thirty-seven times in the book, and, in addition to the King James Version's translation of *hebel* as "vanity," it also gives the sense of emptiness, uselessness, worthlessness, "ephemerality," "meaninglessness," and "absurdity"; most literally, in Hebrew *hebel* means "vapor or breath" (W. Brown 21–22). The phrase "vanity of vanities, all is vanity," is repeated, before a short epilogue, as Qoheleth's final observation in verse 12:8. By framing his narrative with vanity, Qoheleth acknowledges that all of his claims stem from and exist in a world of *hebel*, or meaninglessness.

Furthermore, by challenging the conventional Old Testament deed-consequence wisdom formula, Ecclesiastes privileges real-life experiences over abstract theological dogma. The book of Proverbs, for example, promises God's reward for good actions and punishment for bad ones. Ecclesiastes, however, recognizes that life doesn't work so predictably: sometimes "there [are] just men, unto whom it happeneth according to the work of the wicked; [and] there [are] wicked men, to whom it happeneth according to the work of the righteous" (8:14). Freely challenging the infallibility of traditional wisdom, Qoheleth concludes that the only thing we can know for certain about God is that God encourages people to eat, drink, and work well in a loving community: "Go thy way, eat thy bread with joy, and drink thy wine with a merry heart; for God now accepteth thy works. [. . .] Live joyfully with the wife whom thou lovest all the days of the life of thy vanity" (9:7, 9). Although many Christian readers move away from this conclusion, almost all recognize the general outline of Ecclesiastes as expressed in Alan McNeile's 1904 commentary: "Since the work of the Deity is inscrutable from beginning to end, and no one has any idea of what the future contains, or whether after this life there is any future for man at all, [. . . t]he only course open to him is to make the most of the present" (20). Featuring even this well-known carpe-diem phrasing, Paul Haupt, in 1894, states simply, "The chief maxim of Ecclesiastes is: *There is nothing better than to eat and drink and be merry*" (245; Haupt's emphasis).

If Wharton hoped to avoid a pious allusion in her novel's title, she chose wisely. And yet, as Hemingway would later do in *The Sun Also Rises*, she chose to title *The House of Mirth* after Ecclesiastes, which—despite its secular characteristics—is still a canonized biblical book. Both Wharton and Hemingway were fascinated by religion, but wanted a more demanding, complex, and realistic experience than the religion offered to them in childhood. Wharton biographer Hermione Lee shows that Wharton adopted a position of "skeptical agnosticism" but not one of atheism (62), and Larry Grimes charts what he calls "Hemingway's peculiar religious odyssey. He does not turn to atheism when Protestantism fails him, [but instead] converts to Catholicism and continues to attend mass and say prayers until his death" (3). Wharton, too, developed an interest away from her inherited Protestantism and toward Catholicism. Lee reveals, "Many of Wharton's friends supposed that she might be thinking of converting" (714). Although Wharton doesn't convert and Hemingway's multiple divorces complicate his Catholicism, both authors' lifelong religious journeys meaningfully influenced their literary imaginations. Carol Singley claims readers "can no more separate [Wharton's] religious and philosophical perspectives from her fiction than one can divorce T. S. Eliot's Christianity from his poetry" (xi). Similarly, Grimes sees Hemingway's own seeking after religion reflected in several of his protagonists, and H. R. Stoneback insists that Hemingway's Catholicism "is everywhere in his work, which is fundamentally religious and profoundly Catholic from the earliest good work to the last" (122).

Wharton's and Hemingway's interest in Ecclesiastes and in Catholicism seems to have stemmed from a similar impulse, one especially relevant in light of Catholic Modernism. Before defining a literary or an aesthetic movement, modernism in the twentieth century referred to a liberal movement within the Catholic Church. Though they disliked the label—in part because modernism was condemned in 1907 by Pope Pius X as the "synthesis of all heresies"—two particularly famous excommunicated priests, Alfred Loisy and George Tyrrell, explained the modernist impulse in terms of understanding the relationship between the contemporary world and traditional religion. Loisy, responding to his excommunication in 1908, claimed that the "so-called modernists" are those who "share the desire to adapt the Catholic religion to the intellectual, moral, and social needs of the present time" (15). In 1905, Percy Gardner outlines Loisy's position as an attempted synthesis: "M. Loisy supposes himself to have discovered a way of reconciling intellectual faithfulness to the principles of historic science and Biblical criticism with dutiful submission to the authorities of the Roman Church wherever religious and moral teaching comes in" (126). Tyrrell, in his posthumously published 1910 book *Christianity at the Crossroads*, explains, "By a modernist, I mean a churchman of any sort, who believes in the possibility of a synthesis between the essential truth of his religion and the essential truth of modernity" (5). He also repeatedly emphasizes, "by Modernism I always mean a synthesis of Catholicism and Science—not the supremacy of the latter" (*Letters* 119). Essentially, the modernist impulse was to adapt, rather than abandon, the dogmas of the Church to the insights of the modern world.

In France, Wharton maintained a close friendship with the Catholic abbé Arthur Mugnier and knew a lesser-known modernist, Henri Bremond, who spoke at Tyrrell's funeral and corresponded with Loisy after his excommunication. Wharton dined with Mugnier and Bremond and felt comfortable enough to ask them questions about theology. As R. W. B. Lewis indicates, "Abbé Bremond was a much treasured acquaintance of EW" (Wharton, *Letters* 478).[3] Wharton developed these relationships after the publication of *The House of Mirth*, but the ideas were reaching their apex as she wrote the novel: the papal condemnation of modernism coming in 1907. While writing *The Sun Also Rises,* Hemingway lived in Paris—an important site in the development of Catholic Modernism—and was, as Stoneback reveals, even more invested in Catholicism than Wharton was. Like Catholic Modernism, Ecclesiastes plays a potential role in taking both the modern world and religious traditions seriously. Ecclesiastes couldn't have anticipated its compatibility with turn-of-the-twentieth-century science and philosophy, but the book's attempt to update the wisdom of Proverbs is an effort to square new realities with received ideas: Qoheleth doesn't dismiss traditional wisdom entirely, but he demands that wisdom account for lived experiences. As Wharton and Hemingway attempted to accommodate modern philosophy and science to their religious curiosity, both authors found solidarity in the biblical skepticism of Ecclesiastes. Evoked in the titles of *The House of Mirth* and *The Sun Also Rises,* Ecclesiastes offers the main characters in each novel a potentially satisfying philosophical option—of enjoying life reflectively in a loving relationship—that they cannot, in the end, realize.

Given its appeal for skeptics and pessimists, Ecclesiastes' call to enjoy life could seem potentially at odds with the overriding disposition of the book. Vanity, sorrow, uncertainty, and death pervade Ecclesiastes, and, in Wharton's title allusion in verse 7:4, Qoheleth claims that the house of mourning is superior to the house of mirth. These conclusions stem from his insistence on the finality of death and the primacy of suffering. But death also inspires Qoheleth's claims to enjoy life in the moment: eating, drinking, and loving before humans can no longer do so. The proper relationship for Qoheleth between enjoyment, sorrow, mourning, and mirth depends on self-awareness and reflection. The house of mirth represents empty distractions and drunken forgetfulness; the house of mourning reminds people of their limited lives and encourages reflective joy in the moment. Wharton's characters living perpetually in the house of mirth, the Dorsets, Trenors, and Brys, never seem to reflect on their own mortality. Rather than a tempered enjoyment accounting for the somber realities of existence, their mirth manifests a shallow, thoughtless escapism focused on exclusionary social status and increasing material wealth.

According to Ecclesiastes, however, status, money, and possessions cannot ultimately satisfy. In amassing a great fortune, many maidens, and widespread fame as a wealthy man, Qoheleth comes to realize the meaninglessness of working only toward a reward, and becomes disenchanted with living: "Therefore I hated life; because the work that is wrought under the sun is grievous unto me: for all is vanity and vexation of spirit. [. . .] For what hath man *of* all his labor, and of the vexation of his heart, wherein he hath labored under the sun?" (2:18–22; my emphasis). On the other hand, Qoheleth finds value in enjoying work for its own sake: "There is nothing better for a man, than that he should eat and drink, and that he should make his soul enjoy good *in* his labor. This also I saw, that it was from the hand of God" (2:24; my emphasis). The distinction depends on the prepositions "of" and "in." When Qoheleth expects a reward to come out *of* or *from* his labor—in the form of monetary gain and the potential for delayed enjoyment—he hates life. When he accepts that a reward can only come *in* his labor, by enjoying the work itself and doing it well, he praises labor as a gift from God. Wharton's critique of expecting a reward *from* work is most apparent in the transactional-marriage mentality pervading New York high society. Rather than finding a reward *in* marriage in the form of love, protagonist Lily Bart is expected to earn a reward *from* such a marriage in the form of social capital. If she could be satisfied with a marriage to Gryce or even to Rosedale, Lily would prove successful in securing an upwardly mobile marital transaction. But Lily foundationally distrusts marrying for money just as Qoheleth distrusts working frantically to amass possessions without taking time to enjoy. And yet, even though Wharton's title allusion encourages readers to praise Lily for rejecting the marriage marketplace, Lily is left with few other options.

She must, therefore, seek an alternative life. But "what manner of life," Lily asks herself throughout the novel, "would it be?" (*House of Mirth* 39). Using Ecclesiastes as a guide, for Lily to flourish, she needs to embrace the freedom to adopt a personal philosophy that would allow her to love and to be loved, to enjoy life using the money she has without insisting on increasing her material wealth. She might consider dating Lawrence Selden to allow herself an opportunity to experience love *in* her relationship. She could live in a modest apartment that would allow her to enjoy her life responsibly rather than insisting on having the newest dresses, making yearly trips to pricey Mediterranean hotels, and attending extravagant parties to gain social clout. And she could hold intimate gatherings with friends where she might enjoy human interactions without worrying about damning appearances. Lily, though, cannot. Despite their similar views and obvious attraction, Lily and Selden cannot at the same time imagine themselves happy in marriage. By the time Lily sheds her social adherence to a successful transactional marriage and sees Selden as a serious suitor, Selden submits to his own strictures from the sexual marketplace. Lily is judged harshly by a gender double-standard that drives her to unhappiness and to death. Only an alternative set of social circumstances could have allowed her freedom enough to be happy.

Taking Qoheleth's counsel for enjoyment seriously can provide some motivation for such a social change, even if Qoheleth doesn't specifically prescribe it. Ecclesiastes could do more to craft a specific response to the world's social inequalities, but its universal call for joy still points in a progressive direction. Likewise, *The House of Mirth*—while exposing gender inequality—could say more about economic inequality. Still, the socioeconomic critique the novel does provide is significant. Pointing to enjoyment as the highest good of human experience, through the title and thematic allusions to Ecclesiastes, *The House of Mirth* establishes a lofty social vision: everyone should have access to joy. Such a vision would require a socioeconomic revolution. And while Wharton cannot envision the specifics of this kind of mass-scale social change, she gives readers a place to start. Lily's observation of Nettie Struther and her husband's frail happiness is astute:

> her first glimpse of the continuity of life had come to her that evening in Nettie Struther's kitchen. The poor little working-girl who had found strength to gather up the fragments of her life, and build herself a shelter with them, seemed to Lily to have reached the central truth of existence. It was a meager enough life, on the grim edge of poverty, with scant margin for possibilities of sickness or mischance, but it had the frail audacious permanence of a bird's nest built on the edge of a cliff—[. . .] it had taken two to build the nest. (319)

Nettie's poverty and lung trouble kept her from joy before Lily's donation to Gerty Farish's Girls' Club, and Lily recognizes that similar hardships could afflict Nettie again unless socioeconomic circumstances improve for the poor and the potentially destitute. Still, Lily's observation of Nettie's current happiness should not be dismissed: Nettie *has* reached a "central truth of existence" (319). Even, and perhaps especially, without access to the great possessions of Rosedale and Trenor, Nettie experiences individual moments of love and of joy. For "there is nothing better," indeed, "than that a man [and a woman] should rejoice" (Ecclesiastes 3:22).

Wharton provides one further, pertinent clue highlighting the importance of Ecclesiastes in *The House of Mirth*. On Lily's afternoon walk with Selden, on the day she decides to abandon Gryce, the narrator observes that Lily "always carried an Omar Khayyam in her traveling bag" (65). Edward FitzGerald's 1859 translation, *The Rubáiyát of Omar Khayyám*—which shares several themes with Ecclesiastes—saw immense popularity in the late-nineteenth and early twentieth centuries. Genung's 1901 *Ecclesiastes and Omar Khayyám: A Note for the Spiritual Temper of our Time* claims that *The Rubáiyát* was, in 1901, "on every center-table" (4). Like Genung, several early twentieth-century writers explicitly connect *The Rubáiyát* to Ecclesiastes. George Sparks's 1900 essay "The Hebrew 'Rubáiyát'" calls Ecclesiastes "the '*Rubáiyát*' of the Old Testament" (415), and, in 1906 and 1922 respectively, Forbush and F. Crawford Burkitt translated Ecclesiastes into verse modeled on *The Rubáiyát*.[4] E. H. Plumptre elevates Ecclesiastes' philosophy above that of Khayyám, yet cares enough about their similarities to include significant portions of *The Rubáiyát* as an appendix to the 1898 edition of his Ecclesiastes commentary. Even Rothfeld Otto's 1922 *Umar Khayyam and His Age*, a text focused primarily on *The Rubáiyát*, recognizes, "Umar was not the first to express in immortal verse these longings. [. . .] Ecclesiastes is compounded of the same spirit" (64).

Given the variety of camps invested in Ecclesiastes, Wharton's inclusion of *The Rubáiyát* reveals which aspects of Ecclesiastes she intends to highlight and sharpens readers' focus on those themes in Ecclesiastes, particularly in a culture mesmerized by Omar Khayyám. Most notably, *The Rubáiyát* echoes Ecclesiastes' carpe-diem conclusion. Because everything ends with death, Khayyám insists on embracing present opportunities for joy: "Ah, make the most of what we yet may spend, / Before we, too, into the Dust descend; / Dust unto Dust and under Dust to lie, / Sans Wine, sans Song, sans Singer, and—sans End! [. . .] While you live, Drink!—for once dead you never shall return" (lines 49–52, 136). Anticipating Lily and

Selden's rustic walk, Khayyám calls his lover to join him in the wilderness: "But come with old Khayyam, [. . .] Here with a Loaf of Bread beneath the Bough, / A Flask of Wine, a Book of Verse—and Thou / Beside me singing in the Wilderness— / And Wilderness Is Paradise enow" (lines 33, 41–44). Evoking its parallels to *The Rubáiyát* helps Wharton highlight the worldly recommendations in Ecclesiastes: biblical recommendations for living well on earth. This sacred-secular worldview generates a large part of the appeal of the biblical book for both Wharton and Hemingway.

Consequently, it comes as no surprise that Hemingway took an interest in *The Rubáiyát* as well. On the night he met Carl Sandburg and Sherwood Anderson, in Chicago in 1921, at "the first party Ernest attended, he read aloud from *The Rubaiyat of Omar Khayyam*" (Griffin 152). Bracketing the 1926 publication date of *The Sun Also Rises*, Hemingway also read from *The Rubáiyát* "[d]uring a poetry evening in 1931" (Pustienne 59). Hemingway's sustained interest in *The Rubáiyát*—alongside his interest in Ecclesiastes—is reflected expressly in the character of Count Mippipopolous in *The Sun Also Rises*. In fact, the novel consistently advocates seizing the day. Hemingway's allusion to Ecclesiastes 1:5, in his title and second epigraph, structures the novel and implicitly offers its two main characters—Jake Barnes and Brett Ashley—a potential path toward meaningful happiness. Each of the novel's three books then provides a concrete example of a character embodying Qoheleth's philosophy: in book I, Count Mippipopolous—like Qoheleth and Omar Khayyám—praises the enjoyment of food, wine, and love; in book II, the Pamplona hotel owner Montoya advocates individual moments of passion; and in book III, Jake himself recognizes the simple pleasures of quiet living before being reminded that—because of his inability to perform his heteronormative sexual role—he cannot "[l]ive joyfully with the wife whom [he] lovest" (Ecclesiastes 9:9). In the end, despite multiple elements suggesting the value of Ecclesiastes, Jake and Brett—like Lily and Selden—suffer from their inability to enact fully Ecclesiastes' carpe-diem ethic. *The Sun Also Rises* demonstrates a high level of respect for the biblical book, but still considers that text skeptically, playing with the tensions between the real world and Ecclesiastes. This strategy gives Hemingway's allusion to Ecclesiastes an Ecclesiastes-inspired edge of modern skepticism.

In book I, Count Mippipopolous treats Brett and Jake to a fine dinner during which he reveals his affinities with Ecclesiastes. The count takes a great interest in wine and knows a good deal about it. When Jake suggests that he write a book on wines, however, Mippipopolous answers that he does not expect any lasting gain to come from wine, but wants only joy in the moment: "'Mr. Barnes,' answered the count, 'all I want out of wines is to enjoy them'" (66). The count attributes his ability to enjoy to the variety of his life experiences: "'You see, Mr. Barnes, it is because I have lived very much that now I can enjoy everything so well. [. . .] That is the secret. You must get to know the values.' [. . .] Food had an excellent place in the count's values. So did wine" (67–68). To his praise of food and drink, Mippipopolous adds his commendation to love. When Brett asks whether the count has ever fallen in love, he answers, "I am always in love. [. . .] That, too, has got a place in my values" (67). And it seems to Jake that the count falls in love with his experience during dinner: "The count was in fine form during the meal. So was Brett. It was a good party. [. . .] The count was beaming. He was very happy. 'You are very nice people,' he said. He was smoking a cigar again. 'Why don't you get married, you two?'" (68). With the recommendation that Brett and Jake marry, Count Mippipopolous aligns his view to the foundational elements of Qoheleth's invitation to enjoy. However, the count's Khayyám-infused Ecclesiastes option of enjoying food and wine with a loving spouse fails because the two lovers cannot consummate their love. At the end of book I, Brett and Jake find themselves in their recurring situation: desiring each other without the possibility of fulfillment.

Facing nearly constant reminders of the impossibility of a relationship with Brett, Jake attempts in book II to find meaning elsewhere: in the rituals of Catholicism, bullfighting, and the San Fermin Festival. Although he readily admits that he's not the best Catholic, Jake is drawn to cathedrals and monasteries throughout book II.[5] When he first arrives in Pamplona, he visits the local cathedral, where he prays for everyone he knows: starting with Brett, including the Ecclesiastes-inspired count, and concluding by wishing he weren't "such a rotten Catholic" (103). Brett occasionally attends mass and visits cathedrals with Jake, but in the end, at least for Brett, it seems "praying had not been much of a success" (212). Brett and Jake have more success watching the bullfights together—a passion Jake originally cultivated in his friendship with the bullfighting aficionado Montoya. And it is through Montoya that Hemingway stresses Qoheleth's call for passionate living: "Whatsoever thy hand findeth to do, do it with thy might; for there is no work, nor device, nor knowledge, nor wisdom, in the grave, whither thou goest" (9:10). Montoya teaches Jake about "aficion": "Aficion means passion. An aficionado is one who is passionate about the bull-fights. [. . .] For one who had aficion he could forgive anything" (136–37). Jake's initiation into the aficionado community depends on an "oral *spiritual* examination" (137; my emphasis), and Montoya's passion recalls Jake's earlier observation that "[n]obody ever lives their life all the way up except bull-fighters" (18). Furthermore, Jake's reflection on aficion indicts "commercial bull-fighters" (136) who lack passion and participate only for the money. His warning against putting money above experience echoes Ecclesiastes 5:10 and 5:15: "He that loveth silver shall not be satisfied with silver; [. . . he] shall take nothing of his labour, which he may carry away in his hand." With its emphasis on death's finality and the transience of earthly possessions, Ecclesiastes—like Montoya and his favorite bullfighters—advocates living "life all the way up" while the opportunity remains.

However, when Brett transfers her desire for Jake onto the passionate young bullfighter Pedro Romero, the Catholic bullfighting fiesta leads Jake not toward meaningful joy but into the unreflective house of mirth and a state of serious depression. Montoya, who epitomizes authentic passion, shuns Jake, Brett, and all of their friends for their disgraceful inability to participate reverently in the passion of bullfighting. By the end of book II, the Ecclesiastes option of living "life all the way up," presented through Montoya's definition of aficion, fails. Jake's desire for Brett and his pain at not being able to be with her thwarts this option for giving meaning to his life as well. And so, rejected by Montoya, Jake gets drunk: "Sure. Get tight," Bill encourages him, "Get over your damn depression" (227). While "drunker than [he] ever remembered having been" (227), Jake learns that Brett has left with Romero. He upgrades his intoxication level from "tight" to "blind," and when he finally gets to bed, he feels utterly alone: "Outside in the square the fiesta was going on. It did not mean anything" (227–28). Having been abandoned again by Brett and having severed his friendship with Montoya, Jake finds no meaning or joy in the fiesta.

Nonetheless, after his flurry of drunkenness and a good nap, Jake recovers fairly well. At the beginning of book III, he commits to a quiet week in San Sebastian and nearly becomes the book's Ecclesiastes-inspired character himself. Though he at first regrets not going back to Paris with Bill, Jake quickly realizes that he wouldn't benefit from any more time in the house of mirth: "Paris would have meant more fiesta-ing. I was through with fiestas for a while. It would be quiet in San Sebastian" (236). Knowing nowhere else to turn, Jake reverts to the values he can access in Ecclesiastes' philosophy: "It was pleasant to be drinking slowly and to be tasting the wine and to be drinking alone. A bottle of wine was good company" (236). He spends his time drinking slowly and enjoying the sun: "I swam out to the raft, pulled myself up, and lay on the hot planks. A boy and girl were at the other end. [. . .] I lay on the raft in the sun until I was dry" (239). After swimming, he finds a cool chair and a cold drink to watch the passersby: "I sat out on the terrace and enjoyed the fresh coolness in the hot day, and had a glass of lemon-juice and shaved ice and then a long whiskey and soda. I sat in front of the Marinas for a long time and read and watched the people" (239). And yet, even during these episodes when Jake feels happy, a hint of dissatisfaction remains. He has to experience the pleasures alone. Or worse, he has to share his otherwise satisfying experience on the raft with two people laughing and in love.

Jake can't help but think of Brett and what their life together could have been. And so, when Brett wires from Madrid, he unhesitatingly goes. He even signs his reply telegram, "LOVE JAKE" (243). Soon after arriving in Madrid and being once again disappointed by Brett's plan to renew her relationship with Mike, Jake makes a final test of Ecclesiastes' philosophy. Beginning with his suggestion, "Should we have another Martini?" (249), he eats a good meal with the woman he loves. Ultimately, though, because they can't be together, the experience isn't enough: "I drank my glass and poured out another. Brett put her hand on my arm. 'Don't get drunk, Jake,' she said. 'You don't have to'" (250). Marking the failure of book III's Ecclesiastes option, Jake responds dejectedly, "How do you know?" (250). Even the often-evoked Ecclesiastes cannot provide the war-wounded Jake Barnes with a satisfying life. Consequently, despite Brett's appeal, Jake feels his only option is to become mindlessly drunk. Brett solidifies her love for Jake once more with her final line of dialogue: "'Oh, Jake,' Brett said, 'we could have had such a damned good time together'" (251). There are, of course, good reasons to question whether the pair actually would have been happy together—not least of all Jake's ironic response, presented as the novel's final line: "Isn't it pretty to think so?" (251). Still, Hemingway couches Brett and Jake's search for meaning in terms of an Ecclesiastes-endorsed love they cannot consummate. Taking his cue from the skeptic in scripture to consider Ecclesiastes' own philosophy skeptically, Hemingway leaves readers questioning whether anyone—particularly those in a generation torn apart by World War I—can find sustainable meaning in life at all.

Despite this conclusion, Hemingway very clearly valued Ecclesiastes. He sets up his Ecclesiastes epigraph "*versus* G[ertrude] Stein" (*Selected Letters* 366; his emphasis) to stress "that all generations were lost by something and always had been and always would be" (*A Moveable Feast* 30). He considered two other Ecclesiastes quotations for the title of *The Sun Also Rises* and nine Ecclesiastes-inspired titles for his 1929 novel *A Farewell to Arms.*[6] And perhaps most significantly, in 1925, while writing *The Sun Also Rises,* Hemingway wrote Ezra Pound to ask, "How long since you've read Ecc[lesiastes]? [. . .] Don't let your just disgust with the so called Christian religion keep you from reading Ecclesiastes. The only preachers who ever use it as texts do so to show that it was all wrong and a great mistake to have been allowed to stay in the bible" (*Letters* 2:396). In terms of the Christian reception of Ecclesiastes, Hemingway was at least partially right. There are several examples of sermons and commentaries suggesting Ecclesiastes should not have been included in the Bible. In a 1901 sermon titled "The Layman's Use of the Bible," Charles Brown advocates a shorter Bible "for ordinary use," which—among other books—would not include "the shrewd, bitter, skeptical sayings in Ecclesiastes" (4). Similarly, Haupt, in 1894, insists, "There can be no stronger condemnation of the teachings of Ecclesiastes than these words of our Saviour [cf. Luke 12.15–31 in which Jesus advises, "seek ye the kingdom of God" instead of food and merriment]; and it seems to me, this ought to settle the question whether Ecclesiastes has any claims to canonical authority" (246).

More often, and with approximately the same goal, many turn-of-the-twentieth-century sermons on Ecclesiastes dilute Qoheleth's original message by seeing in him a prodigal son who eventually returns to a traditional faith. In each of his twelve sermons on Ecclesiastes collected in 1905, Herbert Alleman concludes that at the end of his quest Qoheleth abandons his claims that life is vanity and takes solace in the traditional religious formula: "The preacher, as you know, came to himself after his quests, and found peace in the old simple faith of the peasants and children of Judah, in fearing God and keeping His commandments" (115). Frederick Knecht in 1894 goes so far as to imply that he knows Qoheleth's intention better than Qoheleth himself: "These words he meant to say: 'All earthly possessions and joys are passing and cannot make a man really happy. Only the fear and love of God can bring happiness on earth and joy in eternity.' We should not therefore set our hearts on the good things of this earth, but should strive with all our hearts after those which are eternal" (261). Both readings depend on viewing the final six verses as original—in which a later editor writes, "Let us hear the conclusion of the whole matter: Fear God, and keep his commandments" (12:13)—when these verses have long been considered a pious epilogue.[7] Even some commentators who celebrate the epilogue's endorsement of traditional wisdom as an improvement acknowledge it as a later addition. McNeile, in his 1904 commentary, for example, writes, "And it may be gladly admitted that, under these successive hands, Koheleth's *Journal* has been not spoilt but enriched" (27). This exegetical strategy of elevating the final six verses over the previous twelve chapters, however, too easily dismisses the complexity of Qoheleth's hard-won philosophy for living well on earth.

Other readers accept Ecclesiastes' unorthodoxy, but see Qoheleth only as a necessary example exposing the vanity of existence for anyone who lacks hope in the afterlife. Henry Scott Holland titles a series of 1888 sermons *Christ or Ecclesiastes*, and sets up the two voices—Christ and Ecclesiastes—in opposition, concluding that much in the New Testament definitively refutes the teachings of Ecclesiastes: life on earth may be vanity, Holland claims, but there is more for which to hope in a life to come. George Barton, in his 1908 commentary, presents a nuanced understanding of Ecclesiastes, only then to reject it as insufficient and in need of replacement: "Qoheleth preaches a gospel of healthy work and the full enjoyment of life's round of duties and opportunities. Let a man fulfill these while he bravely faces the real facts of life—this is the sum of Qoheleth's teaching. It is a teaching which is to a Christian chilling and disappointing, but Qoheleth's negative work had, no doubt, a function to perform in clearing away outworn conceptions before a new, larger, truer, and more inspiring faith could have its birth" (50).

F. B. Denio, in 1892, argues similarly: "It is well that there is in the Bible a book like this for the purpose of teaching the vanity of all earthly things in themselves to meet the deep need of mankind. It is when this conviction has been attained that God's way of happiness will be sought" (102). And A. J. Grieve asserts, in 1920, "Not without the Divine Providence has this book been included in the Canon of Scripture. It shows better than any other the need for the Incarnation, it forms a most effective background for the Good News" (412). This perception of Qoheleth as a foil to Christian hopefulness may advance a certain New Testament, eschatological theology, but it clearly doesn't take the book of Ecclesiastes seriously on its own terms.

Such interpretations seem to confirm Hemingway's view, expressed in his letter to Pound, that the Church undervalues Ecclesiastes. Indeed, T. K. Cheyne's entry on Ecclesiastes in the 1901 *Encyclopaedia Biblica* recognizes "a certain desire to tone down the thoughts of the Preacher" (1155). Interpretation of Ecclesiastes has not always focused primarily on the value of Ecclesiastes itself. On the other hand, Cheyne charts the beginnings of exegetical progress: "The ancients were too timid to allow the Preacher to speak his mind. Modern interpreters recognise a strong individuality in the book, and are more ready to accept its natural meaning" (1155). One early twentieth-century commentator who celebrates Ecclesiastes for its own insights, tellingly also engages *The Rubáiyát of Omar Khayyám*. Forbush, in the introduction to his 1906 *Ecclesiastes in the Metre of Omar*, outlines not only the book's value but its necessity:

> But why does Ecclesiastes appeal to any one? It is precisely because, like the Rubáiyát, it speaks to men in their questionings. Neither book has any message to the piously omniscient. The deeper one goes into life, the harder he finds it to be patient with ready-made faith. John Morley has spoken of the detestableness of "the complacent religiosity of the prosperous." Thoreau once remarked, "Our sadness is not sad, but our cheap joys." It is of infinite comfort to youth to know that even in the Bible there is a book written by a man who was freely permitted to think. (11)

Most attractive about Wharton's and Hemingway's readings of Ecclesiastes is this kind of emphasis on the book's own value. If the modern period inaugurated a shift in the interpretative focus regarding Ecclesiastes, these novelists played an important role in that shift.

Wharton and Hemingway join the reception history of Ecclesiastes to advance interpretations that value Qoheleth's own recommendations for living in the world. Rather than dismissing it or even balancing the book with other voices, these authors reveal the contemporary urgency of the book of Ecclesiastes, a book that advocates joy in the present moment, elevates lived experience over abstract theology, and resonates with the modernist impulse. Titling their novels after Ecclesiastes reflects the contemporary popularity of the biblical book, while at the same time—through the popularity of their own novels—bringing an additional degree of attention to Ecclesiastes. The religious questions raised in both novels are not, in opposition to some contemporary sermons and commentaries, about whether Ecclesiastes belongs in the Bible or how to square its skepticism with mainline biblical theology. Instead, Wharton and Hemingway present Ecclesiastes as a model for living a life of flourishing and as a catalyst to critique the failings of contemporary society. *The House of Mirth* embraces Qoheleth's warning against a transactional mentality that willingly sacrifices authentic joy in the moment for an unsatisfying future of financial success and social status. *The Sun Also Rises* follows Qoheleth's endorsement of passionate living in the face of death, while exposing destructive world circumstances that too often interfere with human happiness. Ultimately, both novels evoke Ecclesiastes to ask readers to reflect on how social systems and political conflicts have kept some people from accessing a thoughtful carpe-diem philosophy. In a literary period frequently considered antithetical to religion, Wharton and Hemingway not only participated in religious conversations surrounding Ecclesiastes, but also pushed the prevailing view of Ecclesiastes in bold directions: challenging safe, comfortable interpretations of the book, acknowledging its skepticism and unorthodoxy, and embracing its call for reflective joy. As Paul Fiddes has claimed of modern poets, Wharton and Hemingway, in their Ecclesiastes-inspired novels, "seem to have been better exegetes of biblical [. . .] texts than the theologians" (41).

NOTES

1. See also Eric Christianson's essay on Voltaire's 1759 *Precis de l'Ecclesiaste* and Herbert Alleman's 1905 *The Gist of the Sermon*: "It was a manual of that coarse scoffer, Frederick the Great, while Volney and Voltaire appealed to it in support of their philosophy" (30).

2. The Hebrew תלהק is pronounced Ko-hell-et and variously spelled "Qohelet," "Koheleth," "Coheleth," and "Qoheleth." While the King James Bible—which had effectively no mainstream competitors until the 1952 Revised Standard Version of the Old Testament—translates תלהק as "Preacher," I follow most biblical scholars in preferring "Qoheleth," especially because Ecclesiastes' speaker is a complex literary character generally less interested in preaching than in philosophizing.

3. A 1915 letter from Mugnier reads, "Had lunch at Mrs. Wharton's with the Abbé Bremond" (Foata 398), and Lewis notes, "EW had known [Mugnier] since 1908" (Wharton, *Letters* 313). In a 1927 letter, Wharton promises John Hugh Smith that she will "try to find out from the Abbé Bremond where the supposed book on the Dissolution of the Jesuits can be found" (*Letters* 502). On Bremond's relationship to modernism, see Darrell Jodock's *Catholicism Contending with Modernity*, especially page 23.

4. Forbush's title *Ecclesiastes in the Metre of Omar: With an Introduction Essay on Ecclesiastes and The Rubáiyát* clearly illustrates his intention to translate Ecclesiastes in verse resembling *The Rubáiyát;* Burkitt foregrounds his intention in his introductory remarks: "I have ventured on a version in the metre and style of FitzGerald's rendering of Omar Khayyam's Quatrains" (v).

5. See Jake's arrival with Bill in Burguete: "away off on the shoulder of the first dark mountain was the gray metal-sheathed roof of the monastery of Roncesvalles" (114); an afternoon with Bill and their friend Harris in the monastery: "Harris was there and the three of us walked up to Roncesvalles. We went through the monastery" (133); philosophizing with Bill after fishing: "'Listen Jake,' he said, 'are you really a Catholic?' 'Technically'" (128–29); during multiple walks with Brett in Pamplona, specifically before she asks him about Romero: "Behind were the trees and the shadow of the cathedral, and the town silhouetted against the moon" (186); and in a conversation with Brett, in which Jake acknowledges, "I'm pretty religious" (213).

6. Matthew Nickel reveals that, on a "trip to Chartres in September 1925, [Hemingway] wrote out several title choices, [including] *Rivers to the Sea* [from Ecclesiastes 1:7, and] *Two Lie Together* [4:11]" (63). Paul Smith notes that of forty-three titles Hemingway considered for *A Farewell to Arms*, nine are either direct quotations or paraphrases of Ecclesiastes: "'Thing that Has Been' (1:9), 'Knowledge Increaseth Sorrow' (1:18), 'The Peculiar Treasure' (2:8), 'One Event Happeneth to them All' (2:14), 'One Thing for them All' (3:19), 'Nothing Better for a Man' (2:24), 'A Time of War' (3:8), 'One Thing is Certain' (cf. 2:14, 3:19), and 'The Long Home' (12:5)" (75).

7. G. Currie Martin, in 1908, writes, "Every reader feels that the closing section is dif-

ferent in tone from all that precedes it. Particularly is this true of xii, 13, 14. The moral is forced, and it certainly does not appear to be a clear inference from all that has preceded it to say that the conclusion of the argument is 'fear God and keep His commandments, for this is the whole duty of man.' Much more appropriate would be the eighth verse, 'Vanity of vanities,' saith Koheleth, 'all is vanity.' [. . .] The majority of students consequently consider this closing paragraph to be by a different hand from that which composed the bulk of the book" (215–16).

WORKS CITED

Alleman, Herbert C. *The Gist of the Sermon: An Old Message for Young Men.* Philadelphia: Lutheran Publication Society, 1905. Print.

Barton, George Aaron. *A Critical and Exegetical Commentary on the Book of Ecclesiastes.* New York: Scribner's, 1908. Print.

The Bible: Authorized King James Version with Apocrypha. Ed. Robert Carroll and Stephen Prickett. New York: Oxford UP, 2008. Print.

Brown, Charles Reynolds. *Sermons, 1900–1902.* Oakland, CA: Baker Printing Co., 1902. Print.

Brown, William P. *Ecclesiastes: An Interpretation Bible Commentary for Teaching and Preaching.* Louisville, KY: John Knox P, 2000. Print.

Burkitt, F. Crawford. *Ecclesiastes Rendered into English Verse.* London: Christian Knowledge, 1922. Print.

Cheyne, T. K., and J. Sutherland Black, eds. *Encyclopaedia Biblica: A Critical Dictionary of the Literary, Political and Religious History, the Archaeology, Geography, and Natural History of the Bible.* Vol. 2. New York: Macmillan, 1901. Print.

Christianson, Eric S. "Voltaire's Précis of Ecclesiastes: A Case Study in the Bible's Afterlife." *Journal for the Study of the Old Testament* 29.4 (2005): 455–84. Print.

Cox, Samuel. *The Book of Ecclesiastes: With a New Translation.* New York: Armstrong, 1903. Print.

Denio, F. B. "The Book of Ecclesiastes." *The Old and New Testament Student* 14.2 (1892): 98–104. Print.

Fiddes, Paul S. "Versions of the Wasteland: The Sense of an Ending in Theology and Literature in the Modern Period." *Modernism, Christianity and Apocalypse.* Ed. Erik Tonning, Matthew Feldman, and David Addyman. Leiden: Brill, 2015. 27–52. Print.

Foata, Anne. "Edith Wharton and the Faubourg Saint-Germain: The Diary of the Abbé Mugnier." *Twentieth Century Literature* 43.4 (1997): 394–405. Print.

Forbush, William Byron. *Ecclesiastes in the Metre of Omar.* Boston: Houghton, 1906. Print.

Gardner, Percy. "M. Alfred Loisy's Type of Catholicism." *Hibbert Journal* 3.1 (1905): 126–38. Print.

Genung, John Franklin. *Ecclesiastes and Omar Khayyám: A Note for the Spiritual Temper of Our Time.* New York: Crowell, 1901. Print.

———. *Ecclesiastes: Words of Koheleth, Son of David, King in Jerusalem.* Boston: Houghton Mifflin, 1904. Print.

Grieve, A. J. "Ecclesiastes." *Arthur Peake's Commentary on the Bible.* New York: Thomas Nelson, 1920. 411–17. Print.

Griffin, Peter. *Along with Youth: Hemingway, the Early Years.* Oxford: Oxford UP, 1987. Print.

Grimes, Larry E. *The Religious Design of Hemingway's Early Fiction.* Ann Arbor, MI: UMI Research, 1985. Print.

Haupt, Paul. "The Book of Ecclesiastes." *A Selection of Papers Read Before the Oriental Club of Philadelphia, 1888–1894.* Boston: Ginn, 1894. 242–78. Print.

Hemingway, Ernest. *Ernest Hemingway: Selected Letters, 1917–1961.* Ed. Carlos Baker. New York: Scribner's, 1981. Print.

———. *The Letters of Ernest Hemingway.* Vol. 2: *1923–1925.* Ed. Sandra Spanier, Albert J. DeFazio III, and Robert W. Trogdon. Cambridge: Cambridge UP, 2013. Print.

———. *A Moveable Feast.* New York: Scribner's, 1964. Print.

———. *The Sun Also Rises.* 1926. New York: Scribner's, 1954. Print.

Holland, Henry Scott. *Christ or Ecclesiastes: Sermons Preached in St. Paul's Cathedral.* London: Rivingtons, 1888. Print.

Jastrow, Morris, Jr. *A Gentle Cynic: Being a Translation of the Book of Koheleth, Commonly Known as Ecclesiastes . . .* Philadelphia: Lippincott, 1919. Print.

Jodock, Darrell, ed. *Catholicism Contending with Modernity: Roman Catholic Modernism and Anti-Modernism in Historical Context.* Cambridge: Cambridge UP, 2011. Print.

Khayyám, Omar. *The Rubáiyát of Omar Khayyám.* Ca. 1100. Trans. Edward FitzGerald, 1859. Garden City, NY: Garden City, 1937. Print.

Knecht, Frederick Justus. *A Practical Commentary on Holy Scripture for the Use of Those Who Teach Bible History.* 1894. Trans. Michael Glancey. 3rd English ed. London: Herder, 1910. Print.

Lee, Hermione. *Edith Wharton.* New York: Knopf, 2007. Print.

Loisy, Alfred. *Simple Reflections on the Decree of the Holy Office.* Ceffonds, France: Self-published, 1908. Print.

Martin, G. Currie. *The Century Bible: Proverbs, Ecclesiastes, and Song of Songs*. Edinburgh: Jack, 1908. Print.

McNeile, Alan Hugh. *An Introduction to Ecclesiastes with Notes and Appendices*. Cambridge: Cambridge UP, 1904. Print.

Nickel, Matthew C. *Hemingway's Dark Night: Catholic Influences and Intertextualities in the Work of Ernest Hemingway*. Wickford, RI: New Street, 2013. Print.

Otto, Rothfeld. *Umar Khayyam and His Age*. Bombay: Taraporevala, 1922. Print.

Plumptre, E. H. *Ecclesiastes; or, The Preacher*. Cambridge: Cambridge UP, 1898. Print.

Pustienne, Jean-Pierre. *Ernest Hemingway*. Paris: Fitway, 2005.

Singley, Carol J. *Edith Wharton: Matters of Mind and Spirit*. Cambridge: Cambridge UP, 1995. Print.

Smith, Paul. "Almost All Is Vanity: A Note on Nine Rejected Titles for *A Farewell To Arms*." *Hemingway Review* 2.1 (1982): 74–6. Print.

Sparks, George Downing. "The Hebrew '*Rubáiyát*.'" *Sewanee Review* 8.4 (1900): 415–24. Print.

Stoneback, H. R. "In the Nominal Country of the Bogus: Hemingway's Catholicism and the Biographies." *Hemingway: Essays of Reassessment*. Ed. Frank Scafella. New York: Oxford UP, 1991. 105–40. Print.

Tyrrell, George. *Christianity at the Crossroads*. London: Longmans, 1910. Print.

———. *George Tyrrell's Letters*. Ed. Maude D. Petre. London: Unwin, 1920. Print.

Wharton, Edith. *A Backward Glance*. New York: D. Appleton-Century, 1934. Print.

———. *The House of Mirth*. 1905. New York: Penguin, 1985. Print.

———. *The Letters of Edith Wharton*. Ed. R. W. B. Lewis and Nancy Lewis. New York: Scribner's, 1988. Print.

Modernism Delayed, Not Denied

Wharton, Hemingway, and Scribner's Magazine

CAROLINE CHAMBERLIN HELLMAN

Founded in 1846, Charles Scribner's Sons was a tastemaker and storied publishing house that disseminated the work of authors such as Henry James, Teddy Roosevelt, and Robert Louis Stevenson to a well-heeled readership. Similarly, *Scribner's Magazine*, published monthly by Scribner's from January 1887 to May 1939, was an elegant periodical.[1] Edith Wharton and Ernest Hemingway were two of Scribner's most-celebrated and highly remunerated authors. Wharton's and Hemingway's respective relationships and literary successes with the publishing house bracketed the beginning and end of its magazine's reign and were especially lucrative in part because of the serialization of novels in *Scribner's Magazine*. The authors' arrivals at and departures from the publishing house are well documented; after almost thirty years, Wharton reluctantly left Scribner for D. Appleton & Company, commanding a higher price for her work from the latter, whereas Hemingway arrived at Charles Scribner's Sons after leaving Boni & Liveright on the advice of his friend F. Scott Fitzgerald. Publishing with Scribner's offered Wharton and Hemingway a dignified venue and opportunities to work with renowned editors. Wharton enjoyed longstanding relationships with the House of Scribner, editor-in-chief and literary advisor William Crary Brownell, and magazine editor Edward Burlingame. Subsequently, Hemingway worked closely with editor Maxwell Perkins and magazine editors Alfred Dashiell and Robert Bridges. The Scribner's editors in turn deferred to Charles Scribner II, whose tastes guided the firm for many years.

While scholars have treated the politics between these authors and the publishing house, less has been written about reading the work of the writers in the context of particular magazine issues. One decade, the 1920s, found both Wharton and Hemingway publishing in *Scribner's Magazine* and treating the same subject, World War I. Wharton's novel *A Son at the Front* was serialized in *Scribner's Magazine* from 1922 to 1923, and Hemingway's novel *A Farewell to Arms* in 1929. The respective serial histories reveal how Wharton fought an uphill battle to publish a somewhat didactic polemic, whereas Hemingway benefited from a phalanx of editors and publishers defending his fictionalization of the war. Reading these works in their original contexts illustrates shifts in both readership and literary culture, in addition to the evolving role that *Scribner's* played, first as a protector of cultural conservatism and later as a purveyor of modernism.

WHARTON AND THE MAGAZINE

When the first installment of *A Son at the Front* appeared in the December 1922 issue of *Scribner's Magazine*, it was two decades after Wharton's first novel, *The Touchstone*, had appeared in a two-part serial in 1900. Other significant fiction by Wharton serialized in the magazine included *The House of Mirth* (January–November 1905), *The Fruit of the Tree* (January–November 1907), *Ethan Frome* (August, September, and October 1911), and *The Custom of the Country* (January–November 1915). During World War I, the author dealt with the financial pressures of maintaining two residences, fundraising for her war charities, and traveling. As a result, she became more prolific than what *Scribner's* could publish in the pages of its magazine. Departing from *Scribner's* meant attaining higher prices for her work in both serial and novel form, but there were also disadvantages. After the publication of *Summer* (1917), she wrote William Crary Brownell at Scribner's:

> I believe I forgot to have a copy of "Summer" sent for [you]—or rather what I really forgot was, that it was not published by Scribner! I never can get used to any other origin, and always sit down and weep under the willow tree when I remember Jerusalem. I don't know why Mr. Scribner didn't want "Summer," but I'm glad he does want the article on "The French" that I'm doing now, for I can't

> imagine where else, in the vast "fatras" of American magazinery, it would find even one comprehending reader.[2] (qtd. in Bell 309)

Here the author indicates her clear discomfort and chagrin with the change in her relationship with Scribner's, perceived as a standard. What Wharton did not know was that at the same time her expenses had increased, *Scribner's* profits had decreased. In 1912, the author published her novel *The Reef* (sans serialization) with D. Appleton & Company, at a time when *Scribner's Magazine* was losing subscribers and advertisers. While Charles Scribner attempted to hold onto the author, he had to admit that the magazine could no longer offer her the same prices for her work (Bell 310). As a result, Wharton branched out to other periodicals that offered her greater sums, including *McClure's Magazine*, which serialized *Summer* (1917); *The Pictorial Review*, which serialized *The Age of Innocence* (1920), *The Glimpses of the Moon* (1922), *The Mother's Recompense* (1925), *Twilight Sleep* (1927), and *The Children* (1928); *Delineator*, which serialized *Hudson River Bracketed* (1929) and *The Gods Arrive* (1932); and *Ladies' Home Journal*, which serialized her autobiography *A Backward Glance*.[3] While the women's magazines paid Wharton handsomely for her work and boasted broad circulation numbers, material running alongside Wharton's work was typically lowbrow, focused on figure enhancement and physical appearance (not unlike contemporary women's magazines). In contrast, *Scribner's Magazine* was a venerable institution whose journal reached educated, affluent subscribers interested in, judging from the advertisements, antique silver, transatlantic crossings, elite preparatory schools, and Fifth Avenue art exhibitions.

A Son at the Front was not Wharton's only foray into writing about the war and its discontents. In 1915, she reported from the front for *Scribner's* in a series of articles that would become *Fighting France: From Dunkerque to Belfort* (1915). Her testaments described ruined civic and religious structures, exhausted and traumatized refugees, and a civilization torn asunder. She also conceived of and edited *The Book of the Homeless* (1916), which featured contributions from writers, musicians, and artists, and raised $15,000 for the hostel rescue organizations. She intended for the war reportage and high-profile fundraising efforts to compel public sentiment toward the United States' entry into the war; when this failed to transpire, in 1918, the frustrated author turned to fiction to offer a different kind of window into the war.

Set in Paris, *A Son at the Front* chronicles life for expatriate Americans and their circle during the First World War. The novel begins on 30 July 1914, mere days before the declaration of war. John Campton, an American portrait painter, thinks only of his son George's impending visit and fantasizes about their travels together. Immediately after arriving, however, George must report for military duty, as he was born in France. Though his parents and stepfather wield their influence to protect George from battle, Wharton makes it clear that George's sympathies lie with the infantry rather than the privilege of his background. Ultimately, he is injured twice at the front, the second injury proving fatal. At the onset of the war, John Campton espouses isolationist politics and resents his son's conscription in addition to the effect of war on his career as a portrait painter. He evolves to admire his son's courage, decry America's neutrality, and volunteer his service as an artist to aid charitable organizations. The war provokes a variety of responses from both French and Americans within Campton's circle. His ex-wife, Julia Brant, has only a superficial understanding of the conflict, while her husband, Anderson Brant, is an honorable man who wishes to help his stepson; Campton's friends Adele Anthony and Boylston devote their entire existences to war charity work; his cousin Harvey Mayhew, a delegate to a Peace Council, and his associates manipulate charity operations in order to serve their own social agendas; and his servant, Madame Lebel, loses all her sons to the war, in addition to a grandchild, and is likely the novel's most sympathetic character. Instead of following George to the front and immersing readers in battle and destruction, Wharton chooses to chronicle the effect of war on those left behind, waiting for the latest communiqué from the front. George himself is allotted relatively little dialogue; he is more a symbol than a man. The story is told in third person and focuses on John Campton's inner thoughts.

While *A Son at the Front* is not considered a modernist work, it contains modernist themes: the disillusionment with war, the fragmenting of time and space, the relationship of art to war, the breakdown of traditional hierarchies of value. As Jennifer Haytock contends, "In *A Son at the Front*, Wharton engages in modernist conversations about the isolation and alienation of the self, the trauma of war, and the nature of civilization, and she does so using an ironic narrative voice that leaves the reader questioning perceptions and authority" (129). Like other modernists, including Hemingway almost a decade later, Wharton was aware that language came up short in chronicling war's effect on humanity. She embraces this notion more as the narrative progresses.

The first installment begins with an emphasis on time and place: "John Campton, the American portrait-painter, stood in his bare studio in Montmartre at the end of a summer afternoon contemplating a battered calendar that hung against the wall. The calendar marked July 30, 1914" ("A Son at the Front" 643). At the beginning of Book 2 (February 1923), Wharton begins to experiment with language and time. "The war was three months old—three centuries. By virtue of some gift of adaptation which seemed forever to discredit human sensibility, people were already beginning to live into the monstrous idea of it, acquire its ways, speak its language, regard it as a thinkable, endurable, manageable fact; to eat it by day, and sleep on it—yes, and soundly—at night" (149). This experimentation continues in the April 1923 installment. Julia Brant and John Campton repeat the indefinite, somewhat abstract phrases "a son in the war" and "a son at the front" throughout the story. Wharton employs frequent dashes and ellipses to disrupt language, as when Julia tells a fortune teller, "We're his parents—a son at the front . . ." (400). But it is John Campton's return to art that causes the most explicit modernist turn. "For a month Campton painted on in transcendent bliss. The first stroke carried him out of space and time, into a region where all that had become numbed and atrophied in him could expand and breathe. Lines, images, colours were again the sole facts" (394). While Campton is a realist painter, Wharton highlights his modernist approach.

Rutger Jewett, Wharton's editor at Appleton who also functioned as her literary agent for more than a decade, counseled her against publishing the material when she submitted it to him for serialization in 1919. "War Books Dead in America," he wired her in response (qtd. in Lee 458). Jewett advocated for Wharton with magazine editors from the popular market, who often requested happy endings and less taboo (modern) subject matter such as divorce and adultery, both of which are present in *A Son at the Front*. As Shari Benstock notes, "She adamantly refused to temper her social criticism, to turn away from the depressing, often grim, subjects of her fiction, or to alter the narrative structure of her stories to accommodate the magazine trade. In holding firm to the line of artistic integrity, she knew she risked turning away the very readership she wanted to educate as well as losing the monies on which she had become increasingly dependent" ("The Word" 154).

Serialization connoted different things for different texts and authors. Wharton wrote *The House of Mirth* and *The Custom of the Country* on a serialization schedule, crediting then-*Scribner's* editor Edward Burlingame for spurring her transition from a "drifting amateur, into a professional" able to write with discipline for a deadline (qtd. in Benstock, "Introduction" 149). Both novels were enormously successful, in part due to Wharton's shrewd marketing via serialization. *A Son at the Front* was not executed in the same way, as it took several years for Wharton to finish the manuscript, by which time the war was not a popular subject. As a result, it is likely that there was little attention paid to installment divisions. The first installment from December 1922 concludes with a scene that foreshadows George Campton's death in a hospital bed, his father looking on.[4] Campton gazes at his son sleeping and thinks, "Like a statue of a young knight I've seen somewhere," then realizes that "what he had really thought was: Like the *effigy* of a young knight" (659; Wharton's emphasis). Because George Campton is at the front for the majority of the story, many other installments end with John Campton conversing with others about the ongoing nature of the war, or attempting to visualize his son unharmed. After George is injured the first time and recuperates in Paris, he participates in several discussions about the politics of the war, albeit with banal dialogue and little passion. For example, the June 1923 installment concludes with George's comment to his father, "Old Adele's coming presently. Do you suppose we could rake up some fresh tea?" (700). Only the penultimate August installment ends on a note of suspense, with concurrent news of George's critical injury and America's entry into the war.

Considered alongside the material rounding out the rest of *Scribner's* 1922–23 issues, Wharton's text, despite being published several years after the conclusion of the war, seems ahead of its time. Absent *A Son at the Front*, the majority of the magazine contents harkened back not only to the prewar era but often to the nineteenth century. Though 1922 is often heralded as the most significant year in modernist literature, given the publications of Joyce's *Ulysses* and T. S. Eliot's *The Waste Land*, the December 1922 *Scribner's* issue, in which *A Son at the Front* first appeared, demonstrates the magazine's entrenchment in the academy, from its recommendations for art exhibits at the National Arts Club, to inclusions of sentimental children's Christmas poems, to a heartwarming story by Edward Bok, "What Else Did Father Do?" exploring civic and financial responsibility.[5] The cover itself advertises Wharton's novel in the style of an illuminated medieval manuscript, invoking the high culture of antiquity.[6]

By the second installment, in January 1923, war had arrived. *Scribner's* included illustrations by Frances Rogers depicting "before" and "after" the mobilization. The former, on the first page (19) of the text, portrays Campton and his son George enjoying a leisurely breakfast, taking pains not to acknowledge what they both feel to be imminent, George's departure for duty. *Scribner's* dedicated the frontispiece illustration to the notice of mobilization, showing John Campton (looking, incidentally, like James Joyce) huddled with other Parisians of various backgrounds and occupations in front of a war-mobilization sign (2).

Several texts anchor the January 1923 issue in the past, at a safe remove from the uncertainty of the modern era. Adjacent to Wharton's piece is Perry Barlow's "Sketches from an Old French Town," depicting Avignon. The artist recounts a Frenchman's observation that the people of Avignon "were terribly provincial, and behind the times" (36). The latter part of this description pertains to the magazine issue in its entirety, as it seems firmly rooted in the prewar years. The illustrations of idyllic Avignon, with quaint shops and cafés, a market square, peasants in donkey carts, and citizens riding bicycles with baskets filled with baguettes (42) speak to a bygone era untouched by either industrialization or trench warfare. The sole modern attraction in the portrayal of the former papal capital is a poster for a Charlie Chaplin film. The artist observes that Chaplin "is the most popular attraction, and, though his films are usually two or three years old, 'ce ne fait rien,' to the numerous and enthusiastic 'Charlot' fans" (43). Preservation of culture prior to the war extended to tributes to Robert Louis Stevenson and Thomas Nelson Page, authors associated with the late nineteenth century. Though Page's career extended into the twentieth century, and he actually wrote *Italy in the World War* (1920), the biography focused extensively on the Reconstruction years and his work in dialect short stories.

However, the modern era was not entirely struck from historical record. The March 1923 issue included Amy Lowell's poem "Fact" (305), concerning tired poetic imagery. "Young paper birches, with their lustred stems / Brightening old woods. . . . But similes like these / are stock in trade with all poets. If you please, / Therefore, we'll put aside such brummagems" (lines 7–10). With the dismissal of birches, Lowell seems to take a swipe at Robert Frost, but more importantly, seems to push for new language, a modernist tenet. In addition, in the same issue, adjacent to "A Son in the Front" are sketches of Chicago by Frederick Polley, prominently featuring the engineering triumphs of various drawbridges on the Chicago River, in addition to the city's skyscrapers (283). Though the first skyscrapers dated to the 1880s, the Chicago School evolved at the turn of the century, in tandem with European modernism. Just a few pages before, Wharton wrote about Boylston, Campton, and Dastrey walking in a city flung back into the past. "The three went out into the winter blackness. They were all used by this time to the new Paris: to extinguished lamps, shuttered windows, empty streets, the almost total cessation of wheeled traffic" (269). The inclusion of Chicago's modernist architecture has the effect of rendering antiquated and outdated Wharton's defense of a crumbling civilization in France, the war a distant memory.

In the May 1923 issue, Wharton shared billing with Mrs. Schuyler Van Rensselaer (née Mariana Griswold), an art, architecture, and landscape critic from Wharton's social set. Like Wharton, Mariana Griswold hailed from Old New York. Her piece, titled "Painters' Architecture," concerns architectural perspective in sixteenth-century Flemish and Italian painting. The issue also included a poem by Evelyn Lawson, "John Constable Goes Sketching," about the nineteenth-century landscape painter; published letters of Victorian novelist and poet George Meredith; and a profile of the "German Shepherd-Dog." Considered together, these features render the magazine apolitical, as well as outside of time and place. The following month's issue was entrenched in nostalgia, featuring James L. Ford's "New York of the Seventies." He yearns for the New York of memory, when "this overgrown metropolis shrinks to its former size; the automobiles disappear; the noise of the elevated roads ceases, the vast swarms of aliens melt away, leaving the native-born once more in evidence" (748). He concludes on a note of anti-immigrant sentiment all too familiar in today's political landscape. In each issue, Wharton's discussion of war seems almost anachronistic—far more modern than the vast majority of other subject matter. If she devoted attention to the texts surrounding *A Son at the Front*, the author must have been puzzled about the noticeable lack of response to the war. In a letter to her friend Bernard Berenson, she wrote, "Before the war you could write fiction without indicating the period, the present being assumed. The war has put an end to that for a long time, and everything will soon have to be timed with reference to it. In other words, the historical novel, with all its vices, will be the only possible form for fiction" (qtd. in Lewis 423–34). This sentiment reveals the author's distance from the interests of the reading public.

Ultimately, Wharton returned to her first publisher. But the New York society that Wharton explored so incisively in her lauded best seller *The House of Mirth* did not age well in *A Son at the Front*. Many of the expatriate wealthy Americans from Utica, New York, are initially uninvolved and indifferent to the war effort, and later involved under false or fraudulent, self-serving pretenses. At the conclusion of *A Son at the Front*, these characters grow tired of the war and resume moneyed frivolity. It was perhaps unsurprising that Jewett did not want to publish the novel, not only because readers had grown weary of the war but also because Wharton indicted such indifference. The United States declares war on Germany on 6 April 1917, the same day that the protagonist's son, George Campton, lies in a hospital dying from an injury. The author's frustration with her native country's procrastination extended to her relationship with the House of Scribner. In 1919, she wrote Charles Scribner about the difficulty of returning to writing, now that the war had changed her. "I should feel ashamed of these hesitations if I did not find that all novelists I know are much in the same predicament. . . . [A]t present, between the objection of the public to the so-called war-stories and the difficulty of the author to send his imagination backward, the situation is a bewildering one" (qtd. in Bell 312).[7]

Despite Wharton's knowledge of the front, on which she reported extensively, she chose to focus her narrative on the "rear," those who were left behind when the youth of France deployed. Shari Benstock offers useful insight into the author's decision, arguing: "The most fundamental change in our collective experience of war, however, is a truth long repressed in western culture: war—and its cultural products (literature, film, music, painting, and sculpture)—was never the sole province of men. Edith Wharton understood this truth, and in *A Son at the Front* she pictures for us the 'other side' of World War I—the 'world at the rear,' a world composed of women, children, the aged, infirm, ill, and homeless" ("Introduction" xv).

As a result of this focus, it is likely, on gender, her novel did not receive the dramatic billing that Hemingway's work would almost a decade later. The July contributor biography noted, "Those who have followed her absorbing account of a group of Americans in Paris during the war will realize that her skill lends itself admirably to a most difficult task—the portrayal of a father's emotions. . . . Mrs. Wharton sees and interprets her group of characters, with the convincing reality only possible to a writer who was in Paris at the time" (5). The reader notices that *Scribner's* pays considerable attention to sentiment and interior psychology here, rather than larger social issues Wharton confronts in the text. Rather than being characterized as a writer intimately aware of the darkness of the war, as a reporter from the front and as an administrator of numerous war charities, she is simply described as "a writer who was in Paris at the time."

HEMINGWAY AND THE MAGAZINE

When Fitzgerald and Hemingway arrived at Scribner's, it was not known for publishing many contemporary writers. As A. Scott Berg characterizes it, "The Scribner list was a backwater of literary tastes and values. . . . Indeed, most of Scribners' important books were by writers they had been publishing for years, whose manuscripts required no editing" (11). Max Perkins made it a priority to recruit newer, younger writers; his 1920s work with Fitzgerald, Hemingway, and Wolfe, among others, signaled a sea change at the institution. As Matthew Bruccoli writes, "There are no brand names in publishing; but a Scribners writer was something special in American literature during the Perkins decades" (xiii).

By the time *Scribner's* serialized *A Farewell to Arms* in 1929, there were other accounts of World War I, as well as the acknowledgment of and engagement with modernism in other disciplines. Because of Perkins's advocacy with Charles Scribner, the magazine itself had become more modern, too.[8] As Hemingway expanded upon the short story that would become *A Farewell to Arms*, *Scribner's* underwent a format revision. While the magazine cover in December 1922 projected nostalgia for an earlier time, the May 1929 *Scribner's* featured a very different image on its cover, designed by Rockwell Kent.[9]

Other articles in the May 1929 issue testify to scientific and industrial advances. In other words, by the time *A Farewell to Arms* appeared, *Scribner's*, with magazine sales in mind, had relinquished some of its traditional bent. Part of this effort involved pursuing popular authors like Hemingway, who could reach disparate audiences.[10] As Hemingway had explained to Horace Liveright regarding the publication of *In Our Time*, "My book will be praised by highbrows and can be read by lowbrows. There is no writing in it that anybody with a high school education cannot read" (qtd. in Trogdon 1). Perkins alluded to a similar audience breadth for *A Farewell to Arms* in a letter to Charles Scribner II that extolled the virtues of the novel: "Its quality is that of 'The Sun,' though its range is much larger and its implications consequently more numerous and widely scattered" (qtd. in Trogdon 68).

The experience of reading *A Farewell to Arms* in the magazine is quite different from reading the work in novel form. Because Wharton trained her lens on the civilian war effort, largely static and interior, installments ended with rather staid action, such as conversation over tea. In contrast, Hemingway captured the action of the Front, arguably more compelling to readers. As Robert W. Trogdon notes in his astute work *The Lousy Racket: Hemingway, Scribner's, and the Business of Literature* (2007), Hemingway wrote the novel without installments in mind. Though *Hearst's Magazine* proposed acquiring the serial rights for $10,000, and the movie rights for $15,000, Hemingway noted, "I do not want to take an advance which might even unconsciously affect the writing of a novel because of the necessity of submitting it for serialization" (qtd. 61).

The first installment, in May 1929, ended with Frederic Henry's injury and his ambulance ride with a soldier's blood dripping down on him. June 1929 concluded with Catherine's submissive reminder to Henry, subsequent to consummation: "You see? I'm good. I do what you want" (106). July ended with Henry's return to war, sleeping on the floor of a crowded train. The August issue concluded with Henry's vehicle immovable in the mud, and little cover for Henry, Bonello, Piani, and Aymo as they navigate the incongruous landscape of an apple orchard and the Italian sergeant lying in the road. "We walked along together all going fast against time," are the last words of the installment (208). The penultimate, September, issue concluded with Henry and Catherine's escape to Switzerland, "going with the wind" (269). The reader lies in a stretcher alongside Henry in the ambulance; traverses the Italian countryside, altered by war; submerses herself in a river to escape gunfire; and rows across a lake to Switzerland under cover of darkness. As Hemingway did not direct *Scribner's* regarding where to begin and end installments, credit is due to Perkins's editorial skill.

Just as Rutger Jewett had advocated for Wharton, Perkins advocated for Hemingway. It is clear from Perkins's correspondence that he served as a mediator between the more decorous tastemakers at *Scribner's* and an author who balked at the bowdlerization of his book. Several words (*balls, cocksucker, shit, Jesus Christ, son of a bitch, whore, whorehound,* and *fuck*) and a few lines of dialogue were ultimately omitted from the serialization (Reynolds 72).[11] Hemingway responded in a letter, "My point is that the operation of emasculation is a tiny one—It is very simple and easy to perform on men—animals and books—It is not a Major operation but its effects are great—It is *never* performed *intentionally* on books—What we must both watch is that it should not be performed unintentionally—" (qtd. in Trogdon 69).

Though Perkins opposed compromising Hemingway's artistic vision, his advocacy could only go so far. Sending the galleys for the first installment, Robert Bridges wrote, "You will note that in accordance with your talk with Perkins, we have in several places put in dashes instead of the realistic phrases the soldiers of course use. This is not done from any particular squeamishness. . . . In these things we have to consider a constituency that has followed the Magazine for a great many years" (qtd. in Trogdon 70). Bridges also noted that the magazine was often taught in schools. As usual, Perkins the diplomat attempted to mollify the author and convince him that the edits were in his best interest and would achieve a greater audience for his work. Perkins noted that they did not want to dissuade readers from the work because of "words and passages which have on account of conventions, an astonishingly exaggerated importance to them . . . If you know a few of the genteel!" (qtd. in Trogdon 71). As Trogdon writes, "Against the conservatism of the magazine and its editors, Perkins contrasted his commitment to the artist and his art" (72). The editor sought to reassure the author that the excisions were minor and, moreover, that the book would not encounter the same restrictions. In actuality, however, Bridges made cuts and revisions to the second controversial installment, in June, without Hemingway's permission, and editorial tensions continued with preparation of the book for publication.[12]

In the first installment of the novel, in May 1929, Scribner's went to considerable lengths to advertise Hemingway's work.

> A new novel by Ernest Hemingway is an event. *The Sun Also Rises* was an amazing performance, and naturally every one is wanting to know what his second novel will be like. It is gratifying to the editors that we are able to present *A Farewell to Arms* in Scribner's. Proclaimed with enthusiasm by the critics of both England and America, his first novel was objected to by some on the curious theory that because he wrote of vice and dissipation he thereby registered approval. Others declared the book to be frivolous. In that respect *A Farewell to Arms* will certainly satisfy them: no novel could have a more serious or significant motif . . . nor a treatment more profoundly sincere. (43)

Yet because Scribner imagined readers' objections to *The Sun Also Rises* being applied to *A Farewell to Arms*, the company was careful to issue a disclaimer. "The method and material of *A Farewell to Arms* will quite possibly awaken criticism on the part of certain readers. But those who read more than words will see the underlying meaning, will understand that, as a whole, it is an expression of beauty" (43). In addition, Hemingway clarified with his signature humor, it was "no more intended as a picture or criticism of Italy or Italians than was 'Two Gentlemen of Verona.'" Finally, *Scribner's* included extensive supporting testimony: numerous excerpts from favorable reviews of *The Sun Also Rises* and *The Torrents of Spring*. The *Scribner's* team dedicated almost two pages to mounting a preemptive vigorous defense of their author, leaving other contributors' biographies a scant page.

Reading across each issue of *Scribner's* in which *A Farewell to Arms* appeared reveals ways in which *Scribner's* editors attempted to soften the blow of modernism for readers acclimated to realism. One way they accomplished this concerned the content and writing style of the text synopses preceding each installment. The first summary reads: "This is the first novel by Mr. Hemingway since the great success of *The Sun Also Rises.* Most of the action takes place on the Italian front during the period of greatest disaster. It is a love-story woven with such a picture of War as would discourage either victors or the conquered from that terrible solution of international troubles" (493). After reading this synopsis, the story creates a disjunction for the reader. The notes preceding the text provide specifics including geography, time period, and plot that Hemingway does not—or rather, specifics that he apportions carefully as the narrative progresses. The opening sentences are striking for the number of prepositions purporting to deliver information about time and space. "In the late summer of that year we lived in a house in a village that looked across the river and the plain to the mountains. In the bed of the river there were pebbles and boulders, dry and white in the sun, and the water was clear and swiftly moving and blue in the channels" (493). As the reader must work to decipher the location and identity of the narrator, as well as determine who else ("we") is being invoked, the effect is to disarm and displace. In contrast, the summary situates and reassures the reader with descriptive prose, providing a stark departure from Hemingway's language of high modernism.

In a similar vein, the following issue, from June 1929, debriefs readers on the events of the previous installment. "The quiet beautiful Italian country is contaminated by war. . . . Artillery fire has levelled forests and illumines the night sky with ominous lightning. The officers of an Italian ambulance unit, living in a pleasant town less than a mile from the fighting, find their principal amusement with the girls in the house reserved for officers or in baiting the priest in the mess. A young American lieutenant, the narrator, is introduced to an English volunteer nurse, Catherine Barkley, by his roommate, an Italian doctor, Rinaldi" (649). While this overview is factually accurate, the tone is cheerful, the language notable for its overabundance of adjectives and details, antithetical to Hemingway's spare style. After describing Frederic Henry's advances toward Catherine, the synopsis concludes: "The war seems grim, crude, mismanaged, pursued without enthusiasm or courage. The lieutenant seeks food for his men, and as they sit eating cold spaghetti and cheese, a trench mortar shell kills one of the drivers and seriously wounds the lieutenant" (649). Here the notes not only offer a plot summary but also extemporize and explain. The summary valorizes Henry in procuring food for his compatriots, but the mention of cold spaghetti and cheese serves to humanize the men rather than underscore the absurdity of war, as Hemingway does.

The most dramatic disjunction between the synopsis and the text occurs in the September issue. "The turning point of this story of love against the background of death and contamination of war comes in the chapters you are about to read" (272). The sentimental tone of the commentary counters the fragmented, aloof narrative of Hemingway's text. Scribner's utilized the summaries as opportunities to recast the tone and theme and clarify chronology to order the narrative in a way Hemingway did not in the text. This is most evident in the text running prior to the final installment, as the summary encompasses the entire story. The final synopsis served to market the story prior to its publication in book form, characterizing it, for example, as a "much-discussed novel of love and war" (373).

While there was little acknowledgment of war in the magazine's run of *A Son at the Front*, it was a dominant theme come 1929. One way in which *Scribner's* eased its readers into modernism was through pairing Hemingway's text with other perspectives on war, including nonfiction firsthand accounts of World War I and historical studies of the Revolutionary War. Testimonies from Germans and Americans alike buttressed the enormous toll of war that Hemingway underscores in *A Farewell to Arms*. In addition, in the same issues in which *A Farewell to Arms* appeared, readers could rely on a voice that pushed back against modernist leanings. Running alongside several installments of *A Farewell to Arms* were articles by Royal Cortissoz, who served as the art critic for the *New York Herald Tribune* from 1891 until his death in 1948. Cortissoz was steadfast in his dismissal of modernism and notorious for his denunciation of the 1913 Armory Show; sixteen years later, his view of modern art had not evolved significantly.

The first article, which appeared in the May 1929 issue, was entitled "The Contemporary Movement in American Design" and discussed modernist furniture in an industrial arts exhibit at the Metropolitan Museum of Art. "The public is still occupied in making up its mind as to whether in the construction of its home interiors it will be traditional or modernistic. It has been so occupied for several years past," Cortissoz wrote. Explaining away modernism as an unsurprising response to sameness, rather than a recognition of disorder wrought by world war, the art historian noted,

"Mankind from time to time tires of its accustomed environment. Tradition wearies it. It longs for something new" (588). Cortissoz bemoaned the lack of distinction between international and American modernism. "Particularly have I looked in vain for things racy, nationalistic, immediately distinguishable from the sort of decoration and furniture which we have had from abroad. On the contrary, the general effect is of the same fortuitous effort that is characteristic of Europe" (596). Hemingway's words face down Cortissoz on the opposite page. "'Yes,' I said. 'And we have gotten away from the war,'" Frederic Henry tells Catherine during their second meeting (597). The reader thus mulls over modernist design and modernist literature in tandem.

In the September 1929 issue, again adjacent to Hemingway, Cortissoz sustained his counterargument to modernism, writing an ode to Jacques Louis David with the wish for a return to the tenets of classical art. "In a time of artistic transition like our own, when revolutionary impulses make themselves manifest, it is interesting to look back and observe the direction which such impulses have sometimes taken, upon historic occasions. The general impression is, I think, that victory is wont to perch upon the banner of the progressive as distinguished from the reactionary, the individualist versus the academician" (334). With the militaristic fervor found in some of David's compositions, Cortissoz extolled David's academic art. On the opposite page, meanwhile, Hemingway wrote of Frederic Henry's impending desertion, describing him ripping off his military stars after his escape down the river. These juxtaposed images actually illustrate the "individualist versus the academician" conflict that Cortissoz proposes.

Other paratextual information also contributes to our understanding of *Scribner's* careful presentation and marketing of *A Farewell to Arms.* From May to October 1929 there were several articles about the Revolutionary Era, including George Washington and Revolutionary War battles at Stony Point and Yorktown. In addition, the issues featured several editorial pieces on World War I. One, including a firsthand account of detainment in a German prison camp (recalling Harvey Mayhew's story in *A Son at the Front*), was written by an American; others were written by Europeans. These denunciations of war buttress Hemingway's fictional portrayal of the toll of the conflict.

Scribner's maintained its Hemingway marketing throughout the serialization. In the June issue, Hemingway stands with a giant fish ("a large tarpon") nearly matching his height (41). The contributor notes inform us that, when the author was not at work on *Farewell*, he spent his time on leisure pursuits—and remind us that the story is not autobiographical (42). Running alongside the final installment in October is a photograph of Hemingway skiing in Gstaad, Switzerland, in 1927, offering a provocative juxtaposition of the life of the author and the death of Catherine Barkley in the following pages. The September issue offers readers the story behind the story—how Hemingway ended up enlisting in the Red Cross and gaining the experience as an ambulance driver that would later inspire *A Farewell to Arms*. Julian Capers, Hemingway's former colleague at the *Kansas City Star*, wrote to thank the magazine for "many hours of undiluted rapture" (52) brought on by the first three installments of the novel. He revealed that he'd known the great author since he was a seventeen-year-old newspaper writer, "already giving evidence as a reporter of the genius which has since developed in his writing" (53). Capers relates how he signed the affidavit that Hemingway could read, speak, and write Italian and French fluently (despite knowledge to the contrary) to aid acceptance to the Red Cross.

> I next heard from him in Italy . . . advising me that a trench mortar shell had bursted [*sic*] in his lap, and that he had received "considerable tinware" (meaning military medals of several classes) and that one of them "carries a pension for life, which, at the present rate of exchange, amounts to $11.86 a year." Please let me thank Hemingway, and the Magazine, again, for *A Farewell to Arms*. It not only makes little shivers of joy traverse my spine, but it even revives momentarily my cub reporter ambition to write the "Great American Novel." (53)

Capers's unwavering support for his former colleague, along with the endearing history of a youthful Hemingway, humanizes the author.

But, if *Scribner's* walked a fine line in presenting a variety of traditional and *avant garde* material to readers potentially averse to new forms, the editors did not shy away from defending Hemingway's reputation or that of the magazine during the June 1929 censorship saga. Some readers objected to the sex scene (rendered, famously, with very few words) between Frederic Henry and Catherine Barkley; the Boston police took the unusual step of banning the issue from magazine stands. *Scribner's* editor Alfred Dashiell responded with fervor and defiance in the *New York Times*, 21 June 1929:

> The very fact that *Scribner's Magazine* is publishing "*A Farewell to Arms*" by Ernest Hemingway is evidence of our belief in its validity and its integrity. Mr. Hemingway is one of the finest and most highly regarded of the modern writers.
>
> The ban on the sale of the magazine in Boston is an evidence of the improper use of censorship which bases its objections upon certain passages without taking into account the effect and purpose of the story as a whole. "*A Farewell to Arms*" is in its effect distinctly moral. It is the story of a fine and faithful love, born, it is true, out of physical desire.
>
> If good can come from evil, if the fine can grow from the gross, how is a writer effectively to depict the progress of this evolution if he cannot describe the conditions from which the good evolved? If white is to be contrasted with black, thereby emphasizing its whiteness, the picture cannot be all white.

The editors also noted that this was not an antiwar novel. While *Scribner's* had defended Wharton against criticism that *A Son at the Front* constituted prowar propaganda, the magazine defended Hemingway against criticism that *A Farewell to Arms* amounted to antiwar propaganda. Despite the magazine's public defense of the work, the correspondence between Hemingway, Perkins, and Bridges reveals that the editors were far from immune to societal and market pressures. As Scott Donaldson observes, "For better or worse, Hemingway undoubtedly produced a somewhat different novel as a consequence of what happened in Boston and what he feared might happen elsewhere" (91).

The *Scribner's* defense continues the emphasis on morality glimpsed in the magazine's synopses of the story. Yet the love story in *A Farewell to Arms* does not feature the clear delineations—good from evil, fine from gross, white from black—that the publisher wishes to ascribe to it. The decay present throughout *A Farewell to Arms* encompasses everything from the seasons to expired lives to wine that has turned, to Frederic Henry and

Catherine Barkley's relationship. Whatever the attempt to package the narrative in appealing binaries, the editors laid decisive claim to modernism at the conclusion of the story's run. A text box that appeared at the end of the last installment of the story declared, "It is a pleasure to note that Mr. Hemingway's serial has achieved renown similar to the first two Van Dine stories serialized in Scribner's. IMPORTANT MODERN FICTION is a distinctive feature of *SCRIBNER'S MAGAZINE*" (472). The author, Perkins, Dashiell, and Scribner himself ultimately triumphed; the novel was a critical and commercial success. Even before the novel was published, Hemingway's coterie predicted the positive response. From Cannes in early September 1929, Fitzgerald wrote, "Let me say that from Perkins last your book like Pickwick has become a classic while still in serial form. Everything looks bright as day for it and I envy you like hell but would rather have it happen to you than to anyone else" (rpt. Bruccoli 98).

On 27 July 2016 at the Democratic National Convention in Philadelphia, Vice President Joe Biden discussed the loss of his son Beau Biden to cancer, invoking *A Farewell to Arms*: "But as Ernest Hemingway once wrote, the world breaks everyone, and afterward many are strong at the broken places." The vice president concluded his Hemingway quotation on an optimistic note, choosing not to excerpt the following darker lines: "But those that will not break it kills. It kills the very good and the very gentle and the very brave impartially. If you are none of these you can be sure it will kill you too but there will be no special hurry" (249). Broken individuals and the broken world left behind in the wake of the war found themselves reflected in the fragmented narratives of literary modernism. We tend to think of these narratives in novel form, but they were also broken in another way, through installments, when they first appeared in periodical form.

The serializations of *A Son at the Front* and *A Farewell to Arms* reveal a magazine that catered to a divided readership, some of whom were entrenched in prewar values, some of whom yearned to learn about the trenches of World War I. *Scribner's* contributed scant commentary and structural endorsement for Wharton's more realist work, whereas it went to the effort of interpreting and even translating modernism into realism for Hemingway's work, thus ensuring appeal to a more conservative audience.

The comparative study of the two stories illuminates *Scribner's* diffident presentation of Wharton's work and aggressive marketing of Hemingway's text. Wharton's contributor biography focused on her authorial qualification due to her residence in France; Hemingway's biography noted military experience. Wharton was never pictured; Hemingway was featured with skis and giant fish, illustrating his athletic prowess.

The lead text for *A Son at the Front* referenced the author's captivating portrayal of parents' emotions during war mobilization, whereas *A Farewell to Arms* was sold as a story of love and war, life and death. Who wouldn't want to read such a tale? It is possible that *Scribner's* had honed its marketing machine come 1929, but the distinct treatments of the texts and their respective authors represent larger issues concerning gender and war: who was deemed most qualified to tell the story, what sort of story was most compelling, and which new literary genre was worth embracing to advance this agenda. As Bruccoli writes, "When Maxwell Perkins died . . . he had been at Charles Scribner's Sons for thirty-seven years, during which time the canon of American fiction was reconstituted by what critics have since imprecisely categorized as 'modernism'" (xxix). Just as Bruccoli notes the changes that occurred during Perkins's tenure, it must also be noted that Scribner's itself evolved throughout the years. Wharton ended *A Son at the Front* on a hopeful note, with John Campton beginning a sketch of a marble monument for his son's grave; Hemingway ended *A Farewell to Arms* with Frederic Henry turning away from Catherine Barkley's body, which he observes looks like a statue. Monument, statue, realism, modernism: readers learned from the pages of *Scribner's* that the war evoked a variety of artistic responses and forms, some overlooked and some heralded. In the pages of *Scribner's*, one of the more notoriously conservative magazines, readers glimpsed the evolution of American letters, as realism gave way to modernism and a new era began.

NOTES

1. This essay is dedicated to my grandfather, Jo Hubbard Chamberlin, who served as managing editor of *Scribner's Magazine* from 1936 to 1938, corresponded with Hemingway, and (fifty years later) encouraged me to be a writer.

2. Edith Wharton to William Brownell, 20 Aug. 1917, in William Crary Brownell (Am-

herst College 1871) Papers, box 2, folder 3, Amherst College Archives and Special Collections, Amherst College Library.

3. For further information regarding Wharton and the magazines, see Nettels, "Serialization."

4. The language of the scene parallels that of Frederic Henry's last scene with Catherine Barkley in *A Farewell to Arms*: "It was like saying goodbye to a statue" (332).

5. For further discussion of Wharton's response to modernist literature, including Joyce, Woolf, and Eliot, see Olin-Ammentorp's *Edith Wharton's Writings from the Great War* and Haytock's *Edith Wharton and the Conversations of Literary Modernism.*

6. To view the magazine's run of *A Son at the Front*, see library.brown.edu/cds/repository2/repoman.php?verb=render&id=126153028215625&view=pageturner.

7. Letter to Charles Scribner, 12 Sept. 1919, Archives of Charles Scribner's Sons, Firestone Library, Princeton University.

8. For further context, see Berg's *Max Perkins: Editor of Genius*, or Bruccoli's *The Sons of Maxwell Perkins*.

9. To view the magazine's run of *A Farewell to Arms*, see www.manhattanrarebooks.com/pages/books/1554/ernest-hemingway/a-farewell-to-arms/?soldItem=true.

10. Hemingway was paid $16,000 for the serialization of *A Farewell to Arms*; prior to this, Edith Wharton had been *Scribner's* highest-paid author.

11. When Perkins wrote his appraisal of *A Farewell to Arms* to Charles Scribner II, he noted, "P.S. I was somewhat constrained in bringing out the difficult points in 'A Farewell' by dictating this to Miss Wykoff" (qtd. in Trogdon 68). The editor's discomfort with Hemingway's language is apparent.

12. As Reynolds notes, "Hemingway's problems with language were not over with the magazine publication. Words came in two categories: those which could not be used in the magazine and those which could not be used in hardcover." See Reynolds, *Hemingway's First War*, for a comprehensive treatment of the trajectory of *A Farewell to Arms*.

WORKS CITED

Barlow, Perry. "Sketches from an Old French Town." *Scribner's Magazine* Jan. 1923, 36–43. Print.

Bell, Millicent. "Lady into Author: Edith Wharton and the House of Scribner." *American Quarterly* 9.3 (1957): 295–315. Web. Accessed 4 Apr. 2016.

Benstock, Shari. "Introduction." *A Son at the Front*. DeKalb: Northern Illinois UP, 1995. i–xxi. Print.

———. "The Word Which Made All Clear: The Silent Close of *The House of Mirth*." *Edith Wharton's The House of Mirth: A Casebook*. Ed. Carol J. Singley. Oxford: Oxford UP, 2003. 131–62. Print.

Berg, A. Scott. *Max Perkins, Editor of Genius*. New York: Berkeley, 2016.

Biden, Joe. "Vice President Joe Biden's DNC Speech Transcript." *Vox*, 27 July 2016. Web. Accessed 22 Mar. 2017.

Bruccoli, Matthew J., ed., with Judith S. Baughman. *The Sons of Maxwell Perkins: Letters of F. Scott Fitzgerald, Ernest Hemingway, Thomas Wolfe, and Their Editor.* Columbia: U of South Carolina P, 2004. Print.

Capers, Julian. "Letter to the Editor." *Scribner's Magazine*, Sept. 1929, 53. Print.

Cortissoz, Royal. "Sterile Modernism." *TIME*, 10 Mar. 1930. Web. Accessed 12 Apr. 2016.

Curnutt, Kirk. "The Lousy Racket: Hemingway, Scribners, and the Business of Literature." *Hemingway Review* 27.1 (2007): 129–36. Web. Accessed 15 May 2016.

Donaldson, Scott. "Censorship and *A Farewell to Arms*." *Studies in American Fiction* 19.1 (1991): 85–93. Web. Accessed 15 May 2016.

Ford, James L. "New York of the Seventies." *Scribner's Magazine*, June 1923, 748. Print.

Goodman, Susan E. *Civil Wars: American Novelists and Manners, 1880–1940*. Baltimore: Johns Hopkins UP, 2003. Print.

Haytock, Jennifer Anne. *Edith Wharton and the Conversations of Literary Modernism.* New York: Palgrave Macmillan, 2008. Print.

Hellman, Caroline. *Domesticity and Design in American Women's Lives and Literature: Stowe, Alcott, Cather, and Wharton Writing Home.* New York: Routledge, 2011. Print.

Hemingway, Ernest. "A Farewell to Arms." *Scribner's Magazine*, May–Oct. 1929. Print.

———. *A Farewell to Arms.* New York: Scribner's, 1929. Print.

———. *In Our Time: Stories.* New York: Boni & Liveright, 1925. Print.

———. *The Sun Also Rises.* New York: Scribner's, 1926. Print.

Lee, Hermione. *Edith Wharton.* New York: Alfred A. Knopf, 2007. Print.

Lewis, Robert W. *A Farewell to Arms: The War of the Words.* New York: Twayne, 1992. Print.

Lowell, Amy. "Fact." *Scribner's Magazine*, Mar. 1923, 305. Print.

McGrath, Charles. "Wharton Letter Reopens a Mystery." *New York Times*, 21 Nov. 2007. Web. Accessed 22 Mar. 2017.

Nettels, Elsa. "Serialization." *Edith Wharton in Context.* Ed. Laura Rattray. Cambridge: Cambridge UP, 2012. 137–45. Print.

Olin-Ammentorp, Julie. *Edith Wharton's Writings from the Great War.* Gainesville: UP of Florida, 2004. Print.

Peel, Robin. *Apart from Modernism: Edith Wharton, Politics, and Fiction before World War I.* Madison, NJ: Fairleigh Dickinson UP, 2005. Print.

Reynolds, Michael Shane. *Hemingway's First War: The Making of "A Farewell to Arms."* Princeton, NJ: Princeton UP, 1976. Print.

Trogdon, Robert W. *The Lousy Racket: Hemingway, Scribners, and the Business of Literature.* Kent, OH: Kent State UP, 2007. Print.

Tyler, Lisa. *Teaching Hemingway's "A Farewell to Arms."* Kent, OH: Kent State UP, 2008. Print.

Wharton, Edith. *The Age of Innocence.* New York: D. Appleton, 1920. Print.

———. *A Backward Glance.* New York: D. Appleton-Century, 1934. Print.

———. *The Children.* New York: D. Appleton, 1928. Print.

———. *The Gods Arrive.* New York: D. Appleton, 1932. Print.

———. *Hudson River Bracketed.* New York: D. Appleton, 1929. Print.

———. *The Mother's Recompense.* New York: D. Appleton, 1925. Print.

———. "A Son at the Front." *Scribner's Magazine,* Dec. 1922–Feb. 1923. Print.

———. *A Son at the Front.* DeKalb: Northern Illinois UP, 1995. Print.

———. *Summer: A Novel.* New York: D. Appleton, 1917. Print.

———. *The Touchstone.* New York: Charles Scribner's Sons, 1914. Print.

———. *Twilight Sleep.* New York: D. Appleton, 1927. Print.

Wharton to Hemingway to Highsmith

American Noir *Comes of Age*

PARLEY ANN BOSWELL

> What if it were *she* who was dead! If she were going to die—to die soon—and leave him free!
>
> —EDITH WHARTON, *The Age of Innocence* (1920)

> His wife was silent. The doctor wiped his gun carefully with a rag. He pushed the shells back in against the spring of the magazine. He sat with the gun on his knees. He was very fond of it. Then he heard his wife's voice from the darkened room.
>
> —ERNEST HEMINGWAY, "The Doctor and the Doctor's Wife" (1925)

> His hands captured her throat on the last word, stifling its abortive uplift of surprise. He shook her. . . . She made a grating sound in her throat, but he had her too tight for a scream.
>
> —PATRICIA HIGHSMITH, *Strangers on a Train* (1950)

Edith Wharton (1862–1937), Ernest Hemingway (1899–1961), and Patricia Highsmith (1921–1995) were never friends, not even acquaintances. They were born into subsequent generations: Wharton was thirty-seven when Hemingway was born; Hemingway was twenty-two when Highsmith was born. We have no record that any of the three ever met either of the other two. The works they wrote do not suggest that they influenced or had been influenced by the others. Because we know a great deal about all three writers' lives, we know that they all read everything. Wharton most likely read some Hemingway; Hemingway probably read Highsmith and Wharton; and Highsmith probably read both other authors. They share other biographical similarities: they shared a love for works by Edgar Allan Poe, Gustave Flaubert, and Henry James; they all lived outside of the United States for most of their adult lives; their fiction made them all popular (to different degrees) back home in the United States. All three purported to hate literary critics and behaved like old cranks when dealing with their publishers; they all eventually felt betrayed by their American publishers for misrepresenting their fiction to the public.[1]

The fiction that Wharton, Hemingway, and Highsmith wrote also shares characteristics. All three wrote short stories and novels in which detached, manipulative narrators described characters and events so dispassionately that establishing a moral compass, or mooring ourselves to any moral authority, becomes difficult. All three writers created flawed characters who struggle to break out of their ambiguous, powerless lives in a world littered with suggestions of violence and without defined boundaries. All three disguised the central betrayal, guilt, self-delusion, greed, and brutality of their narratives with such deft skill that, when we read them, we rarely know what has hit us, or how to feel about being hit. The works of all three writers are difficult to categorize because what they wrote defies the stereotypical. Realism? Naturalism? Modernism? Postmodernism? Nihilism? Melodrama? Where do these writers belong?

Wharton, Hemingway, and Highsmith are best described as *noir* writers. Their cumulative century's worth of works corresponds to perhaps the most American of all literary and film art movements of the twentieth century, one that developed and flowered during the middle of the century. In his excellent study *American Noir,* David Cochran describes the cultural environment in which *noir* developed: "The uninterrupted series of crises that had befallen Americans—the Depression, World War II, the Cold War—left an underlying sense of doubt" and angst among Americans (3). The *noir* films and fiction of the 1940s, defined by "crime, greed, and jealousy," included tales in which "people meet the most merciless fate for the most mundane reasons" (3).

During the 1950s, much of the American *noir* fiction and film was "gradually isolated or co-opted" as dominant cultural expressions became more binary—capitalism was good and forthright; communism was a contagious and corrupting disease. Through the House Un-American Activities Committee hearings and other public pressures of the era, filmmakers and writers whose works displayed ambiguity or shifting moral compasses were suspect or worse. The "chaos and ambiguity of noir undermined the moral absolutes of the struggle" between the United States and the Soviet Union, and texts and films that suggested doubt or vague values—Wharton, Hemingway, and Highsmith among them—were suppressed or sanitized (Cochran 4). Their brilliant narratives about entrapped characters became themselves entrapped and commodified by literary and film agents in ways that made them all acceptable—or invisible—to postwar middlebrow reading and viewing audiences.

Noir has come to define more than film or "hard-boiled" crime dramas and novels. Through the decades, *noir* has morphed into an artistic expression with its own recognizable tropes, metaphors, and symbols. Once identified as mid-twentieth-century, *noir* has become an elusive organism that moves around and through fiction and film. (The term "neo-noir" sometimes refers to fiction or film generated in the 1970s, 1980s, 1990s, and beyond.) *Noir* represents a cluster of narratives that forces us to move unexpectedly from some predictable situation we recognize into some dangerous, complicated, and subversive situation we know only from nightmares. As scholar Otto Penzler has written, "Like art, love, and pornography, noir is hard to define, but you know it when you see it. . . . [N]oir stories are bleak, existential, alienated, pessimistic tales about losers—people who are so morally challenged that they cannot help but bring about their own ruin" (Ellroy and Penzler x).[2]

To be accurate: Wharton died in 1937, before *noir* fiction or film had a name. Her work *anticipates noir.* Wharton's fiction is our best introduction into the world of *noir,* because her narratives provide an initial imprint for the genre. And, although Wharton was writing before the movement had a name, she certainly understood something about storytelling on film. In fact, Wharton, Hemingway, and Highsmith all made great bundles of money by selling their fiction to American film studios during their lifetimes. They also all hated most of the Hollywood adaptations of their fiction. They had good reasons to be frustrated with the film industry between the 1920s and the 1960s, decades in which literary source material was routinely mutilated and manipulated by studios to fit into certain prescribed genres. In fact, their works' mistreatment by Hollywood studios helps to explain Wharton, Hemingway, and Highsmith as *noir* writers.

During the post–World War II era, the age of conformity and middlebrow culture, their works would not behave properly. For films to survive stringent censors and become successful projects that met the standards of the studio heads, adaptations of Wharton, Hemingway, and Highsmith had to be homogenized, sentimentalized, and romanticized. Wharton's work did not see the light of day on film during the middle of the twentieth century and would not be adapted at all between 1939 and 1990. Studios made money by bowdlerizing Hemingway's novels, and Highsmith attracted attention as well. But the history of these Hollywood adaptations suggests that these three writers' works were almost impossible to tame, which speaks well for them all. Reflecting on the fiction-against-film versions of *The Age of Innocence*; some of the Nick Adams stories, including *The Killers*; and *Strangers on a Train* confirms that Wharton, Hemingway, and Highsmith represent three of the most remarkable literary links in the evolution of American *noir.*

Filmmaker Martin Scorsese read Edith Wharton's *The Age of Innocence* in the 1980s and knew that he wanted to adapt the novel for the screen. Karli Lukas describes Scorsese's attraction to the novel: "Scorsese has often stated that his ultimate reason for choosing to adapt *The Age of Innocence* was that he was so enthralled by Wharton's ability to blind her readers, like Newland, to the various signs of complicit manipulation around them." After several years and other movies to his credit, Scorsese finally secured funding. With his screenplay coauthored with Jay Cocks, a superb creative team, and a stellar cast that included Daniel Day-Lewis, Michelle Pfeiffer, and Winona Ryder, he announced his production of *The Age of Innocence.*

When the film was released in the fall of 1993, Scorsese enthusiasts were initially nonplussed, confused by his choice of source material. After all, Scorsese's body of work included *Mean Streets* (1973), *Taxi Driver* (1976), *Raging Bull* (1980), and *Goodfellas* (1990). His *Age of Innocence* seemed aberrant, dividing his fans "into two camps—those who regarded it as brilliant, full of 'such passionate intelligence and style that one almost feels ravished by its riches'; and those who wished he'd never left the Italian American gangster genre, regarding the film as a tedious and pointless exercise in which Scorsese was 'too busy showing off the furniture'" (Lukas).

As divided as moviegoers—and film critics—felt at the time, Scorsese's film has endured, and is now considered to be not just one of Scorsese's finest films, but a great adaptation of a great novel. In 2005 Roger Ebert included *The Age of Innocence* in his series *Great Movies*, explaining through an apt comparison of *The Age of Innocence* to *Raging Bull* that Scorsese "understood that passion and violence can exist in places where absolute decorum rules; that Jake LaMotta, smashing his fists into the walls of his cell in 'Raging Bull,' found a release that Newland Archer could not discover anywhere in the sitting rooms and dinners and nights at the opera that defined his life in *The Age of Innocence.*" *Raging Bull* has long been considered an example of neo-noir film, and invoking *Raging Bull* suggests that Scorsese—and Ebert—recognized the darkness and instability in *The Age of Innocence.*

Thanks to Scorsese's sharp perceptions, the film adaptation of *The Age of Innocence* privileges and reflects the *noir* characteristics of Wharton's novel: the helplessness and entrapment of Newland Archer, his fantasies of love with Ellen Olenska, his fantasy of his wife's sudden death. Archer knows that he is trapped and manipulated by others. The calm narrator reminds us that, as early as his honeymoon, Archer realizes that he has compromised himself: "He perceived with a flash of chilling insight that in future many problems would be thus negatively solved for him" (Wharton, *Age of Innocence* 166). Scorsese emphasizes Archer's entrapment at this point visually: we watch an iris shot (a dark circle that slowly closes in on an image) that moves in on Archer very slowly, to darkness.

Through Scorsese's camera lens, we understand that by the end of the film Archer has been completely imprisoned by the sly movements of his wife and her tribe, and that he is paying for whatever crimes he has (not) committed: "New York believed him to be Madame Olenska's lover" (276). Archer now realizes that his life moves in ways that he no longer controls: "And so the evening swept on, running and running like a senseless river that did not know how to stop" (276). Through framing and camerawork, Scorsese shows us Archer's final entrapment near the conclusion of *The Age of Innocence.*

Ebert rightly describes Scorsese's adaptation as "improperly appreciated" by critics at the time of its release in 1993 because the film did not meet conventional expectations of a Scorsese film. Ebert might have been describing the reputation of Wharton's fiction as well, and for the same reason. Wharton was most certainly dismissed and diminished from the decade of her death—the 1930s—until the late 1970s. During the middle of the twentieth century several of her works went out of print, and those that did not included back covers that described Wharton flatly as someone who wrote about "the manners and mores of old New York" or who wrote "as a keen observer and chronicler of society." When new generations of readers, scholars, and publishers began to revive Wharton's literary reputation as part of a wave of feminist scholarship in the 1970s and 1980s, readers (among them Martin Scorsese) began recalibrating Wharton's oeuvre.[3]

This recalibration suggests that Wharton's reputation suffered during the mid-twentieth century because her fiction was too dark and complicated. In an America characterized by "standardization, stereotypy, conservatism, mendacity," and vapid consumerism, Wharton was out of step (Cochran 9). The backs of her books did not describe the specific "manners and mores in Old New York" that Wharton included in her work: drug addiction (*The House of Mirth, Twilight Sleep, The Bunner Sisters*); attempted rape (*The House of Mirth*); attempted murder (*Twilight Sleep*); drug overdose (*The House of Mirth*); suicide (*The Custom of the Country*); attempted suicide (*Ethan Frome*); unplanned pregnancy and abortion ("Roman Fever," *Summer,* "The Old Maid"); and mercy killing (*The Fruit of the Tree*). Wharton was indeed a keen observer of society, if that society included powerful middle-aged men who lust after young women (*Summer, The Children, The Reef*), lonely middle-aged women who wander around looking for love (*The Reef, A Mother's Recompense, Twilight Sleep, The Children*), young men who become paid companions of said women (*A Mother's Recompense*), young women who use sex to worm their way into society (*The Custom of the Country, The Reef,* among others), idle rich men who spend most of their time thinking about whom they have slept with and whom they want to sleep with (almost every novel and short story), and men—like Newland Archer—who feel so trapped that they daydream about their young wives' deaths (*The Age of Innocence*). This is just the short list.

Thanks to recent scholarship, and especially to filmmakers like Scorsese and astute film critics like Ebert, we know that Wharton's dark visions of marriage, money, and power were never the stuff of midcentury Book-of-the-Month-Club fare. Her fiction shares much more with the dark, pulp fiction of the middle of the century than it does with either high or middlebrow fiction. The terms "noir fiction" and "noir film" would never have crossed Wharton's mind, of course, but shining a spotlight on her fiction now reveals a healthy subversive streak and defiant resistance to category in her work. Like other writers of the early twentieth century—Henry James, Hart Crane, Kate Chopin—Wharton defies predictability and requires readers to trust her—even as we venture into dark territory. Wharton, James, and others influenced many of the writers we now associate with crime/mystery/noir fiction: Raymond Chandler, James M. Cain, Ray Bradbury, and Dashiell Hammett among them.

But no one among these early twentieth-century writers left a more clearly subversive and darker legacy to later twentieth-century writers than Wharton. Who knows how she might have felt about being considered a *noir* writer? We can only guess. We do know that Wharton had recoiled at the description of *The Age of Innocence* by the Pulitzer jury as "wholesome" fiction, and that she was famously contemptuous of Hollywood and the movies. Near the end of her life in the 1930s, she seemed especially cranky about the work of younger American writers—especially that group of young postwar authors who had settled in Paris—so cranky that she seems to have been obsessed with them. Among these young writers was Ernest Hemingway, whom, along with other midwestern writers (F. Scott Fitzgerald, Sinclair Lewis), she had (perhaps) lampooned as character Vance Weston, an ambitious but thick young midwesterner, in *Hudson River Bracketed* (1929) and *The Gods Arrive* (1932).[4]

Wharton had certainly read Hemingway's fiction by the time she created Vance Weston. Who hadn't? By 1929, Hemingway was famous, and within ten years he would be an international celebrity. During the 1920s, he had published many short stories in various periodicals, which he then published in three collections: *Three Stories & Ten Poems* in 1923, *In Our Time* in 1925, and *Men without Women* in 1927. By the end of the decade, he had published two novels, *The Sun Also Rises* (1926) and *A Farewell to Arms* (1929). The year after Wharton published her second bitter Vance Weston novel, Hemingway published his fourth volume of short stories, *Winner Take Nothing* (1933). Readers could not get enough of Hemingway. From the beginning, his short fiction read like no other in English: startling, stunning, the shock of the new. E. L. Doctorow described Hemingway's early fiction in his essay "Braver Than We Thought," first published in *Esquire* in 1986: "His stuff was new. It moved. There was on every page of clear prose an implicit judgment of all other writing. The Hemingway voice hated pretense and cant and the rhetoric they rode in on" (325).

Hemingway's short fiction seemed to come out of nowhere (which would have irked Edith Wharton). His stories were deceptively simple, and "sought their own level of near perfection without real apprenticeship. . . . It only felt as if modernism in prose had begun with a young husband and father out of the Midwest—a rube, really, no matter that he'd glimpsed war and suffered wounds" (Hendrickson 39). Many of these earliest stories—twenty-four of them—included a recurring character named Nick Adams, also a young rube from the Midwest who had glimpsed war and suffered wounds. In two of the best of the Nick Adams stories, "Big Two-Hearted River" part I and "Big Two-Hearted River" part II, Hemingway created "a new kind of American language. . . . A young man named Nick, who seems vaguely to be troubled, has gone camping alone" (Hendrickson 40). He sets up camp and cooks his supper. "The story is proceeding in such inconsequential fashion, with attentions being paid to the smallest rituals of camping and fishing, as if this is all the story were about" (40).[5]

Camping and fishing are not even the half of it, of course. In his exceptional study *Hemingway's Boat*, Paul Hendrickson quotes a passage from *A Moveable Feast* (1964) in which Hemingway recalls how he had written "Big Two-Hearted River" back in the 1920s: "'The story was about coming back from the war but there was no mention of the war in it'" (40). As with all of his best fiction, Hemingway's power in these stories lay in his silences. Doctorow reminds us that "when composing a story [Hemingway] would withhold mention of its central problem" (325). He withheld more than that. His stories were streamlined, sleek, and sometimes stark because he relied more on dialogue between two characters than on some long-winded narrator who never knew when to shut up. He mimicked "the dynamics of real-life speech. After Hemingway, writers would have the option of making dialogue illustrative or constructive and of having their characters show themselves in ways hitherto only revealed by other methods" (Lamb, *Art Matters* 177–78).

Not just other fiction writers, but screenwriters in Hollywood were paying attention to how Hemingway crafted dialogue. Always on the lookout for adaptations "with a pedigree," Hollywood secured the rights to *A Farewell to Arms* and produced the first adaptation of a Hemingway text only a couple of years after microphones had become standard equipment on stage sets.[6] Released in 1932, directed by Frank Borzage, and starring Gary Cooper and Helen Hayes, the film represents the first of several high-profile Hemingway adaptations to disappoint those viewers who loved Hemingway's fiction. The *New York Times* reviewer lamented that there was "too much sentiment and not enough strength in the pictorial conception of Ernest Hemingway's novel" (Hall). Other critics lamented that the film was too melodramatic. Ironically, the 1932 *A Farewell to Arms* is now considered one of the best adaptations of Hemingway, which tells us just how bad the others must be.[7]

When 20th Century Fox released a boxed set of Hemingway adaptations in 2007, David Haglund wrote about the set in *Slate*. In "Hollywood Hemingway: How the Movies Mangled Great Fiction," Haglund laments that the films in the set, which include *The Snows of Kilimanjaro* (1952), *The Sun Also Rises* (1957), *A Farewell to Arms* (1957), and *Hemingway's Adventures of a Young Man* (1962), are "prime examples of a peculiar subgenre one might call Hollywood Hemingway: widescreen, Technicolor adaptations featuring foreign settings and doomed love, and always at least half an hour too long. . . . [T]hey were made when Hemingway was a living legend."

We can guess that Hemingway would have hated the boxed set. As much as he loved hanging around with movie stars on set, and collecting many thousands of dollars from Hollywood studios, he disliked almost every adaptation made during his lifetime. Haglund recounts a story about Hemingway and one actor from *The Snows of Kilimanjaro*. "Hemingway told Ava Gardner—who plays—wonderfully—Harry Street's doomed lover, that the only things he liked in the movie were her and the hyena." Hemingway's son Patrick confirmed this, writing that "pictures on the silver screen were nothing but pure illusion" to his father (Haglund). With the exception of *The Snows of Kilimanjaro*, the overblown Hemingway duds were adaptations of the novels, including *The Old Man and the Sea* in 1958. Starring Spencer Tracy, and including Hemingway as one of the production consultants, the film was ultimately disappointing to almost everyone involved, including Hemingway.

We know of only two film adaptations of his work that pleased Hemingway, which suggests that he might have disliked the movies, but he certainly understood them. Hemingway loved the two adaptations that were destined to become *noir* classics: *To Have and Have Not,* Howard Hawks's stylish 1944 film starring Humphrey Bogart and Lauren Bacall, and *The Killers,* a 1946 film directed by Robert Siodmak and starring Burt Lancaster and Ava Gardner. Hemingway was especially delighted with *The Killers,* which opens faithfully with his short story and then moves beyond it into original screenplay material for the rest of the film. In his 2015 review of the Criterion edition of *The Killers,* J. R. Jones of the *Chicago Reader* explains that "Hemingway was habitually disgusted with how Hollywood distorted his thematic intentions, yet he was a vocal fan of Robert Siodmak's *The Killers* (1946). 'It is a good picture,' he wrote in 1959."

The film opens with Hemingway's sparse dialogue almost intact:

> *Al:* You got anything to drink?
> *George:* I can give you soda, beer, ginger ale. . . .
> *Al:* I said, "You got anything to drink?"
> *George:* [*intimidated*] No.
> *Al:* This is a hot town. Whatta ya call it?
> *George:* Brentwood.
> *Al:* Did you ever hear of Brentwood?
> *Max:* [*Max shakes his head, no*]
> *Al:* Whatta ya do here nights?
> *Max:* [*sarcastically*] They eat the dinner. They all come here and eat the big dinner.
> *George:* [*showing fear*] That's right.
> *Al:* [*condescendingly*] You're a pretty bright boy, aren't you?
> *George:* [*intimidated*] Sure.
> *Max:* [*contemptuously*] Well you're NOT!
> *Max:* [*to Al*] Is he, Al?
> *Al:* He's dumb!

Jones explains how the screenwriters adapted Hemingway's spare tale. Anthony Veiller was the credited screenwriter, but the real author of *The Killers* was John Huston (*High Sierra, The Maltese Falcon*), who was under contract to another studio. Huston compressed the action of the Hemingway story to about twelve minutes and used it as the jumping-off point for a mystery in which an insurance investigator (Edmund O'Brien) looks into the boxer's murder and can't rest until he uncovers the motive for the crime. As Huston imagines it, the boxer (Burt Lancaster in his screen debut) has gotten mixed up in a robbery to please the woman of his dreams (Ava Gardner) and wound up taking the blame when she and her lover absconded with the loot. Jones concludes: "Siodmak, a master of light and shadow, turned *The Killers* into a landmark film noir, and the invented backstory, told in flashback, was tough and fatalistic enough to satisfy Hemingway."

Flashbacks, like the ones in *The Killers*, are a hallmark of *noir* films of the 1940s as well as neo-noir films of the 1990s and beyond. *The Killers* and Hemingway have been an especially significant influence on neo-noir film. The most iconic of neo-noir films, *Pulp Fiction*, owes a great deal to both the 1946 *noir* classic and to Hemingway's fiction in general. Tom Carson explains:

> *Pulp Fiction* is the greatest—and kookiest—exegesis of the works of Ernest Hemingway on film . . . the Hemingway of "The Killers" (Vincent and Jules are those wisecracking 1927 gunmen's direct descendants) and the boxing story "Fifty Grand" (ditto for Bruce Willis's Butch, the mulishly resourceful prizefighter under orders from Ving Rhames's Marsellus to take a fall). Just for fun, you can even toss *The Sun Also Rises* into the mix to underline the movie's never-to-be-underestimated glamorous side. Not only is [*sic*] Vincent and Mia doing the twist to Chuck Berry's "You Never Can Tell" at Jack Rabbit Slim's a po-mo update on Jake Barnes and Lady Brett Ashley at the *bal musette*, but their pas de deux also had the same effect in redefining our notions of the counterculture.

Hemingway is not a *noir* writer merely because two of his works were adapted into *noir* films, nor because his writing has influenced every other writer since. He represents the most glorious example of mid-century *noir* writing because his fiction—especially his early short stories—cast the mold for *noir*. They remain the most significant *noir* imprint, resisting any predictable narrative in shocking, complicated ways. They have never behaved for Hollywood studios; they almost defy adaptation. Like the fiction of Edith Wharton, the fiction of Hemingway projects as incoherent, embarrassing mush in the wrong (Hollywood studio) hands but as taut, brilliant film art when in the right (*noir* directors' and screenwriters') hands. Some of his best and earliest stories, including "Up in Michigan" (1921), "Indian Camp" (1924), and "The Doctor and the Doctor's Wife" (1925), have been almost impossible, thankfully, to translate to film.[8]

These brilliant early stories anticipate and include *noir* characteristics: a sense of helplessness (clearly every character in "Indian Camp" feels powerless), a distortion of institutional frameworks (what's the deal between the Doctor and his wife, anyway?), and a narrator whose even, minimal storytelling becomes chilling (not even a flinch from the storyteller when Jim rapes Liz in "Up in Michigan"). Before he wrote "The Killers," Hemingway's narrators had calmly told stories in ways that betrayed the portentous acts he described. By the time he created the tale of George and Al looking for Ole Andreson, Hemingway had already hit a kind of stride in his short fiction, creating *noir* landscapes where victims and victimizers looked too much alike.

Also like Wharton, Hemingway eventually developed a high literary profile as a canonical author, and through the decades his image, like his fiction, has suffered ill use by filmmakers, critics, and other writers who ought to know better. If Wharton's reputation diminished through the decades, then Hemingway's image outgrew his writing as time passed. Especially during the 1950s, when "modernist texts were being canonized, and modernism itself was losing most of its critical impetus," Hemingway struggled (Cochran 27). During the years that he "devoted his energies to portraits of heroic elderly fishermen as symbols of humanity writ large," he also fought against a legacy that was tending toward caricature (27). Like Wharton's, Hemingway's fiction regains its power through the dark, unyielding lens of *noir*, where his unadorned language and commanding silences become most accessible. Hemingway's fiction comes alive with the least restriction or prescription, whether in text or on film. Hemingway himself seemed to sense this when he reacted well to Siodmak's *The Killers*: adaptation means much more than fidelity to a text.

Patricia Highsmith knew this, too—she could have written the book on how film can mutate fiction. Instead, twenty-nine-year-old Highsmith, who had published short fiction sporadically and had supported herself for several years by writing comic books, wrote a book about two men who commit murders for each other. This first novel, *Strangers on a Train* (1950), introduces us to Guy Haines, a thoughtful, ambitious twenty-nine-year-old architect, and Charles Anthony Bruno, a twenty-something alcoholic psychopath who tries to befriend Guy as they ride a train from New York toward Texas. As they sit together drinking, Bruno begins to ask Guy questions, and Guy "was aware of an impulse to tell Bruno everything, the stranger on the train who would listen, commiserate, and forget. The idea of telling Bruno began to comfort him" (26–27). After hearing all about Guy's problems extricating himself from an inconvenient marriage, Bruno suggests that they might commit murder for each other—who would suspect?—and Guy plays along, passively. Drunk and tired, he goes to his compartment to sleep it off.

Of course, Bruno does kill Guy's pesky estranged wife, and he now expects Guy to kill his father. Guy can't quite bring himself to come clean about Bruno to his wealthy fiancée, Anne, and Guy begins a slow, spiraling descent from up-and-coming architect to murderer. By the time he tells the police detective to whom he has confessed "take me" at the end of the novel, Guy is relieved to be free of everything—the lies, the pressure, the memories of misery (281). He represents the first of many of Highsmith's male characters who, unlike the "virile men of action who populated Cold War" fiction and film, instead projects a profile as "weak, insufferable, craven" (Cochran 127). Within a deep undercurrent of homoeroticism (reminiscent—not coincidentally—of the homoerotic ghost story "The Eyes" by Edith Wharton), Bruno and Guy are counterpoints to the dominant American male stereotype of the time, with "deep psychological flaws, making them unfit for . . . moral leadership" (Cochran 227).[9] In a popular culture overrun with narratives of simplistic good and evil (including the several bad Hemingway adaptations), Bruno and Guy appeared to be both creepy victims and creepy victimizers. No wonder Alfred Hitchcock took notice.

Within weeks of the book's publication, Hitchcock paid six thousand dollars for the film rights to *Strangers on a Train* (Wilson 168). After much complicated work on the screenplay—which had to adhere to the strict Hollywood film code—and problems with casting, Hitchcock's *Strangers on a Train* was released in 1951. It deviates in details from Highsmith's novel—Hitchcock changed the main character's profession from architect to professional tennis player—and the film ends differently than the novel. But the film remains sound, often considered one of Hitchcock's finest visual efforts. Hitchcock introduces us to trouble through visual correspondence in the very first scene, where "Guy and Bruno's meeting on the train bears all the marks of a pickup—the two men tip feet, light a cigarette together, and retire into Bruno's private car" (Hatch 55).[10]

After *Strangers on a Train,* Highsmith was immediately associated with "suspense" fiction. She tried throughout her career to distance herself from being typed—her many short stories and novels represent a wide expanse of subjects and interests. In interviews, she suggested that being pinned into a genre might have its advantages, however. She thought that, because the "suspense and mystery book has a cheapness hanging about it, a reputation for superficiality, a stigma of inferiority to the straight novel," a suspense novelist actually enjoyed "a great deal of room to raise fundamental questions on the nature of such issues as justice, morality, and courage and, implicitly, to cast a critical eye on the world we live in" (Hatch 117). Throughout her writing career, Highsmith did raise these questions through a remarkable body of work that defies genre. Thrillers? Mysteries? Psychological studies? Even romance?[11] All of the above.

And yes—*noir.* Patricia Highsmith represents the most articulate and elegant of the mid-century *noir* writers. She was a master storyteller with rich command of language and a sharp wit, whose "most sadistic acts . . . are never physical; they're rooted in precise, often economic, exchanges of power, information, or money" (Arn 5). Even with the significant changes to her story in Hitchcock's *Strangers on a Train,* Highsmith's work shines through in ways that continue to influence recent neo-noir films. David Keyes, writing for *Cinemaphile* in 2002, sees the film as seminal: "Aside from its very evident approach as a crowd-pleasing popcorn flick, [Hitchcock's *Strangers on a Train*] is one of the original shells for identity-inspired mystery thrillers, in which natural human behavior is the driving force behind the true macabre rather than supernatural elements. Even classic endeavors like *Fargo* and *A Simple Plan* seem directly fueled by this concept."

Wharton to Hemingway to Highsmith might initially seem like a stretch, but they do not represent a stretch, but a span. These three authors span a century's worth of *noir* fiction and film, much of it beholden to their work. They are all master storytellers who consistently demand that we trust them, while at the same time they disorient and force us to question our assumptions and hypocrisies about how the world works. That is how the best American *noir* behaves. These three authors testify to the versatility and continuing power of American *noir* just as they enrich the genre. As Nicholas Seeley points out in his excellent essay "Noir Is Protest Literature," *noir* "is everywhere these days . . . best exemplified by the popularity and cachet of TV series like *Breaking Bad* and *True Detective*. . . . [T]he images and tropes of that classic noir have melted into broader culture."[12]

Seeley defines *noir* by comparing it to classic crime fiction of Agatha Christie and Sir Arthur Conan Doyle. These writers gave us "the whodunit: it takes place in an essentially orderly universe, with a common understanding of good and evil." Seeley then describes *noir* in a way that Wharton, Hemingway, and Highsmith would all recognize because their writings project worlds like this:

> Noir, as it emerged in the middle of a violent century, said to hell with [a common understanding of good and evil]. Its world was chaotic, baroque and hypocritical. Crime doesn't disturb this world, it's foundational to it. Noir stories gave the stage to criminals and their motivations, which range from unspeakable passions to a firm conviction that their particular crime serves a greater good. A detective may pursue such a criminal, but noir reveals the line between them to be a product of chance and circumstance—if, indeed, such a line exists at all.

The fiction of Wharton, Hemingway, and Highsmith certainly provides narratives of "protest and deconstruction," of weapons "against entrenched and invisible systems of power and privilege," and of havens "of unheard, angry voices" (Seeley). Like other *noir* texts and films, their works reveal that the lines between victim and victimizer, right and wrong, good and evil, are constantly shifting lines. Assumptions we make about anything or anyone in their narratives are always moving. We must question everything. Who did the wrong thing? How do we know? Which one is the victim? Why do we sympathize with this sniveling, whining murderer? How can we like him while we hate him?

Wharton, Hemingway, and Highsmith all provide fiction that is disruptively, unexpectedly, uncomfortably fluid. As Highsmith understood, fiction that is not considered canonical can be experimental, and can move around from genre to genre, from art form to art form. These misfit *noir* texts—Wharton, Hemingway, Highsmith included—have moved from text to screen in challenging, sometimes difficult ways over the last century. The successful adaptations are quirky and complicated, and the relationship of fiction to film forces us to acknowledge a profound integrity to the works of Wharton, Hemingway and Highsmith. Their fiction, through the dark lens of *noir,* looks more substantial because of its difficult relationship to film. This American *noir* and its eccentric antecedents—among them earlier American writers (Charles Brockden Brown, Edgar Allan Poe, Herman Melville, Henry James, and others) have helped usher in new twenty-first-century art forms beyond film.

The fluid, shifting *noir* characteristics that we recognize in Wharton, Hemingway, and Highsmith (and earlier writers as well) anticipate recent nonbinary expressions which move fluidly among fiction, film, anime, gaming, and other art forms in our own century. Through technologically sophisticated lenses of gender-fluid, genre-fluid, nonbinary, and genderqueer narratives, and through the visual power of graphic novels (Highsmith the comic-book writer would approve), we can continue to reconsider the rich narrative legacy of Wharton, Hemingway, Highsmith, and other *noir* writers. As innovative as these twenty-first-century literary/cinematic movements are, they will always be indebted to their antecedents, most pointedly to American *noir,* where we can delight in the perverse and powerful narratives of these three writers. From the overly decorated sitting rooms of *The Age of Innocence,* through the North Woods of "Up in Michigan," to a cross-country train adventure in *Strangers on a Train,* Wharton, Hemingway, and Highsmith help us move us through the currents of American *noir* and into the rapids of our own century.

FILMS REFERENCED

YEAR	TITLE	DIRECTOR
1932	*A Farewell to Arms*	Frank Borzage
1941	*High Sierra*	Raoul Walsh
1941	*The Maltese Falcon*	John Huston
1944	*To Have and Have Not*	Howard Hawks
1946	*The Killers*	Robert Siodmak
1951	*Strangers on a Train*	Alfred Hitchcock
1952	*The Snows of Kilimanjaro*	Henry King
1957	*A Farewell to Arms*	Charles Vidor
1957	*The Sun Also Rises*	Henry King
1958	*The Old Man and the Sea*	John Sturges
1962	*Hemingway's Adventures of a Young Man*	Martin Ritt
1973	*Mean Streets*	Martin Scorsese
1976	*Taxi Driver*	Martin Scorsese
1980	*Raging Bull*	Martin Scorsese
1990	*Goodfellas*	Martin Scorsese
1993	*The Age of Innocence*	Martin Scorsese
1994	*Pulp Fiction*	Quentin Tarantino
1996	*Fargo*	Joel Coen
1998	*A Simple Plan*	Sam Raimi
2002	*Far From Heaven*	Todd Haynes
2013	*The Last Good Country*	Aidan Brezonick
2015	*Carol*	Todd Hayne

NOTES

1. There are great biographies of all three writers. For Wharton, Lee's biography has been useful, as has Singley's *Historical Guide to Edith Wharton.* Hendrickson's *Hemingway's Boat* is a great resource and a great read, as is Baker's definitive biography. Wilson's and Schenkar's biographies of Patricia Highsmith are both excellent.

2. There are many good sources on *noir* fiction and film, among them Cochran's *American Noir*, Sklar's *Film: An International History,* Silver and Ursini's *Film Noir Reader*, and Kaplan's *Women in Film Noir.* Ellroy and Penzler's *Best American Noir of the Century* is valuable, as is Naremore's excellent study, *More Than Night.* For online resources, see especially Seeley,

"Noir Is Protest Literature"; Keyes, "Strangers on a Train"; and Carson, "The Movies of 1994."

3. Several of Wharton's works were adapted in the early years of Hollywood production, beginning with a now lost adaptation of *The House of Mirth* in 1918. For comprehensive information on Wharton and film, see Boswell, *Edith Wharton on Film*, and Marshall, "Media Adaptations of Wharton's Works." For more useful scholarship, see Thomas Doherty's great study *Pre-Code Hollywood* and Peucker's "Scorsese's *Age of Innocence*" and *Incorporating Images.*

4. I am especially grateful to Lisa Tyler for reminding me of the correspondence between Wharton's Vance Weston and Hemingway.

5. Both of Lamb's books *Art Matters* and *The Hemingway Short Story* have been helpful, as has Hendrickson.

6. This is Scorsese's great saying: he wrote about trying to adapt a novel "with a pedigree" in the introduction to the published screenplay of *The Age of Innocence* (vii).

7. The best source for information on the many adaptations of Hemingway on film has been Grissom's *Fitzgerald and Hemingway on Film.* Also see Broer and Holland, *Hemingway and Women,* especially Putnam's "On Defiling Eden" and Sanderson's "Hemingway's Literary Sisters." For more on adaptation, see Elliott's excellent *Rethinking the Novel/Film Debate.* For more on adaptations of the 1950s, see Pomerance's collection *American Cinema of the 1950s.*

8. In 2013 Aidan Brezonick wrote and directed an independent film, *The Last Good Country,* about young Hemingway in Michigan. Kramer described this as an "elegant short film."

9. Several scholars have pointed out the homoeroticism in both Wharton and Highsmith. See especially Crow, "The Girl in the Library."

10. Truffaut's interview with Hitchcock about *Strangers on a Train* in *Hitchcock/Truffaut* is especially interesting. For more on both novel and film versions, see Leitch, *Crime Films.*

11. Highsmith published *The Price of Salt,* or *Carol*, a novel about forbidden love among women, originally under the pseudonym Claire Morgan in 1952. It is her only novel "in which no violent crime occurs" (Talbot 75). Among other things, *The Price of Salt* is a romance. The novel was adapted to the screen in 2015 by director Todd Haynes, who is drawn to *noir* and neo-noir: in 2002 he directed the neo-noir film *Far from Heaven*, and he also adapted James M. Cain's *noir* classic *Mildred Pierce*, starring Kate Winslet, for HBO in 2011. See Talbot, "Forbidden Love." Also see O'Brien's *Hardboiled America.*

12. Seeley's essay on how *noir* functions in American society is the most intelligent and challenging source I have read on contemporary *noir.* He puts *noir* fiction and film into historical context, and suggests that American *noir* is the best potential site for continuing cultural diversity within American arts and letters. I think he's right.

WORKS CITED

Arn, Jackson. "Adaptation: Patricia Highsmith." *Film Comment,* 25 Nov. 2015. Web. www.filmcomment.com/blog/adaptation-patricia-highsmith/.

Baker, Carlos. *Ernest Hemingway: A Life Story.* New York: Charles Scribner's Sons, 1969. Print.

Boswell, Parley Ann. *Edith Wharton on Film.* Carbondale: Southern Illinois UP, 2007. Print.

Broer, Lawrence, and Gloria Holland, eds. *Hemingway and Women: Female Critics and the Female Voice.* Tuscaloosa: U of Alabama P, 2002. Print.

Carson, Tom. "The Movies of 1994: 'Pulp Fiction' and the Making of Quentin Tarantino." *Grantland,* Oct 14, 2014. Web. grantland.com/hollywood-prospectus/movies-of-1994-pulp-fiction-quentin-tarantino/.

Cochran, David. *American Noir: Underground Writers and Filmmakers of the Postwar Era.* Washington DC: Smithsonian Institution P, 2000. Print.

Crow, Charles L., "The Girl in the Library: Edith Wharton's 'The Eyes' and American Gothic Traditions." *Spectral America: Phantoms and the National Imagination.* Ed. Jeffrey Andrew Weinstock. Madison, WI: Popular Press, 2004. 157–68. Print.

Doctorow, E. L. "Braver than We Thought." Wagner, ed. *Ernest Hemingway.* 325–31.

Doherty, Thomas. *Pre-Code Hollywood: Sex, Immorality, and Insurrection in American Cinema, 1930–1934.* New York: Columbia UP, 1999. Print.

Ebert, Roger. "*The Age of Innocence.*" Web. www.rogerebert.com/reviews/great-movie-the-age-of-innocence-1993. Accessed 14 Aug. 2005.

Elliott, Kamilla. *Rethinking the Novel/Film Debate.* Cambridge: Cambridge UP, 2003. Print.

Ellroy, James, and Otto Penzler, eds. *The Best American Noir of the Century.* New York: Mariner Books, 2011. Print.

Grissom, Candace Ursula. *Fitzgerald and Hemingway on Film: A Critical Study of the Adaptations, 1924–2013.* Jefferson, NC: McFarland & Co., 2014. Print.

Haglund, David. "Hollywood Hemingway: How the Movies Mangled Great Fiction." *Slate,* 13 Apr. 2007. Web. www.slate.com/articles/arts/dvdextras/2007/04/hollywood_hemingway.html.

Hall, Mordaunt. "Helen Hayes, Gary Cooper, and Adolf Menjou in a Film of Hemingway's 'Farewell to Arms.'" *New York Times,* 9 Dec. 1932. Web. www.nytimes.com/movie/review?res=9902E0DD1F31E333A2575AC0A9649D946394D6CF.

Hatch, Kristen. "1951: Movies and the New Faces of Masculinity." Pomerance, ed. *American Cinema of the 1950s,* 43–64.

Hemingway, Ernest. *The Complete Short Stories of Ernest Hemingway.* The Finca Vigía Edition. New York: Scribner's, 1987. Print.

———. *A Farewell to Arms.* 1929. New York: Scribner's, 2014. Print.

———. *For Whom the Bell Tolls.* 1940. New York: Scribner's, 1995. Print.

———. *In Our Time.* 1925. New York: Scribner's, 1996. Print.

———. *Men without Women.* 1927. New York: Scribner's, 1997. Print.

———. *A Moveable Feast.* 1964. Restored ed. New York: Scribner's, 2009. Print.

———. *The Old Man and the Sea.* 1952. New York: Scribner's, 1995. Print.

———. *The Sun Also Rises.* 1926. New York: Scribner's, 2006. Print.

———. *Three Stories & Ten Poems.* New York: Amereon, 1923. Print.

———. *Winner Take Nothing.* 1933. New York: Scribner's, 1968. Print.

Hendrickson, Paul. *Hemingway's Boat: Everything He Loved in Life, and Lost.* New York: Vintage Books, 2011. Print.

Highsmith, Patricia. *The Price of Salt, or Carol.* 1952. New York: Norton, 2004. Print.

———. *Strangers on a Train.* 1950. New York: Norton, 2001. Print.

Jones, J. R. "How One Hemingway Short Story Became Three Different Movies." *Chicago Reader,* 30 July 2015. Web. www.chicagoreader.com/chicago/ernest-hemingway-the-killers-criterion-siodmak-don-siegel-tarkovsky/Content?oid=18473617.

Kaplan, Ann, ed. *Women in Film Noir.* Rev. ed. London: British Film Institute, 2008. Print.

Keyes, David. "Strangers on a Train." *Cinemaphile,* Apr. 2002. Web. www.cinemaphile.org/reviews/2002/strangersonatrain.html.

Kramer, Gary M. "Hemingway on Film: 6 Films That Take Him from a WWI Hotshot Almost to the Bitter End." Salon.com. 10 June 2016. Web. www.salon.com/2016/06/10/hemingway_on_film_6_films_that_take_him_from_a_wwi_hotshot_almost_to_the_bitter_end/.

Lamb, Robert Paul. *Art Matters: Hemingway, Craft, and the Creation of the Modern Short Story.* Baton Rouge: Louisiana State UP, 2010. Print.

———. *The Hemingway Short Story: A Study in Craft for Writers and Readers.* Baton Rouge: Louisiana State UP, 2013. Print.

Lee, Hermione. *Edith Wharton.* New York: Alfred A. Knopf, 2007. Print.

Leitch, Thomas. *Crime Films.* Cambridge: Cambridge UP, 2002. Print.

Lukas, Karli. "Creative Visions: (De)Constructing 'The Beautiful' in Scorsese's *The Age of Innocence.*" *Cinémathètique Annotations on Film* 25 (Mar. 2003). Web. sensesofcinema.com/2003/cteq/age_of_innocence/.

Marshall, Scott. "Media Adaptations of Edith Wharton's Works." *Edith Wharton A to Z.* By Sarah Bird Wright. New York: Checkmark, 1998. 287–95. Print.

Naremore, James. *More Than Night: Film Noir in Its Contexts.* Berkeley: U of California P, 1998. Print.

O'Brien, Geoffrey. *Hardboiled America: Lurid Paperbacks and the Masters of Noir.* New York: DeCapo, 1997. Print.

Peucker, Brigitte. *Incorporating Images: Film and the Rival Arts.* Princeton, NJ: Princeton UP, 1995. Print.

Pomerance, Murray, ed. *American Cinema in the 1950s: Themes and Variations.* New Brunswick, NJ: Rutgers UP, 2005. Print.

Putnam, Ann. "On Defiling Eden: The Search for Eve in the Garden of Eden." Broer and Holland, eds., *Hemingway and Women,* 109–30.

Sanderson, Rena. "Hemingway's Literary Sisters: The Author through the Eyes of Women Writers." Broer and Holland, eds., *Hemingway and Women*, 276–94.

Schenkar, Joan. *The Talented Miss Highsmith: The Secret Life and Serious Art of Patricia Highsmith.* New York: St. Martin's Press, 2009. Print.

Scorsese, Martin, and Jay Cocks. *The Age of Innocence: The Shooting Script.* New York: Newmarket, 1995. Print.

Seeley, Nicholas. "Noir Is Protest Literature: That's Why It's Having a Renaissance." *Electric Lit.*, 27 Apr. 2015. Web. electricliterature.com/noir-is-protest-literature-thats-why-it-s-having-a-renaissance-49b0a2ba52e4#.m7mdt1°4i.

Silver, Alain, and James Ursini, eds. *Film Noir Reader 4: The Crucial Films and Themes.* Pompton Plains, NJ: Limelight Editions, 2004. Print.

Singley, Carol J., ed. *A Historical Guide to Edith Wharton.* New York: Houghton Mifflin, 2000. Print.

Sklar, Robert. *Film: An International History of the Medium.* 2nd ed. New York: Prentice Hall, 2002. Print.

Talbot, Margaret. "Forbidden Love: The Passions behind Patricia Highsmith's 'The Price of Salt.'" *New Yorker.* 30 Nov. 2015. 75–79. Print.

Truffaut, François. *Hitchcock/Truffaut.* Rev. ed. New York: Simon & Schuster, 1985. Print.

Wagner, Linda, ed. *Ernest Hemingway: Six Decades of Criticism.* East Lansing: Michigan State UP, 1987. Print.

Wharton, Edith. *The Age of Innocence.* 1920. Ed. Candace Waid. New York: Norton, 2003. Print.

———. *Collected Stories, 1911–1937.* 2 vols. New York: Library of America, 2001. Print.

———. *The Children.* 1928. New York: Scribner's, 1997. Print.

———. *The Custom of the Country.* 1913. New York: Simon & Schuster, 1997. Print.

———. *Ethan Frome* [1911] *and Summer* [1917]. Ed. Denise D. Knight. New York: Houghton, 2004. Print.

———. *The Ghost Stories of Edith Wharton.* New York: Scribner's, 1973. Print.

———. *The House of Mirth.* 1905. Ed. Shari Benstock. New York: Bedford, 1994. Print.

———. *Old New York.* 1924. New York: Scribner's, 1995. Print.

———. *The Reef.* 1912. New York: Penguin, 1995. Print.

———. *Twilight Sleep.* 1927. New York: Scribner's, 1997. Print.

Wilson, Andrew. *Beautiful Shadow: A Life of Patricia Highsmith.* New York: Bloomsbury, 2003. Print.

CONTRIBUTORS

PARLEY ANN BOSWELL is professor emerita of English at Eastern Illinois University, where for thirty years she taught American literature and film studies. In her book *Edith Wharton on Film* (2007) she studies the relationship between Wharton's writings and the films adapted from her works. Most recently, her book *Pregnancy in Literature and Film* (2014) explores the ways in which pregnancy narratives behave in American literature from *The Scarlet Letter* to works by Harriet Jacobs, Chopin, Wharton, Hemingway, Faulkner, Didion, Morrison, and others, and the ways that pregnancy behaves in American film from early melodrama through *Juno* and *Precious.*

DUSTIN FAULSTICK teaches in the Lewis Honors College at the University of Kentucky. His scholarship considers twentieth-century US literature in relation to biblical intertextuality, cultural studies, and critical reflections on the American Dream. He has won an Edith Wharton Society Emerging Scholar Essay Prize, and his articles have appeared in *New Ohio Review, Studies in American Naturalism, Literature and Belief, Edith Wharton Review, Renascence, Re-Markings,* and *Religion and the Arts.*

ANNA GREEN is a doctoral candidate in the English Department at Michigan State University. Her dissertation explores the dialogic relationship between the precarious subject positions of woman artists and their engagements with collage and collage-adjacent methodologies.

PETER HAYS is professor emeritus of English at the University of California, Davis. He has the rare distinction of having served on the Hemingway Foundation and Society Board and also as the token male on the Wharton Society Board; he is a life member of the Wharton Society and recently taught a class on Wharton. His most recent of five books on Hemingway is *Fifty Years of Hemingway Criticism.*

JENNIFER HAYTOCK is professor of English at the College at Brockport, State University of New York. She is the author of *At Home, At War: Domesticity and World War I in American Literature* (2003), *Edith Wharton and the Conversations of Literary Modernism* (2008), *The Middle Class in the Great Depression: Popular Women Writers in the 1930s* (2013), and *The Routledge Introduction to American War Literature* (2018). She has published essays on early twentieth-century writers such as Hemingway, Wharton, and Cather. She is currently coediting (with Laura Rattray) *The New Edith Wharton Studies.*

CAROLINE CHAMBERLIN HELLMAN is professor of English at City Tech, City University of New York. Her book *Domesticity and Design in American Women's Literature: Stowe, Alcott, Cather, and Wharton Writing Home* was published in 2011. Her teaching and research interests concern the connotations of space and place in American literature, in addition to public education policy. She is currently working on a book project on literary inheritance.

ELLEN ANDREWS KNODT is professor of English at Penn State University, Abington, where she teaches modern American literature. She has published articles on Hemingway in the *Hemingway Review, North Dakota Quarterly, Resources for American Literary Study,* and in essay collections from Louisiana State University Press and Kent State University Press. She is a consulting scholar for the Hemingway Letters Project. Conference presentations in addition to those on Hemingway include discussions of Edith Wharton's and Willa Cather's World War I novels. Knodt received Penn State's Atherton Award for Excellence in Teaching.

CECILIA MACHESKI is professor emerita of English at LaGuardia Community College of the City University of New York. As a Fulbright Senior Scholar, she has taught and lectured in New Zealand and Norway. She is coeditor with Mary Anne Schofield of *Fetter'd or Free? British Women Novelists, 1670–1815,* and *Curtain Calls: British and American Women and the Theater, 1660–1820.* She is coauthor with Marian Arkin of *Research Papers: A Guide and Workbook.* Her essays "Architecture" and "Novel of Manners" appear in *Edith Wharton in Context,* edited by Laura Rattray. She has given conference papers on knitting in Wharton's fiction, the importance of A. J. Downing to *Hudson River Bracketed,* and other topics. Most recently, she is developing a study of the impact of Venetian history and culture on the American imagination, 1860–1920.

MILENA RADEVA-COSTELLO teaches at Providence College, Rhode Island. She is the author of *Philanthropy and Early Twentieth-Century British Literature*

(2018). She has also published essays in *Phenomenology and the Arts*, *Philosophy and Children's Literature*, and *Selected Papers from the Eighteenth Annual Conference on Virginia Woolf.*

LAURA RATTRAY is a reader in American literature at the University of Glasgow. She is editor of *The Unpublished Writings of Edith Wharton* (2009), *Edith Wharton's "The Custom of the Country": A Reassessment* (2010), *Edith Wharton in Context* (2012), and Oxford World Classics' *Summer* (2015), and she coedited *Twenty-First Century Readings of "Tender Is the Night"* (2007). With Mary Chinery, she co-wrote an article on Wharton's play *The Shadow of a Doubt*, a work previously unknown to Wharton scholars. The article and play were published in the *Edith Wharton Review* (2017). In 2016 she was the keynote speaker at the Edith Wharton Society Conference in Washington, DC. She has also published on American fiction of the early twentieth century, the Hollywood novel, and neglected women writers.

SIRPA SALENIUS, presently a senior lecturer in English and American literature at the University of Eastern Finland in Joensuu, has taught at the University of Tokyo and at study-abroad programs in Rome and Florence for various American universities. Her courses have focused on analyzing the works of Henry James, Ernest Hemingway, Edith Wharton, and others whose fiction uses Italy as a setting. She has lectured extensively on American writers in Italy, which has also been the topic of her conference presentations and publications, including *Florence, Italy: Images of the City in Nineteenth-Century American Writing* (2007) and *American Authors Reinventing Italy: The Writings of Exceptional Nineteenth-Century Women* (edited by Salenius, 2009). More recently, her work has centered on exploring gender, sexuality, and race. Recent books include *An Abolitionist Abroad: Sarah Parker Remond in Cosmopolitan Europe* (2016), *Rose Elizabeth Cleveland: First Lady and Literary Scholar* (2014), and essay collections (coedited with Beth L. Lueck and Nancy Lusignan Schultz) *Transatlantic Conversations: Nineteenth-Century American Women's Encounters with Italy and the Atlantic World* (2016) and (with Elizabeth T. Kenney and Whitney Womack Smith) *Race and Transatlantic Identities* (2017).

LISA TYLER is professor of English at Sinclair Community College, where she has taught for more than twenty-five years. A member of the editorial advisory board of the *Hemingway Review*, she has published three books: *Student Companion to Ernest Hemingway* (2001), *Teaching Hemingway's "A Farewell to Arms"* (2008), and *Understanding Marsha Norman* (2019). She has also published more than forty essays in edited collections and academic journals, and has presented papers at International Hemingway Society conferences in Sun Valley, Stresa, Key West, Kansas

City, Petoskey, and Venice. In 2017 she received Sinclair's Distinguished Faculty Scholar Award.

LINDA WAGNER-MARTIN, Hanes Professor Emerita of English and Comparative Literature at the University of North Carolina, Chapel Hill, is a recipient of the Hubbell Medal for work in American literature. Among her recent books are *Hemingway's Wars: The Public and Private Battles*, *A History of American Literature from 1950 to the Present*, and *Maya Angelou: Adventurous Spirit*.

INDEX